SEARS

USER INSTRUCTIONS
PRECAUTIONS TO AVOID POSSIBLE EXPOSURE TO EXCESSIVE MICROWAVE ENERGY

(a) DO NOT ATTEMPT to operate this oven with the door open since open-door operation can result in harmful exposure to microwave energy. It is important not to defeat or tamper with the safety interlocks.

(b) DO NOT PLACE any object between the oven front face and the door or allow soil or cleaner residue to accumulate on sealing surfaces.

(c) DO NOT OPERATE the oven if it is damaged. It is particularly important that the oven door close properly and that there is no damage to the:

      (1) DOOR (bent)

      (2) HINGES AND LATCHES (broken or loosened)

      (3) DOOR SEALS AND SEALING SURFACES

(d) THE OVEN SHOULD NOT BE ADJUSTED OR REPAIRED BY ANYONE EXCEPT PROPERLY QUALIFIED SERVICE PERSONNEL.

Kenmore

SPACEMASTER

SEARS

BENJAMIN

Home Economics Director: Virginia Peterson
Senior Home Economists: Thelma Pressman, Betty Sullivan, LuAnne Dugan
Managing Editor: Virginia Schomp
Editor: Naomi Galbreath
Editorial Assistants: Laurie Marzahl, Terry Firkins,
                      Annemarie Erena, Terese Brecklin,
                      Mona Marino, Glen Gilchrist
Project Manager: David P. Stefani
Creative Director: Thomas C. Brecklin
Graphic Artist: Barbara Schwoegler
Typography: A-Line, Milwaukee
Photography Food Stylist: Jean Carey
Photography: Teri Sandison, Los Angeles

Library of Congress Catalog Card Number: 85-73022
ISBN: 0-87502-167-0
Prepared, produced, and published by The Benjamin Company, Inc.
                      One Westchester Plaza
                      Elmsford, New York 10523

Printed in Japan
10 9 8 7 6 5   SRS 13467

CONTENTS

Roast Beef

LOOK WHAT YOU CAN DO!

Let's begin your introduction to microwave cooking with a brief look at just a few of the outstanding foods this oven can help you prepare. Of course, you can cook just about anything in the microwave oven. However, some foods are prepared not only in a fraction of their conventional cooking times but also rate "best ever" quality. Many of those foods take a bow here. The recipes for all the dishes illustrated are included in the book, so feel perfectly free to choose your personal favorites as you browse.

Roast beef (facing page) is just as rare as you like it and has a special succulence when roasted in the microwave oven. And no color enhancers were used on this roast! Meat belongs in the microwave oven for defrosting *and* cooking, and we think this picture is the proof.

Baked chicken (top left), with or without stuffing, cooks in less than 30 minutes. And you can have a frozen chicken ready to cook in just about an hour, thanks to microwave defrosting. A soy-based microwave browning sauce was used on this chicken before it was baked in the microwave oven.

Baked potatoes (left center) can now be last-minute additions to any meal. They are fluffy, have a wonderful texture, and one potato bakes in just four to six minutes.

Classic Quiche Lorraine (bottom left) is so easy to prepare the microwave way that it will soon be one of your favorite luncheons, served up with a simple salad. And it can double as an appetizer anytime. Yes the pastry crust is also a microwave success — and the kitchen remained cool from start to finish. You can also substitute as you wish to create your own quiches.

Cakes (left), whether from a mix or your favorite "from scratch" recipe, are rich, moist, and tantalizingly high when baked in the microwave oven. You'll be so pleased that you may want to turn every cake into a special torte like this one.

Apple pie (top left) is just one of many fruit pies that excel in this oven. We hope you will like the unusual crumb topping on this pie. Most of your favorite pies are in our baked goods chapter and you can easily convert conventional pie recipes to microwave baking.

Seafood (left center) is represented here by poached fish, but all kinds of fish and shellfish cook to perfection in the microwave oven. Cooking occurs so incredibly fast that no moisture is lost and, as all good cooks know, retaining moisture is the secret to just-caught flavor for seafood.

Soup and a *sandwich* (bottom left), that All-American lunch, becomes a gourmet treat in this oven. Soup cooks quickly with very little stirring required, and it can be reheated right in any microwave-safe (microproof) serving bowl or mug. Did we cheat? No, that beautiful burger owes its texture and color to grilling in a special microwave browning dish.

Poached pears (below) are one of our fruit favorites that we hope you will also enjoy. This beauty was poached in a wine and cranberry juice syrup. The result is not only flavorful but also quite attractive.

Bacon and *eggs* (right) have never been so good and so easy to prepare. These shirred eggs were cooked in their serving dish. Imagine, no frying pan to clean. The bacon? No pan required here, either. In the microwave oven, bacon is usually cooked between paper towels placed on a microproof plate. Just throw the used towels away after removing the bacon. That *croissant* will be wonderfully warm, too, with just about a half minute in the microwave oven. Coffee? Although some special microwave brewing cookware is available, we don't see any reason to abandon the timeless conventional methods for brewing coffee. But, if you are a coffee drinker, you will be using your oven to reheat your coffee — right in the microproof cup — several times a day. And that brings us to the orange juice. The oven can be used to thaw frozen juice concentrate if it is removed from its foil-lined container first. Sorry, but while we've taken pretty good care of breakfast, the oven can't provide your wake-up call!

Candy (right center) is a particular favorite of microwave cooks because it is so easy to prepare. Your friends will think that you fussed and fussed. The truth is that the microwave oven enables you to prepare candy without a double boiler, usually in a 2-quart glass measure or bowl, and with a minimum of stirring. Wouldn't it be fun if this was a scratch 'n sniff cookbook and you could sample the aroma of that chocolate fudge? Almond Bark is the other candy displayed here, and you will find many others in the "Candies, Puddings, & Fruits" chapter.

Casseroles (bottom right) can be cooked in the microwave oven in a fraction of the conventional cooking time, and the only ingredient change necessary to convert a conventional recipe is usually a reduction in the amount of liquid. You can defrost and reheat casseroles in the microwave oven, too. Probably the nicest thing of all is the fact that you don't have to worry about food sticking to the bottom of the dish when cooking or reheating casseroles in your new microwave oven. Casseroles stay moist, too, because there is no heat source in the oven to cause rapid evaporation.

Vegetables and *Sauces* (left) are so much better when cooked in the microwave oven that you simply won't prepare them any other way again. That's a pretty bold statement, but we really think you will soon agree with us. Most vegetables cook with little or no water added. As a result, they retain their just-picked color and texture. Usually, the only extra moisture necessary is less than ¼ cup, or whatever water clings to the vegetables when they are washed. Another big microwave plus is the opportunity to cook vegetables in the serving bowl or platter, providing eye-appeal. For example, just look at the squash and pea pods in the photograph. Sauces are a cinch, too. They can be prepared in a glass measure in a matter of a few minutes. The constant stirring characteristic of stove-top cooking is gone forever. With microwave sauces, you seldom need to whisk more than two or three times to create truly elegant sauces whenever you wish.

Rumaki (left center) steps forward from the appetizer chapter to tell us how quickly and conveniently the microwave oven cooks everything from family nibblers to formal party fare. A creative cook's challenge — serving always-hot appetizers — is answered by this oven. You simply prepare them ahead and reheat on microproof serving dishes as guests arrive, or as you need to replenish the supplies!

Reheating dinner (bottom left) for those late arrivals is no longer a nasty affair. It only takes a minute or two in the microwave oven and a plate of food is restored to piping-hot quality. It's so convenient to reheat in the microwave oven that you may find yourself preparing your own TV dinners and freezing them for use as needed later.

As you learn more about microwave cooking and your oven, we hope you will agree with us that this appliance offers you more freedom in the kitchen (or *from* the kitchen) than you have ever experienced in conventional cooking — and everything you cook will have equal or superior quality.

MICROWAVE COOKING

Now that you have had a preview of some of the wonderful things this oven can do, we can set out to explore microwave cooking and the principles behind it. It's not difficult to learn microwave cooking. In fact, you are joining countless thousands of people (about 50% of the homes in America now have a microwave oven) who have discovered the joys in this fast, easy, and efficient method of cooking.

Before you start using your oven, you should take the time to study the information here and in your Use & Care Manual. As with any new appliance, there are many things you need to know to use your new oven without disappointments. In the illustrated chapters that follow, we will tell you all about the way the oven works, why it works the way it does, what it can do, and how you can get the most out of it.

A COOKING SCHOOL

We have selected both traditional and new recipes that will show off this oven to its best advantage. The recipes offer a balanced selection, providing the speed and simplicity we all value, as well as opportunities for more elaborate food preparation when you wish. If you are an innovative cook, you'll find this oven versatile enough to answer your every need.

There is nothing complicated about using this oven. All you need is a little understanding of the special possibilities it offers. We have taken an approach that is best characterized as a "cooking school" in book form. However, you do the grading! We think you will soon find that the microwave way is the best way to cook most foods.

To install your oven, follow the instructions in your Use & Care Manual. A micro-

wave oven operates on standard household current of 110 to 120 volts and does not require a service call to ready it for regular use. You will also be pleased to know that the oven requires little maintenance. Unlike a conventional oven with heat generated in the oven cavity, a microwave oven has no heat that can cause spills to bake on or discolor the interior. No harsh cleaning agents or difficult cleaning tasks are ever necessary. Just a simple wiping is all you need to keep the oven clean. Do keep the door and gasket free of food buildup to maintain a tight seal. Now, let's find out how a microwave oven works.

HOW DOES IT WORK?

In conventional stove-top cooking, food cooks by heat applied to the bottom of the pan. In a conventional oven, food cooks by the hot air that surrounds the food and pan. The energy source is either gas, which produces flame, or electricity, which powers a heat coil. In the microwave oven, that same electricity provides the power for a magnetron vacuum tube. The magnetron converts the electricity into microwaves. The microwaves travel directly to the food. Because they are waves of energy, not heat, the oven remains cool. The magnetron tube is usually located inside the top of the oven. A fan-like *stirrer* helps distribute the microwaves evenly throughout the oven. As a result, food does not need to be constantly rotated by a turntable.

Microwaves are high-frequency waves, just like those that bring television and radio into our homes. They can do one of three things, depending upon the material contacted. They bounce off or are reflected by metal surfaces. They pass through materials such as glass, paper, pottery made from lead-free clay, and microproof plastics. They are absorbed by liquids and by the moisture in food. Very simply, then, the absorbed microwaves cause the moisture molecules in food to vibrate very rapidly against each other, inducing friction. Friction causes heat (to demonstrate this, rub the palms of your hands together very fast). The food is cooked by the friction-produced heat. The *exterior* begins to cook first and the interior then cooks by the heat con-

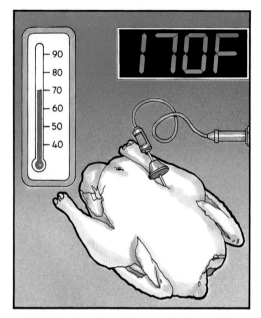

Because there is no heat source in a microwave oven, the interior does not become hot. The internal temperature of the cooked food, however, is the same as that produced by conventional cooking. When cooking with the temperature probe, you can even see the temperature of the food displayed as it cooks.

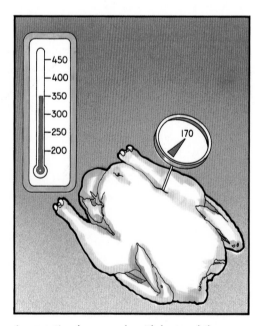

A conventional oven cooks with heat and the oven interior is extremely hot. Much hotter, of course, than the finished temperature of the food itself. The hot air can also cause rapid moisture loss and can dry the surface of the food.

ducted from the surface to the interior (conduction). Don't believe anything you may have heard about microwaves cooking food on the inside first. Food cooks just as it does in a conventional oven. How else could that beautifully-rare Roast Beef on page 6 have been produced?

Because the cooking containers used in microwave cooking do not absorb microwave energy, they do not usually become hot. While the microwaves pass right through the cookware to the food, the cookware can become heated by the food as the food becomes hot. So you will occasionally need to use hot pads. Selection of the correct cookware is quite important in microwave cooking, and is covered fully in the next chapter.

The see-through panel in the microwave oven door is made of a specially prepared material that contains a metal screen. The metal screen prevents the microwaves from escaping the oven by causing them to be reflected and to bounce about the oven interior, doing their efficient cooking job. The special screen also enables you to observe the food as it cooks. The microwaves cannot penetrate the screen and cannot escape from the oven. Opening the oven door turns the unit off automatically and no microwaves are present. You can stir, turn food over, or check doneness just as you do with a conventional oven. Be confident. Your microwave oven is a well-tested, safe, and reliable cooking appliance.

More detailed technical information about microwave energy is available in your Use & Care Manual. At this point, however, you really don't need more specific information unless it is of interest to you. So, let's move forward with the all-important information about cooking times, micro-proof cookware, and cooking techniques.

Microwave cooking calls for new techniques in arranging food. The principles provide many especially-attractive cook-and-serve dishes.

Whole poultry and certain roasts need to be turned over to promote even cooking.

A large beef roast takes longer to cook than the small portion of ground meat. If they were of equal weight, the roast would still take longer because it has a greater density.

TIMING, COOKWARE & TECHNIQUES

In this chapter you will find everything you need to know to make microwave cooking easy, efficient, and pleasurable. Once you know the principles, the techniques will become second nature. Read this basic information with its accompanying illustrations carefully. As you begin to use the oven, you can always refer back to this useful chapter whenever a question arises about a cooking term or technique. Here you will learn why some foods cook faster than others, what you should know about timing and judging doneness, which cooking utensils are appropriate, how to cook most efficiently, and much more. In short, all the basics — and some advanced methods — that you should know to be a skilled microwave cook.

Because of the unique qualities of microwave energy, microwave cooking uses certain terms and techniques that are different from those of conventional cooking. For example, in microwave cooking, many foods complete cooking during standing time, either in the oven or after being removed from the oven. In addition, how food is arranged in the cooking dish is important to its being cooked evenly throughout. You may wonder why you need to know all this when the recipes in this book provide detailed instructions. Fair question. If you restrict your cooking to those recipes, you may not need as much detail. But the fact is that you'll also need to be familiar with this basic information to adapt recipes for personal preferences (do any two people like their scrambled eggs exactly alike?) and to use recipes from magazines, other cookbooks, and those time-honored family favorites you usually prepare from memory. We want you to be a confident microwave cook and, in all likelihood, study now will eliminate frustration later. As we said in the previous chapter, there is nothing complicated about microwave cooking. Let's go to microwave cooking school so you can discover how truly easy it is.

ABOUT TIMING

Timing is crucial in microwave cooking. But isn't that true for all cooking? You, the cook, have to be the judge as you consider your family's preferences and use your own instincts. Chances are, you can tell if a chicken is done simply by looking at it. You might even scoff at the timing chart given on a package because you know that a particular food always seems to need more or less time. It is important to know that even though the microwave oven is a marvel of computer technology, it is no more or less precise than any other cooking device. Nevertheless, because of the speed with which it cooks, timing is more crucial in microwave cooking than in conventional cooking. One minute can make a big difference. When you consider that a cooking task requiring one hour in a conventional oven generally needs only one-quarter of that time in a microwave oven, you can understand why microwave cooking requires a somewhat different approach to timing. Where an extra minute in conventional cooking is seldom critical, that same minute in microwave cooking can spell the difference between overcooked and undercooked food. As you become familiar with your oven, you will recognize when to begin to check for doneness. Remember that it is better to undercook and add more cooking time than to overcook — then it's too late.

Cooking times for the recipes in this book have been determined for you, of course. They are precise, but they can vary according to the quantity of food being cooked, its temperature prior to cooking, and other factors.

Cooking times would always be precise if a way could be found to guarantee that all foods would be exactly the same each time we cooked them, and if the electric company would maintain a constant power output (there are frequent changes in the voltage levels reaching our homes). The fact is that one potato or one steak differs from another in density, moisture or fat content, shape, weight, and temperature. This is true for all food. Consequently, the cook must be ready to adjust to these changes, to be flexible and observant. After all, you, and not the microwave oven, are the cook.

While the oven can measure the internal temperature of a food when the temperature probe is used, it can't make judgments. You must do that. All of the recipes have been thoroughly kitchen tested by expert home economists. As in all fine cooking, however, microwave cooking is enhanced by the personal touch you bring to it. As you cook, feel free to alter the timing.

Quantity

In conventional cooking, it is not always necessary to alter cooking time when increasing the quantity. It takes no longer to bake 4 potatoes than 2 in the conventional oven. In the microwave oven, more food requires more cooking time. One potato cooks in about 5 minutes; 3 potatoes may cook in 11 minutes; and 5 potatoes in about 18 minutes. Therefore, if the quantity in a recipe is changed, an adjustment in the timing is necessary.

When changing the quantity of a recipe, follow this general rule: When doubling, increase the cooking time by approximately 50 percent. When cutting a recipe in half, reduce the time by approximately 40 percent.

Irregularly-shaped food is a special microwave cooking challenge. It should be placed in the dish with the thickest portions toward the outside edge of the dish. The center of the dish receives less microwave energy.

Shape and Size

Thin food cooks faster than thick food; thin sections faster than thick. Likewise small pieces cook faster than large pieces. So that your food cooks evenly, place thick pieces toward the outside of the dish, since the outside areas cook faster than the inside areas. For best results, try to cook pieces of similar size and shape together.

Height

As in conventional cooking, areas that are closer to the energy source cook faster. In most microwave ovens the energy source is at the top of the oven. For food to cook evenly, therefore, those portions that are close to the top may need to be shielded with pieces of aluminum foil. Moreover, the food may have to be turned over once during cooking time.

Density

Dense foods, like potatoes, roast beef, and carrots, take longer to cook than porous foods, such as cakes, ground beef, and apples, because it takes the microwaves longer to penetrate the denser substance. For example, a 2-pound roast will take longer than a 2-pound meat loaf.

Moisture Content

Moist food cooks faster than dry food because microwave energy is absorbed easily by the moisture within the food. One cup of sliced zucchini, for example, will cook faster than 1 cup of carrots because of the higher water content in the zucchini. In short, the amount of free moisture within a food affects how rapidly it cooks.

The high sugar content in the filling of a sweet roll will cause it to become very hot in an extremely short time. A plain roll reheats less quickly.

The amount of free moisture within a food will determine how fast it cooks. With less moisture than zucchini, carrots take a bit longer to cook in the microwave oven.

Storage temperature affects cooking time. Cold food takes longer to reheat than food at room temperature.

Delicate Ingredients

The term "delicate" refers to food that cooks so quickly in the microwave oven that it can easily overcook — toughen, separate, or curdle — mayonnaise, cheese, eggs, cream, and dairy sour cream, for example. Other food may "pop," such as snails, oysters, and chicken livers. For this reason, a lower power setting is often recommended for proper cooking. However, when these ingredients are mixed with other food, as in a casserole, stew, or soup, you may use a higher power setting, because the increased volume automatically slows down the cooking.

Sugar and Fat Content

Because microwave energy is drawn to sugar and fat, food high in these ingredients heats quicker than food which is low. For example, the fruit or cheese filling of a sweet roll will heat faster than the roll itself. And it will be hotter, since sugar and fat reach higher temperatures.

Starting Temperature

As in conventional cooking, the temperature at which food is placed in the microwave oven affects its cooking time. More time is needed to cook food just out of the refrigerator than food at room temperature. It takes longer, for example, to heat frozen green beans than canned green beans. By the same token, hot tap water comes to a boil sooner than cold water. Recipes in this book assume that food is at its normal storage temperature.

ABOUT COOKWARE

A wide variety of cookware and cooking utensils can be used in the microwave oven. To show that an item is safe and recommended for microwave cooking, we have created a new term, *microproof.* The Materials Checklist and *A Guide to Microproof Cookware* on the following pages will assist you in selecting the appropriate microproof utensil. With the exception of metal, most materials are microproof for at least a limited amount of cooking time. Unless specifically approved, however, items made of metal, even partially, are never to be used in the microwave oven, because they reflect microwaves and prevent them from passing into the food. In addition, metal that touches the oven sides will create a static charge and cause sparks, a condition known as arcing. Though arcing is not harmful to you, it will deface your oven. Metal twist ties or dishes and cups with gold or silver trim should not be used. See the Materials Checklist for metals approved for microwave cooking, such as metal clips attached to frozen turkey, or pieces of aluminum foil, used to shield certain areas of food to prevent overcooking.

When selecting a new piece of cookware, first check the manufacturer's directions. Also review the Materials Checklist and the *Guide to Microproof Cookware.* If you are still in doubt, try this test: Pour a cup of water into a glass measure and place in the oven next to the container or dish to be tested. Cook on HI for 1 minute. If the new dish feels hot, don't use it — it is absorbing microwave energy. If it feels warm, the dish may be used only for warming food. If it remains at room temperature, it is *microproof.*

The rapid growth of microwave cooking has created many new products for use in the microwave oven. Among these are microproof replacements for cookware for-

Glass is a superior microwave cooking material. Because glass is always acceptable, microproof is not cited when glass is recommended.

merly available only in metal. You'll find a wide variety at your store — cake, bundt, and muffin pans, roasting racks, etc. When you add these to traditional microproof cookware and the vast number of microproof plastic and paper products, you'll find that microwave cooking enables you to select from many more kinds of cookware than are available for conventional cooking.

Selecting Containers

Containers should accomodate the food being cooked. Whenever possible use round or oval dishes, because square corners in cookware attract higher concentrations of energy and tend to overcook food in those areas. Some cake and loaf recipes call for ring molds or bundt pans to facilitate more even cooking, inasmuch as the center of a round or oval dish generally cooks more slowly than the outside. Round cookware with a small glass inserted open-end up in the center works well to eliminate undercooked centers. When a particular size or shape of container is specified in a recipe, it should be used. Varying the container size or shape may change the results. A 2-quart casserole in a recipe refers to a bowl-shaped cooking dish with its own lid. A 12× 7-inch baking dish refers to a shallow cooking dish. For liquids, large containers are specified to prevent them from boiling over.

For best results, always try to use the dish cited in the recipe rather than substitute a different dish.

Materials Checklist

CHINA, POTTERY: Ideal for microwave use. However, if trimmed or glazed with metal, they are not microproof and should not be used.

GLASS: An excellent microwave cooking material. Especially useful for baking pies, insofar as its transparency allows you to check doneness of pie shells. Since oven-proof glass is always safe, "microproof" is not mentioned in any recipe where a glass item is specified.

METALS: *Not* suitable except as follows:
Small strips of aluminum foil can be used to cover areas on large pieces of meat or poultry that defrost or cook more rapidly than other areas — for example, a roast with exposed bones or thin ends, or the wings or breast bone of poultry. In microwave cooking this method is known as *shielding*.
Shallow aluminum frozen TV dinner trays with foil covers removed can be heated, provided the trays are not more than ¾-inch deep. However, microwaves can reach only the top surface of the food. TV dinners heat

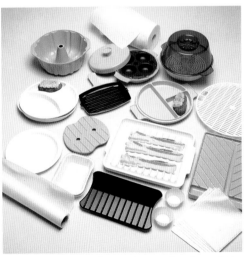

An impressive array of new microproof cookware has been created for microwave cooking. White paper products can also be used.

Many plastic items are safe for microwave cooking use. Be sure to check the manufacturer's recommendations to be sure.

much faster if you remove the food portions and cook them on a microproof dinner plate.

Frozen poultry containing metal clamps may be defrosted in your microwave oven without removing the clamps. Remove the clamps after defrosting.

Any item made of foil or metal must be kept at least 1 inch from oven walls.

WICKER AND WOOD: Can be used for quick warming, so long as no metal is present in the utensil. A word of caution: In some cases what appears to be wicker may actually be made of plastic-coated wire. Such materials are not approved for use in the microwave oven.

A GUIDE TO MICROPROOF COOKWARE

ITEM	GOOD USE	GENERAL NOTES
China plates, cups	Heating dinners and drinks.	No metal trim.
Cooking pouches (plastic)	Cooking meat, vegetables, rice, other frozen food.	Slit pouch so steam can escape.
Corelle® Livingware	Heating dinners, soups drinks.	Closed-handle cups should not be used.
Corning Ware® or Pyrex casseroles	Cooking main dishes, vegetables, desserts.	No metal trim
Microwave browning dishes or grills	Searing, grilling, and frying small meat items; grilling sandwiches; frying eggs.	These utensils are specially made to absorb microwaves and preheat to high temperatures. They brown food that otherwise would not brown in a microwave oven.
Microwave roasting racks	Cooking roasts and chickens, squash and potatoes.	Special racks are available for cooking bacon.
Oven film and cooking bags	Cooking roasts or stews.	Substitute string for metal twist ties. Bag itself will not cause tenderizing. Do not use film with foil edges.
Paper plates, cups, napkins	Heating hot dogs, drinks, rolls, appetizers, sandwiches.	Absorbs moisture from baked goods and freshens them. Paper plates and cups with wax coatings should not be used.
Plastic wrap	Covering dishes.	Fold back edge to ventilate, allowing steam to escape.
Pottery and earthenware plates, mugs, etc.	Heating dinners, soups, drinks.	Some pottery has a metallic glaze. To check, use dish test (page 16).
Soft plastics, sherbet cartons	Reheating leftovers for very short periods.	Used for very short reheating periods.
Thermometers	Measuring temperature of meat, poultry, or candy.	Use only approved microproof meat or candy thermometer in microwave oven. Microwave temperature probe is available with oven (see page 26).
TV dinner trays (aluminum)	Frozen dinners or homemade dinners.	No deeper than ¾ inch. Food will receive heat from top surface only. Foil covering food must be removed.
Waxed paper	Covering casseroles. Use as a tent.	Prevents splattering. Helps contain heat where a tight seal is not required. Food temperature may cause some melting.
Wooden spoons, wooden skewers, straw baskets	Stirring puddings and sauces; for shish kabobs, appetizers, warming breads.	Can withstand microwaves for short cooking periods. Be sure no metal fittings on wood or straw.

PAPER: Approved for short-term cooking and for reheating at low settings. These must not be foil-lined. Extended use may cause the paper to burn. Waxed paper is a suitable covering.

PLASTICS: Excellent products have been designed for microwave use. For best results, use only plastic utensils marked for microwave use and follow the manufacturer's instructions.

Use plastic wrap specifically recommended for microwave use. Plastics which melt from the heat of the food should not be used.

PLASTIC COOKING POUCHES: Can be used as long as they are marked for microwave cooking. Slit the pouch so steam can escape.

Browning Dish

Designed for microwave use only, a browning dish sears, grills, fries, or browns food. A special coating on the bottom of the dish absorbs microwave energy and becomes very hot when preheated empty in the microwave oven. A variety of such dishes are available. Follow the manufacturer's instructions for care and use and for the amount of time needed to preheat the dish.

After the dish is preheated, vegetable oil or butter may be added to enhance browning and to prevent food from sticking. Once food is placed on the preheated browning dish, microwave energy is attracted to the food, rather than to the dish itself. Since the hot surface of the dish browns the food, the food can be turned over to brown all sides. When cooking hamburger or moist foods, you may wish to pour off any juices before turning the food over. Because the dish cools rapidly, the longer you wait to turn the food, the less it will brown. You may need to drain the dish, wipe it out, and preheat it again. In doubling a recipe, such as for fried chicken, wipe out the browning dish after the first batch, preheat the empty dish, and repeat the process. A word of caution: The browning dish becomes *very* hot. Be sure to use potholders whenever a browning dish is in use.

Used as a grill, the browning dish reduces cooking time. However, if you wish to use the dish to brown certain foods prior to adding them to a recipe, your time will remain about the same. Some foods, such as eggs or sandwiches, require less heat for browning than do other foods, such as chicken or meat.

Glass Tray

The glass tray on the bottom of your microwave oven is the primary cooking level. It is made of glass to allow microwaves to pass through it and bounce off the oven bottom, thereby cooking the underside of the food. Glass is also easy to clean. Never operate the oven without the glass tray in place on the oven bottom.

Wire Rack

The wire rack provided with your oven is used mainly in whole meal cooking or when certain double quantities are desired. Made of specially engineered metal, the rack is safe for the microwave oven. The microwaves bounce off it and are absorbed by the food. When the wire rack is used, it must be placed on the upper or lower guides in the oven. Generally, for faster and more even cooking, it is best to cook in stages rather than on two oven levels at the same time. The rack should be removed from the oven when not in use.

ABOUT TECHNIQUES

The evenness and speed of microwave cooking are affected not only by the characteristics of the food itself, but also by certain techniques, which are described here. Some of these techniques are used in conventional cooking as well, but they have a particular application in microwave cooking because of the special qualities of microwave energy. Also included in this section are discussions of the many variables which affect cooking, defrosting, and reheating in the microwave oven. Becoming familiar with these variables, terms, and techniques will make microwave cooking easy and successful.

Rolled fish fillets and chicken legs are shown properly arranged for microwave cooking.

In microwave cooking, less microwave energy reaches the center of a dish. When possible, leave the center of a dish open for more even cooking results. Apple-Stuffed Acorn Squash (page 136) illustrates this principle.

Arrangement

How food is arranged in the oven and in the dish is directly related to how evenly and quickly your oven will defrost, heat, and cook. Since microwaves penetrate the outer portions first, foods should be arranged so that the denser, thicker areas are near the edge of the dish, and the thinner, more porous areas are near the center. When cooking broccoli, for example, split the heavy stalks to expose more area to the microwaves and then overlap with florets. Or you can alternate florets of cauliflower with broccoli. This will not only distribute the density of the food, which allows it to cook more evenly, but it creates an attractive dish as well. A nice touch. Similarly, place shrimp in a ring with the tails toward the center. Arrange chicken legs in a spoke-like fashion with the bony ends toward the center.

In microwave cooking, most items are arranged in a circle, rather than in rows. Muffins and potatoes are good examples of this principle.

Arrange potatoes end to end in a ring.

Turning Over

As in conventional cooking, large roasts, whole poultry, hams, or hamburgers may have to be turned over to brown each side and heat evenly. Food seared on a browning dish should be turned over. Microwave defrosting also frequently calls for food to be turned over.

Food that cannot be stirred, such as Swiss steak, may need to be rearranged in the dish to achieve the most uniform cooking results.

When a recipe recommends, rotate a baking dish one-quarter turn. rotate only if baked goods are rising unevenly.

Rearranging

Sometimes food that can't be stirred must be rearranged in the dish to allow it to heat evenly. Move the center food to the outside of the dish and outer food toward the center. Some poultry and beef recipes profit when the food is rearranged halfway through the cooking time.

Stirring

Less stirring is required in microwave cooking than in conventional cooking. When a recipe so indicates, however, stir from the outside to the center, because food on the outside cooks faster. In addition to helping food heat more evenly, stirring blends flavors.

Shielding

Certain thin or bony areas cook faster than thicker areas — the wing tips of poultry, the head and tail of fish, the breastbone of a turkey. Covering these parts with pieces of aluminum foil shields these areas from overcooking, since aluminum foil reflects microwaves. In addition to preventing thin parts of food from cooking more rapidly than thicker ones, shielding may be used during defrosting to cover those portions that defrost more quickly than others. Use aluminum foil only when recommended in recipes. Be careful to keep the foil at least 1 inch from the oven walls.

Rotating

A few foods, such as pies and cakes, that cannot be stirred, turned over, or rearranged, need to be given one-quarter or one-half turn in the oven to allow for even distribution of the microwave energy. Rotate only if the baked food is not cooking or rising evenly. Most foods do not need to be rotated.

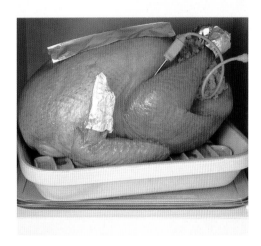

To prevent breast bone, wing tips, and leg tips of poultry from overcooking, shield them with small strips of aluminum foil.

Browning

Many foods do not brown in the microwave oven as much as they do in the conventional oven, and some do not brown at all. Depending upon the fat content, however, food that cooks longer than 15 minutes will brown somewhat in the microwave oven but it usually will not become crisp. However, bacon browns and crisps in minutes because of its high fat content. Poultry will not brown even after 15 minutes. As a general guideline, the longer the cooking time, or the higher the fat content, the more the food will brown.

For food that cooks too quickly to brown, such as hamburgers, fried eggs, steaks, or cutlets, a special browning dish is available (page 19). You can also create a browned look on roasts, poultry, steaks, and other foods by brushing on a browning agent, such as gravy mix, soy sauce, dehydrated onion soup mix, paprika, etc. Cakes, bread, and pie shells do not brown as they do in conventional cooking. Using chocolate, spices, or dark flour, however, gives them a browned appearance. In addition, you can create appealing color by adding frostings, toppings, glazes, or dark spices such as cinnamon.

Covering

Covers are used to trap steam, prevent dehydration, speed cooking, and help food retain its natural moisture. Suitably tight coverings include microproof casserole tops, glass covers, plastic wraps, oven bags, and microproof plates and saucers. Boilable freezer bags may be used as cooking containers for the frozen food inside. Pierce top with a knife to ventilate before cooking. When doing so, keep your face at a safe distance to prevent steam burns. Paper towels are especially useful as a light covering to prevent splatter and to absorb moisture. Waxed paper helps to retain heat and moisture.

Piercing

Because the skins and membranes of such foods as egg yolks, potatoes, liver, chicken giblets, eggplant, and squash retain moisture, it is necessary to pierce them before cooking. This allows steam to escape and prevents bursting during cooking time. For example, pierce sausage casing in several places before cooking. A toothpick may be used for egg yolks; a fork is best for potatoes. Pierce squash deeply several times with a long-tined fork.

Glass casserole lids are the most convenient covers for microwave cooking when you want to trap steam. Plastic wrap approved for microwave use by the manufacturer is used on dishes without lids.

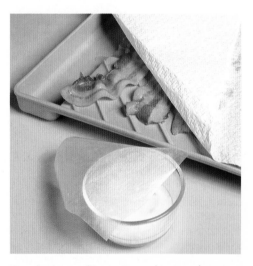

Waxed paper or white paper towels are used as covers in microwave cooking when splatters need to be contained but steam is not wanted.

Standing Time

This term refers to the time needed to cook or thaw food completely, once microwave time has ended. During the standing time, heat continues to be conducted from the outside to the center of the food. Food may remain in the oven during standing time, or it may be placed on a heatproof counter. This procedure is an essential part of food preparation with the microwave oven. Some foods, such as roasts, require standing time to reach their desired levels of doneness — rare, medium, or well done. Casseroles need standing time to allow the heat to spread evenly and to complete reheating or cooking. With cakes, pies, and quiches, standing time permits the center to finish cooking. During standing time outside the oven, place food on a flat surface, such as a heat-resistant breadboard or countertop, not on a cooling rack as you would if cooking with a conventional oven.

A flat surface is usually preferred for standing time following microwave cooking. Traditional cooling racks are seldom used.

Piercing allows steam to escape from items such as squash, potatoes, and egg yolks.

Beef roasts of the same weight illustrate the effect of standing time. The roast on the left was sliced immediately after the cooking time ended. The roast on the right was given its recommended 10-minute standing time and continued to cook to medium doneness.

Adjusting for High Altitudes

As in conventional cooking, microwave cooking at high altitudes requires adjustments in cooking time for leavened products like breads and cakes. Other food may require a slightly longer cooking time to become tender, since liquids boil there at a lower temperature. Usually, for every 3 minutes of microwave cooking time you must add 1 minute to compensate for the higher altitude. Therefore, a recipe calling for 3 minutes needs 4 minutes, and a recipe requiring 6 minutes needs 8 minutes. The wisest way to proceed is to start with the time given in the recipe and then check for doneness before cooking further. Remember: You can always add time, but you can't subtract it once a food is overcooked. Here, again, your judgment is vital.

It may be advisable to consult your local utility for specific information about your area.

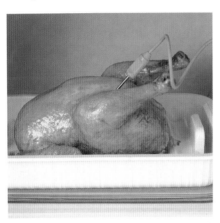

The temperature probe is one of the most convenient special features of your oven. Proper positioning for ham (any large roast) is illustrated.

The temperature probe is inserted into the inside thigh muscle of poultry without touching bone. Probe spacer helps maintain proper position.

Soups, casseroles, and similar dishes can be cooked using the temperature probe. Cover with plastic wrap and tuck wrap around the probe.

The oven's control panel has been designed for ease of operation and accuracy. A display window at the top of the oven monitors the time of day, cooking time, and other functions of the oven, selected by using the touch pads below.

Your microwave oven gives you the ability to select from many power settings from 0% to HI (100%). These settings give you flexibility and control, just as in conventional cooking. Selection of the appropriate power settings is not difficult. You simply touch the POWER CONTROL touch pad, followed by the numbered touch pads for the power setting you want. The maximum power setting, HI, appears automatically as soon as you touch POWER CONTROL. Obviously, the oven does not operate at 0% power but you can use this setting when you want to set standing time as part of a cooking sequence. (You can also use the 0% setting when you simply want to use the clock as a timer to remind you about an errand, or other needs.)

The control panel lists the main power control settings and gives them familiar cooking terms. We have also included a guide on page 26 with more complete descriptions. You may find, however, that other settings work best for you. You may want to warm certain foods on 13 or 15, for example.

Touch Pads

The touch pads on the oven control panel need only to be touched to be activated. A beep tone assures that the setting is being entered. In addition to the POWER CONTROL touch pad and the numbered pads, the TIME, TIME OF DAY, MEMORY/RECALL, PAUSE, TEMP CONTROL, CLEAR, START, and STOP pads enable you to select the many features of your oven.

The TIME touch pad is used to set the actual cooking time desired, in combination with the numbered pads. The maximum time setting possible is 99 minutes and 99 seconds. Keep in mind, for example, that "10" means ten seconds; you must set 10:00 for ten minutes.

The PAUSE touch pad is used in setting multiple-stage cooking procedures when a pause is desired between cooking functions. The MEMORY/RECALL touch pad is used in multiple-stage cooking when a pause is not desired between cooking functions, although there is a change in the power setting.

The TEMP CONTROL touch pad is used in temperature probe cooking only, in combination with the numbered pads. The TIME OF DAY touch pad is only used to set or change the digital clock. Like all electric clocks, it must be reset after a power failure.

The CLEAR touch pad removes any previously set data. It is used, for example, if you decide to stop cooking before the programmed time has ended, or if a mistake is made when entering cooking time, power setting, etc. Finally, the START and STOP touch pads do exactly what they say. Before any cooking can begin, you must touch

START. However, you can also stop the oven simply by opening the oven door. To resume cooking, simply close the door and touch START again. You might use the STOP touch pad, for example, if you want to put a "hold" on the food being cooked without opening the oven door. When you touch START, the oven will resume cooking where it left off. Isn't that convenient!

Your oven may also be equipped with touch pads for special features such as STOP TIME, AUTO DEFROST, or PROGRAMMED DEFROST. Please consult your Use & Care Manual for information about their use.

TEMPERATURE PROBE

When inserted into the food, the temperature probe enables you to cook food to a preselected internal temperature. When the desired temperature is reached, the oven automatically holds food warm up to 1½ hours. Instead of setting the oven to a certain number of minutes, you set the probe at the exact temperature you want the food to reach prior to standing time to

GUIDE FOR POWER CONTROL SETTINGS

Main Setting	Suggested Cooking Uses
1	Raising bread dough
10 (warm)	Softening cream cheese; keeping casseroles and main dishes warm.
20 (low)	Softening chocolate; reheating breads, rolls, pancakes, tacos, tortillas, and French toast; clarifying butter; taking chill out of fruit; heating small amounts of food.
30 (defrost)	Thawing meat, poultry, and seafood; finish cooking casseroles, stews, and some sauces; cooking small quantities of most food.
40 (braise)	Cooking less tender cuts of meat in liquid and slow cooking dishes, finish cooking less tender roasts.
50 (simmer)	Cooking stews and soups after bringing to a boil; cooking baked custards and pasta.
60 (bake)	Cooking scrambled eggs; cakes
70 (roast)	Cooking rump roast, ham, veal, and lamb; cooking cheese dishes; cooking eggs, and milk; cooking quick breads and cereal products.
80 (reheat)	Quickly reheating precooked or prepared food; heating sandwiches.
90 (sauté)	Quickly cooking onions, celery, and green peppers; reheating meat slices quickly.
HI (max. power)	Cooking tender cuts of meat; cooking poultry, fish, vegetables, and most casseroles; preheating the browning dish; boiling water; thickening some sauces; cooking muffins. Cooking whole meal, i.e. two or three dishes at once.

attain desired doneness. The oven must also be set for the power level at which the food is to be cooked. The probe provides accuracy in cooking almost any food, from instant coffee and sauces to beef casseroles and roast chicken. You can even watch the display window as the food reaches the selected temperature.

The probe must be carefully and properly inserted in the food for the best results. The probe tip should be in the center of the dish, cup, or casserole or in the thickest portion of the meat. Do not allow the probe to touch bone, fat, or any metal foil being used as a shield. After using the probe, remove it from the oven. Use warm, soapy water to wash the part that contacted the food. Rinse and dry. Do not immerse the probe in water or wash it in a dishwasher.

The *Suggested Temperature Probe Settings* guide provides a range from 120°F to 180°F. Follow the directions in the recipes for placement of the probe and covering of the dish, if specified, and consult the "Tips for Probe Use" for step-by-step directions.

Standing Time

Standing time is essential for most food to reach its optimum serving temperature. Because of the nature of microwave energy, during standing time the temperature of most food rises about 5°F to 15°F. For example, after 10 minutes of standing time, the temperature of rare beef will reach 135°F; well done lamb will reach its proper serving temperature of 170°F to 180°F. The temperature of beverages, however, drops in 10 minutes from 150°F to 135°F.

Tips for Probe Use

The temperature probe is not difficult to use. Place food in container, as recipe directs. Position temperature probe in the food with the first inch of the probe secured in the center of the food. Probe should not touch bone or a fat pocket. Probe should be inserted from the side or the front, not from the top of the food, except when inserting into casseroles, a cup of soup, etc. Try to insert probe as close to a horizontal position as possible.

Suggested Temperature Probe Settings
120°F Rare Beef, Fully Cooked Ham
130°F Medium Beef
140°F Fish Steaks and Fillets, Well Done Beef
150°F Vegetables, Hot Drinks, Soups, Casseroles
155°F Veal
165°F Well Done Lamb, Well Done Pork
170°F Poultry Parts
180°F Well Done Whole Poultry

Refer to individual Cooking Guides (see index) for specific instructions.

Plug the probe into the receptacle on side wall of oven cavity. Make sure the end of the temperature probe, inserted in the food, does not touch the cooking container, or the sides of the oven.

Touch CLEAR. Touch TEMP CONTROL. Enter desired internal temperature of the food. Touch POWER CONTROL. Set power desired. Touch START. That's all there is to it.

Never operate the oven with the temperature probe in the cavity unless the probe is plugged in and inserted into food.

COOKING CASSEROLES

The microwave oven is exceptionally good for cooking casseroles. Vegetables keep their bright fresh color and crisp texture. Meat is tender and flavorful. There is no heat source in the microwave oven, of course, so you can look to easier clean-up with no food stuck to the bottom of the casserole dish. If you follow the information here and the specific instructions given with the many casserole recipes in this book, you will find yourself looking to the microwave oven for all your casserole cookery.

Casseroles are usually covered with plastic wrap or glass lids during cooking. That's because you usually want to trap moisture within the dish, in the form of steam. But be sure to leave the dish uncovered if you have added a cheese topping, crushed potato chips, or similar casserole toppings.

Allow casseroles to stand 5 to 10 minutes before serving, according to size. Standing time allows the center of the casserole to complete cooking.

You will obtain best results if you make ingredients uniform in size, stirring occasionally to distribute heat. If the ingredients are of different sizes, stir more often.

Casseroles containing less tender meats should be cooked on a low power setting, such as 50 or 30, for longer than usual microwave times. This provides an effect much like simmering on a stove top, providing tenderizing and flavor development.

Reheating Casseroles

Most casseroles can be made ahead of time, refrigerated or frozen, then reheated later in the microwave before serving. A few general guidelines are all you need to know to thaw and reheat casseroles. This information also applies to soups, stews, or any food you would cook in a casserole and then freeze in the casserole or in one- or two-serving containers.

Broth-based soups or casseroles high in liquid content are thawed/reheated by starting on HI and reducing the microwave power to 50 halfway through the recommended time. Stir twice.

Thick or cream-based soups and stirrable casseroles should begin thawing at 70. The power setting should be reduced to 30 halfway through the recommended time.

Recommended times are: 1 pint, 10 to 15 minutes; 1 quart, 25 to 35 minutes. For 2 quarts, thaw/reheat 35 to 40 minutes. And for 4 quarts, the time is 45 to 55 minutes.

If your casserole is at refrigerator temperature, reheat for one-third the time recommended above for frozen casseroles. Or, you can use the temperature probe. Cook on 70 with the temperature probe set at 130°F. Stir and continue to reheat on 70 with the temperature probe set at 150°F.

REHEATING DINNER PLATES

How nice it will be to no longer worry about a hot meal for those late arrivals. A plate of food reheats quickly and there is virtually no moisture loss, so food retains its just-cooked appeal. Arrange food on a microproof plate with dense food, like meat and potatoes, around the outside edge of the plate, and less dense food, like green vegetables, toward the center. Cover plate with waxed paper. Cook on 80 for 1½ to 2 minutes. If the plate feels warm, the food is probably heated through. (The warmth of the food, *not the microwaves* produces the warm plate.) If the plate of food has been refrigerated for a while, cook on 80, 2 to 2½ minutes before checking.

Other Reheating Tips

As you can see, reheating is one of the major assets of this oven. Not only does most food reheat quickly, but it also retains moisture and its just-cooked flavor. Throughout the book, you will find charts that provide reheating information for many of the popular convenience foods. There are so many variances, however, that the best general guide will be the package itself. Always reheat for the minimum recommended time, then check.

Use 80 except when otherwise specified. You can use the temperature probe for reheating casseroles, beverages, and other appropriate food. Insert temperature probe into the largest or most dense piece of food and cook with the temperature probe set at 150°F to 160°F.

Dense food, such as mashed potatoes and casseroles, cooks more quickly and evenly if a depression is made in the center, or if the food is shaped in a ring.

To retain moisture during reheating, cover food with plastic wrap or a microproof lid.

Spread food out in a shallow container, rather than piling it high, for quicker and more even heating.

There is no better way to learn than to do it yourself. Now it's time for some practical experience using your Kenmore microwave oven. Let's turn our "cooking school" into a traveling kitchen for the preparation of some simple recipes to acquaint you with the easy features of your new oven. First, a quick hot drink, then a continental breakfast, and, finally, an easy and nutritious lunch. You should have read the introductory chapters and checked your Use & Care Manual. Aprons on! Let's begin.

LESSON ONE

Uses the HI power setting because it is best when you want to heat liquids quickly.

Take your favorite mug or cup, making sure it has no gold or silver trim. (If you are not certain your mug is microproof, test it as directed on page 16.) Follow these step-by-step directions:

1. Fill mug with water and place on the glass tray, in the center of the oven. Close the oven door.

2. Touch CLEAR. (This is usually not a necessary step unless previously set information remains.)

3. Touch TIME. Then touch 2-0-0. Your oven is now set to cook on HI for 2 minutes. *It was not necessary to touch POWER CONTROL because your oven is automatically on HI unless changed to another setting.*

4. Now touch START.

5. The oven will signal with a tone when the 2 minutes are up. The oven turns off automatically. Open the door.

6. Remove the mug. The handle will be cool enough to hold and the cup warm from the heated water.

7. Stir in instant coffee, tea, or soup.

Enjoy as you graduate to Lesson Two.

LESSON TWO

Power settings HI and 20 bring us a simple continental breakfast.

Frozen Orange Juice
Sweet Roll
Instant Coffee

1. Spoon frozen juice into a microproof serving pitcher and place in the oven.

2. Touch TIME. Touch 3-0. Touch START. Oven will soften juice concentrate on HI for 30 seconds. (Recall that it is not necessary to touch CLEAR or POWER CONTROL to cook on HI.)

3. At the signal, remove serving pitcher from the oven. Set aside.

4. Prepare coffee as directed in Lesson One.

5. Set sweet roll on napkin-lined paper plate and place in the oven.

6. Touch TIME. Touch 3-0. Touch POWER CONTROL. Touch 2-0. Touch START. The oven will warm the sweet roll on 20% power setting for 30 seconds.

7. Add required amount of water to juice concentrate and stir briskly. Pour juice.

8. At signal, remove sweet roll from the oven and relax with the morning paper and your first microwave breakfast.

Bakery products should be just warm to the touch because they will be hotter just below the surface. Be conservative in setting reheating time for bakery. The microwaves are especially attracted to the sweet filling, so be careful. While the roll will be nicely warm, the filling may be very hot.

LESSON THREE

The temperature probe helps prepare a quick and easy soup-and-sandwich luncheon.

1 bowl (12 ounces) soup
1 hot dog
1 hot dog bun

1. Pour soup into microproof serving bowl and place in oven. Insert temperature probe into center of bowl. Cover loosely with plastic wrap (not shown), tucking around probe.

2. Touch TEMP CONTROL. Touch 1-1-5. Touch POWER CONTROL. Touch 8-0. Touch START. Oven will reheat soup to 115°F at 80% power setting.

3. At signal, stir soup, using care not to remove temperature probe. Touch TEMP CONTROL. Touch 1-5-0. Touch POWER CONTROL. Touch 8-0. Touch START.

4. At signal, soup will be heated through to 150°F. Set aside. (Be sure to remove the temperature probe from the oven.)

5. Score hot dog and place on a microproof plate. Set plate in the oven. Let's set the oven for a two-stage cooking procedure.

6. Touch TIME. Touch 4-5. Touch PAUSE. Touch TIME. Touch 1-5. Touch START. The oven will cook the hot dog, then pause so you can add the bun.

7. At signal, "1-5" will appear in display window. Open door and place hot dog in bun. Close door and touch START.

8. At signal, bring on the mustard and enjoy the classic American lunch.

ADAPTING YOUR RECIPES

You will undoubtedly want to cook some of your favorite conventional recipes in the microwave oven. With a little thought and experimenting you can convert many recipes. Before converting a recipe, study it to determine if it will adapt well to microwave cooking. Look for a recipe in the book that matches your conventional one most closely. For example, find a recipe with the same amount, type, and form of main ingredient, such as 1 pound ground meat or 2 pounds beef cut in 1-inch pieces, etc. Then compare other ingredients, such as pasta or vegetables. The microwave recipe will probably call for less liquid, because there is so little evaporation in microwave cooking.

At the beginning of each recipe chapter, hints on adapting recipes are provided. Of course, each recipe contains detailed instructions and timing recommendations. You can use that information as a guide in determining timing and power settings for those recipes you wish to adapt. Also use the additional suggestions here.

Candies, bar cookies, meat loaf, and certain baked goods may not need adjustments in ingredients.

In puddings, cakes, sauces, gravies, and some casseroles, liquids should be reduced.

Most converted recipes will require adjustments in cooking time. Although a "rule of thumb" always has exceptions, you can generally assume that most microwave recipes are cooked in about one-quarter to one-third of the conventional recipe time.

Check for doneness after one-quarter of the time before continuing to cook.

Now let's try converting a conventional recipe to the microwave oven. Suppose you have a favorite recipe for Chicken Marengo that you would like to prepare in your microwave oven. The closest recipe in this book turns out to be Chicken Cacciatore (page 85). Let's take a detailed look at both recipes and the conversion process.

CHICKEN MARENGO
(Conventional Style)

4 to 6 servings

   ½ **cup flour**
   1 **teaspoon salt**
   ½ **teaspoon pepper**
   1 **teaspoon tarragon**
   1 **chicken (3 pounds), cut up**
   ¼ **cup olive oil**
   ¼ **cup butter**
   1 **cup dry white wine**
   2 **cups canned tomatoes**
   1 **clove garlic, finely chopped**
   8 **mushrooms (½ pound), sliced**
      Chopped parsley

Preheat oven to 350°F. Mix flour, salt, pepper, and tarragon, and dredge chicken with seasoned flour. Reserve remaining flour.

In skillet, heat oil and butter, and brown chicken. Place chicken in large casserole. Add reserved flour to the fat in skillet and, using a wire whisk, gradually stir in wine. When sauce is thickened and smooth, pour over the chicken and add the tomatoes, garlic, and mushrooms. Cover casserole and bake until chicken is tender, about 45 minutes. When done, sprinkle with parsley.

Checking the Chicken Cacciatore recipe, you'll notice that the amount of liquid is quite a bit less than in the conventional Chicken Marengo recipe. That's because liquids do not reduce in microwave cooking, and we don't want a thin sauce. Notice, too, that the onion is cooked first to be sure it is tender and that the flavor of the dish is fully developed. In converting, the Chicken Marengo recipe has the liquid reduced, and the garlic is cooked first. Since the volume of food is about the same, the cooking times and power settings for Chicken Cacciatore are followed for Chicken Marengo, converted to microwave cooking. Here's the converted recipe:

CHICKEN MARENGO
(Microwave Style)
Cooking Time: 31 to 36 minutes

- 1 **chicken (3 pounds), cut up**
- 1 **teaspoon salt**
- ½ **teaspoon pepper**
- 1 **teaspoon tarragon**
- 1 **clove garlic, minced**
- 1 **tablespoon butter**
- 1 **tablespoon olive oil**
- ¼ **cup all-purpose flour**
- ½ **cup dry white wine**
- 2 **cups canned tomatoes**
- 8 **mushrooms (½ pound), sliced**
   Chopped parsley

Rub chicken with salt, pepper, and tarragon and set aside. Place garlic, butter, and olive oil in 3-quart microproof casserole. Cover with casserole lid and cook on HI, 1 minute. Add flour and stir until smooth, gradually adding wine. Stir in tomatoes and mushrooms. Cook, covered, on HI, 5 minutes; stir. Add chicken, immersing pieces in sauce. Cover and cook on HI, 25 to 30 minutes, or until chicken is tender. Sprinkle with chopped parsley. Let stand, covered, 5 minutes before serving.

4 to 6 servings

Butter, olive oil, and flour have been reduced, since browning is not part of the microwave recipe. If you wish, however, add more butter and olive oil, dredge chicken in flour, and brown chicken in preheated browning dish. The white wine has been reduced to enable the sauce to thicken.

ABOUT LOW CALORIES

Scattered throughout the book are reduced-calorie suggestions and naturally low-calorie recipes. In general, you can reduce calories in many recipes by making the following substitutions.

You can significantly reduce calories by

substituting bouillon or water for butter when sautéing onions or cooking vegetables and other foods.

Many vegetables can be substituted for rice, potatoes, or pasta. Spaghetti squash, for example, can fool almost anybody, and mashed cauliflower is a fine potato stand-in.

Well-trimmed meat not only offers far fewer calories than fatty cuts but also reduces cholesterol intake.

A wide variety of skim milk-based cheeses are available today, and you'll never know the difference when substituting for whole milk cheeses.

If you take advantage of the natural juices produced when cooking rather than using flour, cream, or butter-based gravies and sauces, you can significantly reduce your calorie intake.

Fruits cooked in their natural juices are the "natural choice" for the calorie-counters among us. In fact, some people think sugar masks the taste of good fruit.

Removing the skin and fat from poultry is also a good way to cut calories. And, today, we are fortunate to have turkey and chicken, skinned and boned, readily available in a wide variety of packages at the market.

BY THE WAY . . .

To get the greatest pleasure out of your microwave oven, keep in mind that certain food is best cooked by conventional cooking methods. The following paragraphs present comments on several foods that you should continue to prepare with a conventional cooking appliance.

Eggs should not be cooked in the shell, because the light membrane surrounding the yolk collects energy, which then causes a steam build-up that could explode the egg. Don't experiment. It's a mess to clean up!

We don't approve of using the oven for deep-fat frying, because the confined environment of the oven is not suited to the handling of the food or oil, and it is not a safe procedure.

Pancakes should not be cooked from batter in the oven because no crust forms. (But the oven is great for reheating pancakes, waffles, and similar items.)

Popovers belong in the conventional oven because of the slow steam development necessary to make them rise.

Home canning should not be attempted in the oven because it is impossible to judge exact boiling temperatures inside a jar and you cannot be sure that the temperature and length of cooking are sufficient to prevent contamination of the food.

Chiffon and angel food cakes do not bake well in the microwave oven because they require steady, dry heat to rise and be tender.

Do not heat bottles with small necks, like those for syrups and toppings, because they are apt to break from the pressure build-up.

Large items and quantities, such as a 25-pound turkey or a dozen baking potatoes should not be cooked in the oven because the space is not adequate and no time is saved.

Finally, do not attempt to make popcorn in a paper bag. The corn may dehydrate and overheat, causing the paper bag to catch on fire. If you use a special microwave popcorn device, carefully follow the instructions provided with that product.

School's out. Well, not quite. We will continue to help you along the way with brief "refresher courses" to start off each chapter. We hope your experiences with this oven will bring you your most successful cooking results. And now, LET'S GET COOKING!

Large poultry may need some areas to be shielded during defrosting. If an area feels even slightly warm, cover with small strips of foil.

Fish fillets and similar items should be separated halfway through microwave defrosting time. Return unthawed pieces to the oven.

To defrost ground meat without having portions cook, scrape off thawed pieces with a fork once or twice during defrosting time.

DEFROSTING

One of the most important functions designed into this microwave oven is its superior ability to defrost food. It uses all the latest technology to speed and simplify one of our most frequent and aggravating kitchen chores. Well, yes, often the aggravation is our own fault because we forgot to take something out of the freezer. But that doesn't matter anymore. Detailed defrosting guides are provided throughout the book to aid in your preparation of the food discussed in the recipe chapters. Here, as a special convenience, many common and important microwave defrosting techniques have been presented to acquaint you with the basics. You'll also want to spend more time reviewing the defrosting instructions in your Use and Care Manual, especially if your oven is equipped with the Auto Defrost or Programmed Defrost features. Many of the same principles and techniques that apply to microwave cooking also apply to microwave defrosting and heating.

Microwaves are attracted to water or moisture molecules. As soon as microwaves have thawed a portion of the item, they are more attracted to the thawed portion. The frozen portion continues to thaw, but this is due to the warmth produced in the thawed portion. Special techniques, such as shielding and rotating, are helpful to be sure the thawed portion does not cook before the rest defrosts. It is often necessary to turn, stir, and separate to assist the defrosting process. Defrosting requires standing time to complete. Because food differs in size, weight, and density, recommended defrosting times can only be approximate. Additional standing time may be necessary to defrost completely. Read the defrosting guides throughout the book for times, power control settings, and special instructions about defrosting specific foods. Here are some tips to aid you toward fast and easy defrosting.

Helpful Tips

Plastic-wrapped packages from the supermarket meat department may not be wrapped with a plastic wrap recommended for microwave use. Regardless, we recommend removing all meat, poultry, and seafood packaging before defrosting. This is because steam can develop inside the closed package and cause portions to begin cooking.

Metal clips in poultry may be left in until it becomes possible to remove them. They should always be removed before cooking. Metal twists on bags should be replaced with rubber bands.

Vegetables are usually packaged to go right into the microwave for defrosting and heating to serving temperature. It is not necessary to use a defrost power control setting (usually 30) for frozen vegetables. They defrost/reheat on HI.

Poultry wings, legs, and the small or bony ends of meat or fish may need to be covered with pieces of aluminum foil for part of the thawing time to prevent cooking while the remainder thaws.

Large items should be turned and rotated halfway through defrosting time to provide more even thawing.

Food textures influence thawing time. Because of air space, porous foods like cake and bread defrost more quickly than a solid mass, such as a sauce, or roast.

Do not thaw food wrapped in aluminum or in foil dishes. Traditional TV dinners in foil trays may be reheated, if desired, with top foil covering removed. Keep tray l-inch from oven walls.

The edges will begin cooking if meat, fish, and seafood are completely thawed in the microwave oven. Therefore, food should still be icy in the center when removed from oven. It will finish thawing while standing.

Remove portions of ground meat as soon as thawed, returning frozen portions to the oven.

Thin or sliced items, such as fish fillets, meat patties, etc., should be separated as soon as possible. Remove thawed pieces and allow others to continue thawing.

Casseroles, saucy foods, vegetables, and soups should be stirred once or twice during defrosting to redistribute heat.

Frozen fried foods may be defrosted but will not be crisp when heated in the microwave oven. Of course, new products are introduced every day and we have even seen French fries specially packaged for microwave reheating.

Freezing Tips

It is helpful to freeze in small quantities rather than in one large piece. This will promote more even microwave defrosting.

When freezing casseroles, it's a good idea to insert an empty paper cup in the center so no food is present there. This speeds thawing. Depressing the center of ground meat when freezing also hastens thawing later.

The microwave oven is an excellent appliance to use in preparing vegetables for freezing. A special microwave blanching guide is provided in the vegetables chapter.

The wire rack offers a convenient option in reheating appetizers quickly. Reheat on 80, 2 to 3 minutes. Reverse dish positions at 1½ minutes.

BBQ Baby Back Ribs (page 39) are prepared for microwave cooking in a glass baking dish. Glass is always safe for microwave cooking.

The familiar circular arrangement of food for microwave cooking is illustrated with Honey-Sesame Chicken Wings (page 39).

APPETIZERS

Appetizers can be the most creative food of today's entertaining. They can be hot or cold, simple or fancy, light or hearty, depending upon the occasion. There are no rules, so you can let your imagination soar. Until now, hot appetizers were the most troublesome and time-consuming part of a special event for the host or hostess. But that's no longer true with the microwave oven. Parties are much easier and more enjoyable because the microwave eliminates all that last-minute hassle and lengthy cooking over a hot stove, or tending a hot oven. You can assemble most appetizers and nibbles in advance, and at the right moment, just coolly "heat 'n serve!" This chapter presents many recipes for entertaining your guests, but you'll also be tempted to prepare delicious snacks and munchies just for the family. There's no doubt about it — appetizers cooked in the microwave oven are fun to make, fun to serve, and fun to eat. We hope you enjoy the collection provided here.

ADAPTING YOUR RECIPES

Most of your favorite hot appetizers will adapt well to microwave cooking, except for those wrapped in pastry. The microwave oven simply cannot provide the hot, dry environment pastry requires to become crisp. However, you can certainly reheat them quickly in the microwave.

The recipe for Rumaki (page 39) is an ideal guide for countless skewered appetizers containing seafood, chicken, vegetable, and fruit combinations. Trader Bob's Kabobs (page 39) is another guide you can use for similar finger foods. There are probably more than 25 different popular approaches to stuffed mushrooms, too, and we invite you to let the Mozzarella Mushrooms (page 38) be your guide to cooking them in the microwave oven. Dips, of course, also adapt easily and microwave defrosting on HI can bail us out of those unexpected moments when guests just drop in.

Helpful Tips

Appetizers and dips that contain cheese, mayonnaise, and other such delicate ingredients are usually heated on 70. A higher setting might cause separation or drying.

The temperature probe set at 130°F on 70 provides an excellent alternative for heating hot dips containing seafood, cheese, or food to be served in a chafing dish or fondue pot.

Because of its very delicate nature, a sour cream dip should be covered and heated on 10.

Toppings for canapés can be made ahead, but do not place on bread or crackers until just before heating to assure a crisp base.

Cover appetizers or dips only when the recipe specifies doing so. Use fitted glass lids, waxed paper, plastic wrap, or paper towels.

You can heat two batches of the same or similar appetizers at one time by using both oven levels, the wire rack and bottom glass tray, for almost double the time of one batch. Watch closely because those on top may cook more quickly than those on bottom.

BURGUNDY-BAKED BRIE

Cooking Time: 3 minutes

    1 **small wheel (8 ounces) Brie cheese**
    2 **tablespoons Burgundy wine**
    ½ **teaspoon grated lemon peel**
       Grapes
       Apple wedges
       Crackers

Place cheese in center of round microproof serving platter. Score top with sharp knife in criss-cross fashion, cutting about ¼ inch deep. Pour wine over cheese. Sprinkle with lemon peel. Cover with waxed paper and cook on 50, 3 minutes. Surround with grapes, apple wedges, and crackers, and serve at once.

2 to 4 servings

If necessary, return to oven and reheat on 50, 1 to 1½ minutes while serving to keep cheese warm and slightly melted.

REHEATING GUIDE — APPETIZERS*

Food	Power	Cook Time	Special Notes
Dips, cream ½ cup	10	1½ — 2½ min.	Cover with plastic wrap.
Eggrolls, 6 oz. (12)		follow package directions	
Meat spread 4 oz. can	80	30 — 45 sec.	Use microproof bowl.
Sausages, 5 oz. can	80	1½ — 2 min.	Use microproof casserole. Cover.
Tacos, mini, 5½ oz.		follow package directions	

* Due to the tremendous variety in convenience food products available, times given here should be used only as guidelines. We suggest you cook food for the shortest recommended time and then check for doneness. Be sure to check the package for microwave instructions.

MOZZARELLA MUSHROOMS

Cooking Time: 12 to 14 minutes

    24 **large fresh mushrooms (about 8 ounces)**
     2 **slices bacon, chopped**
     2 **green onions, chopped**
     ½ **cup seasoned dry bread crumbs**
     1 **tablespoon chopped fresh parsley**
     6 **ounces mozzarella cheese, cut into 24 cubes**

Wipe mushrooms with a damp towel. Remove caps and set aside. Finely chop stems. In a 4-cup glass mesure, combine mushroom stems, bacon, and green onions. Cover with plastic wrap and cook on HI, 1½ minutes. Pour off fat. Stir in bread crumbs and parsley. Mound bread crumb mixture in mushroom caps. Arrange half the mushrooms in a ring on microproof plate. Cover with waxed paper. Cook on HI, 3½ to 4 minutes.

Push cheese cube into center of each mushroom. Cook on HI, 1 to 1½ minutes or until cheese melts. Repeat with remaining mushrooms.

24 appetizers

BBQ BABY BACK RIBS

Cooking Time: 26½ to 27 minutes

 **2 pounds pork loin back ribs,
cut into 2-inch pieces**
 ¼ cup honey
 2 tablespoons ketchup
 1 tablespoon soy sauce
 ½ teaspoon celery seed

Place ribs in 2½-quart microproof casserole and set aside. Combine honey, ketchup, soy sauce, and celery seed in 2-cup glass measure. Cover with plastic wrap and cook on HI, 1½ to 2 minutes, or until bubbly. Stir sauce and pour over ribs. Cover and cook on HI, 5 minutes. Rearragne ribs. Cover and cook on 50, 20 minutes. Let stand, covered, 5 minutes.

about 40 appetizers

Ask your butcher to cut the ribs for you. When prepared, these ribs are wonder finger food for any party. Provide those handy finger wipes, available in the paper goods section of your market, and your guests will dig in with gusto.

RUMAKI

Cooking Time: 14 to 16 minutes

 **½ pound chicken livers,
rinsed and drained**
 ¼ cup soy sauce
 ¼ teaspoon garlic powder
 18 thin slices bacon, cut in half
 **1 can (8 ounces) sliced water
chestnuts, drained**

Cut chicken livers into 36 1-inch pieces. Discard membranes; set livers aside. Combine soy sauce and garlic powder; set aside. Place 1 piece liver on 1 piece bacon. Top with water chestnut. Roll up and fasten with wooden toothpick. Repeat with remaining liver pieces. Dip each into soy sauce mixture. Place 18 rumaki on microproof baking sheet and cover with paper towel. Cook on HI, 7 to 8 minutes. Repeat for remaining rumaki.

36 appetizers

HONEY-SESAME CHICKEN WINGS

Cooking Time: 29½ to 31½ minutes

 12 chicken wings (about 1½ pounds)
 ½ cup honey
 1 teaspoon Dijon-style mustard
 ½ cup sesame seed

Cut chicken wings apart at both joints; discard tips. Pat dry with paper towels; set aside. Combine honey and mustard in 1-cup glass measure. Cover with plastic wrap. Cook on HI, 1½ minutes.

Brush wings with honey mixture, then roll in sesame seed. Arrange 12 pieces in a spoke pattern on 10-inch microproof plate, with thickest parts toward outside of plate. Cover with paper towel. Cook on HI, 14 to 15 minutes, depending on thickness of wings. Repeat with remaining pieces.

24 appetizers

TRADER BOB'S KABOBS

Cooking Time: 8 to 12 minutes

 **1 whole chicken breast, skinned,
boned, and cut into 1-inch chunks**
 **1 medium green pepper,
cut into 1-inch chunks**
 **1 can (8 ounces) pineapple chunks,
drained**
 Citrus Sauce (page 148)
 Peanut Colada Sauce (page 152)

Alternate chicken chunks with green pepper and pineapple on 12 6-inch wooden skewers. Place kabobs in shallow dish. Pour Citrus Sauce over kabobs. Cover with plastic wrap and refrigerate 2 hours.

Arrange kabobs in spoke pattern on microwave roasting rack. Cook on 50, 8 to 12 minutes, or until chicken is done. Rearrange and baste once during cooking time. Serve with Peanut Colada Sauce.

12 kabobs

ALMOND CHICKEN LIVER DIP

Cooking Time: 4 to 4½ minutes

- 1 **pound chicken livers**
- 1 **medium onion, chopped**
- 2 **tablespoons butter or margarine**
- ½ **teaspoon rosemary**
- ½ **teaspoon thyme**
- 1 **cup chopped almonds**
- 2 **tablespoons dry sherry**

Rinse chicken livers and pat dry. Pierce each with toothpick. In 4-cup glass measure, combine livers, onion, butter, rosemary, and thyme. Cover with plastic wrap. Cook on HI, 4 to 4½ minutes, or until livers are no longer pink, stirring once. Pour off all but 2 tablespoons of the juices. Place liver mixture in food processor or blender. Add nuts and sherry. Purée until mixture is smooth.

2½ cups

A steamed artichoke (Guide, page 129) with choke removed makes an attractive, edible container for this lovely dip. Surround with raw vegetables.

CHILI CON QUESO DIP

Cooking Time: 5 to 5½ minutes

- 1 **can (8 ounces) tomatoes, drained and chopped**
- 1 **large onion, chopped**
- 2 **tablespoons chopped green chilies**
- 1 **small clove garlic, minced**
- 1 **tablespoon Worcestershire sauce**
- 1 **pound Cheddar cheese, shredded**

Combine tomatoes, onions, peppers, garlic, and Worcestershire in 1-quart microproof casserole. Cover with casserole lid and cook on HI, 3 minutes. Stir in cheese. Cover and cook on 70, 2 to 2½ minutes, stirring once. Serve hot with corn chips.

3 cups

SPINACH YOGURT DIP

Cooking Time: 6 minutes

- 1 **package (10 ounces) frozen chopped spinach**
- ½ **cup mayonnaise**
- ½ **cup yogurt**
- ½ **cup chopped fresh parsley**
- ⅓ **cup coarsely chopped green onion**
- ¼ **cup chopped water chestnuts**
- 2 **tablespoons chopped pimiento**
- 1 **clove garlic, minced**
- 1½ **teaspoons pepper**
- 1 **tablespoon lemon juice**

Place unopened spinach package on microproof plate. (If spinach is in a foil-wrapped package, remove foil.) Cook on HI, 6 minutes. Let stand 5 minutes. Drain and squeeze dry. Place spinach in medium bowl and add remaining ingredients. Stir until well blended. Chill several hours.

3 cups

Remove center portion of a small red cabbage or purple kale to make an unusual and attractive container for this dip.

Almond Chicken Liver Dip, Spinach Yogurt Dip

OYSTERS ROCKEFELLER

Cooking Time: 12 to 14 minutes

36 large oysters in the shell
1 package (10 ounces)
   frozen chopped spinach
3 tablespoons minced fresh parsley
2 tablespoons butter or margarine
1 tablespoon minced onion
½ teaspoon salt
¼ teaspoon cayenne
1 cup half and half
1 tablespoon Worcestershire sauce
   Parmesan cheese

Carefully remove oysters from shells. Set aside. Select 36 shell halves; those that will sit level are best. Rinse well. Place, open-side up, in two 12 × 7 × 2-inch microproof baking dishes. Set aside.

Place unopened package of spinach in 1½-quart microproof casserole. (If spinach is in foil-wrapped package, remove foil.) Cook on HI, 6 minutes. Drain well. Place spinach between paper towels and squeeze dry. Combine spinach, parsley, butter, onion, salt, cayenne, cream, and Worcestershire in bowl. Divide half the spinach mixture among shells. Add one oyster to each shell. Top with remaining spinach mixture and generous sprinkling of Parmesan. Cover each baking dish with waxed paper. Place wire rack in oven. Place one dish on wire rack and one on bottom glass tray of oven. Cook on 80, 3 minutes. Reverse dishes and continue to cook on HI, 3 to 5 minutes, or until oysters are plump and edges curled. Let stand 5 minutes before serving. Garnish with lemon wedges.

6 servings

This recipe can be halved. Place one dish on the bottom glass tray and cook on 70, 5 minutes.

TACO SURPRISE

Cooking Time: 7 minutes

1 pound lean ground beef
1 medium onion, chopped
1 small green pepper, chopped
4 to 6 jalapeño peppers, chopped
1 tablespoon chili powder
1 envelope (1¼ ounces)
   taco seasoning mix
1 package (8 ounces) cream cheese,
   softened
1 small head lettuce, torn into
   bite-size pieces
2 medium tomatoes, coarsely chopped
½ cup sliced black olives
2 green onions, finely sliced
½ to 1 cup shredded Cheddar cheese

Crumble ground beef into 2-quart microproof casserole. Add onion, green pepper, jalapeño peppers, add chili powder. Cover with casserole lid and cook on HI, 6 minutes, stirring once to break up beef. Drain and set aside.

Stir taco seasoning mix and cream cheese together in small microproof bowl. Cook on 50, 1 minute. Spread evenly on 10-inch serving platter. Arrange lettuce on top of cream cheese mixture. Spoon meat mixture over center of lettuce. Arrange tomatoes, olives, and green onions around meat. Sprinkle with Cheddar cheese. Serve with corn chip rounds.

4 to 6 servings

As a preparation alternative, place a large tortilla on the serving platter before adding the cream cheese mixture. Top with a second tortilla after adding Cheddar cheese. Using a sharp knife, cut into small wedges before serving.

SWEET 'N SOUR MEATBALLS

Cooking Time: 16 to 18 minutes

2 pounds lean ground beef
1 envelope (1¼ ounces) dry onion soup mix
2 eggs
1 teaspoon Worcestershire sauce
1 teaspoon pepper
½ teaspoon salt

Sauce:

2 cups Western-style salad dressing
1 jar (18 ounces) currant or grape jelly
1 envelope (1¼ ounces) brown gravy mix

Combine beef, onion soup mix, eggs, Worcestershire, pepper, and salt. Mix until well blended. Form mixture into 1-inch balls. Arrange meatballs in a single layer on microwave roasting rack in microproof baking dish. Cook on 90, 5 to 6 minutes. Place meatballs in chafing dish and cover. Repeat with remaining meatballs.

Combine salad dressing, jelly, and brown gravy mix in 2-quart glass measure. Stir to blend. Cover with waxed paper and cook on 90, 6 minutes, stirring once. Pour sauce over meatballs.

50 meatballs

Offer your guests pretzel sticks — they're perfect for spearing these appetizer meatballs!

PITA PIZZAS

Cooking Time: 9 to 12 minutes

6 pita breads, split and separated
1 can (8 ounces) pizza sauce
1 package (4 ounces) sliced pepperoni
12 black olives, sliced
1 cup (4 ounces) shredded mozzarella cheese

Spread each pita half with pizza sauce. Top each with pepperoni and black olive slices. Sprinkle each with cheese. Place 4 halves in ring on microproof serving plate. Cook on 70, 3 to 4 minutes, or until cheese is melted. Let stand 3 minutes before serving. Repeat with remaining pizzas.

12 small pizzas

TOASTED MIXED NUTS

Cooking Time: 8 to 9 minutes

½ pound pecan halves
¼ pound chshews
¼ pound almonds
1 tablespoon seasoned salt
¼ cup buter or margarine

Place pecans, cashews, and almonds in 1½-quart microproof casserole. Sprinkle with seasoned salt. Cut butter into 8 pieces and arrange evenly on top of pecans. Cook, uncovered, on HI, 8 to 9 minutes, stirring once or twice during cooking.

1 pound

You can make your own seasoned salt by combining garlic powder, paprika, cayenne or curry powder, and salt. Incidentally, we don't recommend roasting nuts in the shell.

Fish and Vegetable Bisque

You can use the temperature probe method to cook soup in a casserole. Set temperature probe at 150°F to 160°F and cook on HI.

Mugs of hot chocolate or soup can be reheated using the temperature probe. Place temperature probe in 1 mug and cook on HI to 150°F.

The browning dish is excellent for burgers. For varying doneness, simply form the patties thickly for rare, and thinly for medium.

SOUPS, SANDWICHES & HOT DRINKS

Microwaves perform at their very best with sandwiches, hot drinks, soups, and chowders. For a quick pick-me-up all you need is a minute or two and a mug full of water for a cup of instant soup, or coffee. And, if you like to make soup from scratch without those endless hours of simmering and hovering that are required by conventional cooking, follow these microwave recipes.

Rise and shine with breakfast cocoa and wind down your day with after-dinner instant coffee swiftly and easily made in your microwave oven. What a convenience for fresh-brewed coffee lovers! No more of that bitterness when coffee is kept warm for more than 15 minutes in the conventional way. Brew your coffee as you normally do and pour what you want to drink now. Refrigerate the rest — yes, refrigerate. Then, throughout the day, pour single cups as you wish. Place in the oven and reheat on HI, 2 minutes. In a moment, truly fresh coffee.

ADAPTING YOUR RECIPES

To convert your soup or hot drink recipes to the microwave method, find a similar recipe in this chapter and follow the time and power level settings used here. Most soup is cooked on HI for an initial cooking sequence to heat the liquids rapidly. It is then usually reduced to 50, providing slower cooking for flavor development and tenderization.

Helpful Tips

Soup is usually cooked covered. Large casseroles with lids are best, as the lids can be removed easily to check on the food.

It is always permissible to interrupt cooking by opening the oven door to stir or add ingredients. Simply touch START after closing the door.

Instead of soaking dried beans overnight, rinse beans in water. Place in a microproof casserole. Add water. Cover with the casserole lid and place in the oven. Cook on HI, 20 minutes, or until water comes to a full boil. Set aside, covered, for 1 hour. Proceed to cook soup according to your recipe.

Remember, since there is no heat in the microwave cavity, there is less evaporation of liquid than with stove top simmering.

Be careful with milk-based liquids and 2-or 3-quart quantities. They can boil over quickly. Always choose a large microproof container. Fill individual cups of milk-based liquids no more than two-thirds full.

Reheating Soup

To reheat canned soup, use a 1½- or 2-quart microproof casserole. Add milk or water as directed on the can. Cover with casserole lid and cook according to the guide below. Stir cream-style soup halfway through the cooking time. Let stand, covered, 3 minutes.

Instant soups and soup mixes are also easily prepared. Use a microproof soup mug or casserole. Add water, according to the guide. Cover with waxed paper or casserole lid and cook on HI, according to the guide. Let stand, covered, 5 minutes. (If noodles or rice are not tender, return to oven and cook another 1 to 1½ minutes.)

Sandwiches

With the renewed interest in bread baking, as well as the whole grain and wonderful French and Italian breads available commercially, the enormous variety of sandwich combinations you can create will tickle your imagination. They are easy to heat in the microwave oven.

If you want a grilled effect, a microwave browning dish is a good companion.

The best breads to use for sandwiches warmed in the microwave oven are day-old, full-bodied breads such as rye and whole wheat, and breads rich in eggs and shortening.

It is best to heat sandwiches on paper towels to absorb the steam and prevent sogginess. You will also discover that several thin slices of deli-style meat heat more quickly and evenly than one thick slice. The thick slice may also cause the bread to overcook before the meat is hot. Heat thick slices separately, then add the bread for a quick warming. The same is true for moist fillings, such as barbecued beef. The bread will overcook or become soggy if the filling and bread are heated together.

A general guide to reheating sandwiches is to reheat on HI, 45 to 50 seconds for 1 sandwich. For 2 sandwiches, increase the time to 1 to 1½ minutes, and for 4 sandwiches, to 2 to 2½ minutes.

REHEATING GUIDE — CANNED SOUP

Soup	Amount	Power Control	Time (in minutes)	or	Probe Method	Special Notes
Broth	10¾ oz.	80	3½ - 4½	or	150°	Use 1½-quart casserole
Cream Style: Tomato	10¾ oz. 26 oz.	80 80	6 - 7½ 9 - 11	or or	140° 140°	Use 1½-quart casserole Use 2-quart casserole
Bean, Pea, or Mushroom	10¾ oz.	70	7 - 8½	or	150°	Use 1½-quart casserole
Undiluted chunk-style vegetable	10¾ oz. 19 oz.	80 80	3 - 4½ 6 - 7½	or or	150° 150°	Use 1-quart casserole Use 1½-quart casserole

REHEATING GUIDE — QUICK SOUP

Soup	Number of Envelopes	Power Control	Time (in minutes)	or	Probe Method	Special Notes
Instant soup 1¼-ounce envelope	1	HI	2 - 3	or	150°	Use ⅔ cup water in 8-ounce mug.
	2	HI	3 - 4	or	150°	Use ⅔ cup water per 8-ounce mug.
	4	HI	6 - 7	or	150°	Use ⅔ cup water per 8-ounce mug.
Soup mix 2¾-ounce envelope	1	HI	8 - 10	or	160°	Use 4 cups water in 2-quart casserole. Cover.

TOMATO CITRUS SOUP

Cooking Time: 5 to 5½ minutes

- 1 **can (10½ ounces) condensed tomato soup, undiluted**
- 1 **cup orange juice**
- ⅓ **cup chicken broth**
- 1 **teaspoon lemon juice**
- ½ **teaspoon sugar**

Combine tomato soup, orange juice, chicken broth, lemon juice, and sugar in 4-cup glass measure. Cook on HI, 5 to 5½ minutes, or until hot.

Serve with croutons, Parmesan cheese, or a dollop of sour cream.

2 servings

Give this unusual combination of ingredients a try — you'll be surprised and very pleased.

EGG FLOWER SOUP

Cooking Time: 8½ minutes

- 4 **cups chicken broth, divided**
- 2 **stalks celery, thinly sliced**
- 1½ **tablespoons cornstarch**
- 1 **egg, beaten**
- 2 **green onions, chopped**

Place 3¾ cups broth and celery in 2-quart microproof casserole. Cover with casserole lid and cook on HI, 6½ minutes, or until boiling.

Stir remaining broth and cornstarch together in a separate bowl until blended. Add to hot broth and mix well. Cover and cook on HI, 2 minutes, or until mixture becomes clear.

Pour beaten egg in a slow, steady stream into hot broth while stirring constantly. Stir in green onions.

4 servings

NEW ENGLAND CLAM CHOWDER

Cooking Time: 17 minutes

    2   **strips bacon, diced**
    1   **small onion, chopped**
    1   **stalk celery, sliced**
    1   **medium potato, peeled and cut
          into ¼-inch cubes**
    ⅛   **teaspoon thyme**
    2   **cups milk, divided**
    2   **tablespoons flour**
    1   **can (6½ ounces) minced clams,
          drained**

Place bacon in 2-quart casserole and cook on HI, 2 minutes.

Pour off fat. Stir in onion, celery, potato, and thyme. Add ½ cup of the milk. Cover with casserole lid and cook on HI, 10 minutes.

Add flour to remaining milk, and stir to blend. Add clams and flour mixture to casserole. Cover and cook on 60, 5 minutes, stirring once.

2 to 4 servings

TOMATO WARMER

Cooking Time: 6 to 7 minutes

    2½ **cups tomato juice**
    1   **can (10½ ounces) condensed
          beef broth**
    ¼   **cup lemon juice**
    1   **teaspoon prepared horseradish**
    1   **teaspoon parsely flakes**
    ½   **teaspoon celery salt**
    4   **tablespoons dry sherry**

In a 4-cup glass measure, combine tomato juice, broth, lemon juice, horseradish, parsley, and celery salt. Cook on HI, 6 to 7 minutes, until hot but not boiling. Stir.

Pour into 6 mugs and stir 2 teaspoons sherry into each mug.

6 servings

FRESH TOMATO SOUP

Cooking Time: 25 minutes

    2   **pounds ripe tomatoes, peeled and
          cut into eighths**
    2   **cups dry white wine**
    ½   **cup chopped onions**
    1   **tablespoon sugar**
    2   **teaspoons paprika**
    1   **teaspoon salt**
    1   **strip (2 inches) lemon peel**
    1   **to 2 teaspoons lemon juice,
          to taste**
        Dairy sour cream

Combine tomatoes, wine, onions, sugar, paprika, salt, and lemon peel, in 4-quart microproof casserole. Cover and cook on HI, 10 minutes.

Stir through several times. Cover and cook on HI, 15 minutes.

Discard lemon peel. Pour soup into blender or food processor and mix until smooth. Blend in lemon juice. Return to casserole and cook on HI, 1 to 2 minutes, or until hot. Pour into serving bowls and top each with dollop of sour cream.

4 to 6 servings

CORN CHOWDER

Cooking Time: 16 to 22 minutes

    1   **can (17 ounces) cream-style corn**
    1   **cup chicken broth**
    1   **cup milk**
    ¼   **cup diced potato**
    2   **large eggs**
        Salt and pepper to taste
    1   **green onion, finely chopped**

Combine corn, broth, milk and potatoes in 2-quart microproof casserole. Cover with casserole lid and cook on 80, 12 to 14 minutes, or until potatoes are tender.

Break eggs into small bowl. Gradually stir 1 cup hot corn mixture into eggs. Blend back into hot corn mixture. Cover and cook on 80, 4 to 8 minutes, or until hot.

4 servings

CHICKEN AND SAUSAGE GUMBO

Cooking Time: 17 to 20 minutes

- ¼ **pound Polish sausage, cut into ½-inch pieces**
- 1 **to 2 stalks celery, chopped**
- 1 **medium green pepper, chopped**
- 1 **medium onion, chopped**
- 1 **clove garlic, minced**
- 3 **cups chicken broth**
- 1 **teaspoon Worcestershire sauce Dash hot pepper sauce**
- 2 **cups cubed cooked chicken**
- 1 **cup hot cooked rice**

Combine all ingredients except chicken and rice in a 3-quart microproof casserole. Cover with casserole lid and cook on HI, 15 to 17 minutes.

Stir in chicken. Cover and cook on HI, 2 to 3 minutes.

Spoon hot cooked rice into soup bowls. Fill bowls with hot gumbo.

4 servings

FRENCH ONION SOUP

Cooking Time: 30 to 33 minutes

- 2 **pounds onions, thinly sliced**
- 2 **tablespoons butter or margarine**
- 1½ **teaspoons oil**
- ¼ **teaspoon sugar**
- 1½ **tablespoons all-purpose flour**
- 4 **cups beef broth**
- ¼ **cup dry white wine**
- 4 **to 6 pieces buttered toast Garlic powder**
- 1 **to 1½ cups grated Parmesan cheese**
- ½ **cup shredded Swiss or Monterey jack cheese**

Combine onions, butter, and oil in 3-quart microproof casserole. Cook on HI, 8 minutes, or until onions are transparent, stirring once during cooking.

Stir in sugar and cook on HI, 10 minutes, or until onions just begin to brown. Stir in flour.

Stir in broth and wine. Cover with casserole lid and cook on HI, 10 minutes.

Lightly sprinkle garlic powder over buttered toast. Nearly fill individual microproof soup bowls with soup. Float one piece of toast in each bowl. Cover toast generously with a combination of Parmesan and Swiss cheeses. Place up to 3 bowls in oven. Cook, uncovered, on 80, 2 to 3 minutes, or until cheese is melted.

Repeat with remaining soup, toast, and cheese.

4 to 6 servings

CREAM OF BROCCOLI SOUP

Cooking Time: 27 to 28½ minutes

- 3 **tablespoons butter or margarine**
- ¼ **cup all-purpose flour**
- 4 **cups chicken broth**
- 1 **pound broccoli, cut into florets, stalks removed**
- ¼ **cup half and half**
- 1 **egg yolk Slivers of lemon peel**

Place butter in 2-quart microproof casserole and cook on HI, 1 to 1½ minutes, or until melted. Stir in flour and mix until smooth. Blend in stock. Cover with casserole lid and cook on HI, 7 minutes. Add broccoli and blend well.

Cover and cook on HI, 15 minutes, or until tender. Let stand 10 minutes.

Transfer soup to blender or food processor in batches and purée. Return to casserole; cover and cook on HI, 4 to 5 minutes, or until heated through. Beat half and half with egg yolk in small bowl. Add a little warm soup and blend well. Beat mixture into remaining soup a little at a time; blend well. Cook on 60, 1 to 2 minutes. Garnish with lemon peel.

4 servings

The fibrous broccoli stalks are not suitable for a soup of this kind. However, they can be combined with carrots for a delicious and colorful side dish.

FISH AND VEGETABLE BISQUE

Cooking Time: 23 to 29 minutes

- ¾ **pound fish fillets, cut into 1-inch chunks**
- ¼ **pound ham, cut into ½-inch cubes**
- 1 **can (8 ounces) whole kernel corn, drained**
- 2 **stalks celery, cut into julienne strips**
- 2 **carrots, cut into julienne strips**
- 1 **small red pepper, cut into julienne strips**
- 1 **small green pepper, cut into julienne strips**
- 2 **small red potatoes, cubed**
- 3 **tablespoons flour**
- 3 **cups hot milk**
- 1 **tablespoon chopped fresh parsley**
- ½ **teaspoon tarragon**
  Salt and pepper to taste

Place fish and ham in 3-quart microproof casserole. Cover with casserole lid. Cook on 50, 5 minutes.

Stir in corn, celery, carrots, peppers, and potatoes. Stir flour into milk until blended. Add to vegetable mixture. Cover and cook on HI, 10 to 12 minutes.

Stir. Add parsley, tarragon, salt, and pepper. Cover and cook on 80, 8 to 12 minutes, or until vegetables are tender-crisp.

4 servings

MINESTRONE SOUP

Cooking Time: 38 to 43 minutes

- 1 **pound beef for stew, fat and gristle removed**
- 1 **medium onion, chopped**
- 1 **clove garlic, minced**
- ½ **teaspoon basil**
- ¼ **teaspoon pepper**
- 1 **can (16 ounces) tomatoes**
- ½ **cup thinly sliced carrots**
- ½ **cup uncooked vermicelli, broken into 1-inch pieces**
- 1 **cup sliced zucchini**
- 1 **can (16 ounces) kidney beans, drained**
- ¾ **cup shredded cabbage**
- 2 **tablespoons chopped fresh parsley**
- 1 **teaspoon salt**
  Graded Parmesan or Romano cheese

Cut beef into ½- to ¾-inch chunks. Place in 3-quart microproof casserole with 4 cups hot water. Add onion, garlic, basil, and pepper. Cover with casserole lid and cook on HI, 20 to 25 minutes, or until meat is tender.

Add tomatoes and carrots. Cover and cook on HI, 8 minutes. Stir in vermicelli, zucchini, kidney beans, cabbage, parsley, and salt. Cover and cook on HI, 10 minutes, stirring once.

Remove from oven and let stand 5 minutes before serving. Sprinkle generously with cheese.

6 servings

The temperature probe may be used after all ingredients have been added. Cook on 60 with temperature probe set at 150°F.

MUSHROOM SOUP FOR TWO

Cooking Time: 6½ to 8 minutes

- **1 cup sliced fresh mushrooms**
- **1 small onion, thinly sliced**
- **1½ cups milk**
- **1 egg, beaten**
- **1 teaspoon instant chicken bouillon**
- **⅛ teaspoon white pepper**

Place mushrooms and onion in 1-quart microproof casserole. Cover with casserole lid and cook on HI, 2 minutes.

Add milk and egg, and stir until well mixed. Stir in bouillon and pepper. Cover and cook on 80, 4½ to 6 minutes, stirring once.

2 servings

This recipe makes a light soup, thickened only with egg. If you would like a thicker soup, sprinkle mushrooms and onions with 1 tablespoon flour before adding milk. Stir thoroughly. Proceed as directed above.

BEEFY VEGETABLE SOUP

Cooking Time: 40 minutes

- **1½ pounds beef chuck blade steak, trimmed**
- **2 medium tomatoes, peeled and chopped**
- **2 carrots, sliced**
- **2 stalks celery, sliced**
- **2 medium red potatoes, cubed**
- **2 small zucchini, sliced**
- **2 medium onions, chopped**
- **2 bay leaves**
- **1 teaspoon basil**
- **1 teaspoon Italian herb seasoning**
- **Salt and pepper to taste**
- **3 cups beef broth**

Combine all ingredients in 3-quart microproof casserole. Cover with casserole lid and cook on HI, 20 minutes. Stir.

Cover and cook on 50, 20 minutes.

Remove from oven and let stand, covered, 5 minutes. Remove meat from bone and add to soup. Discard bone and bay leaves before serving.

4 servings

HOT SPICED DAIQUIRI

Cooking Time: 6½ to 7½ minutes

- **1½ cups hot water**
- **¼ cup sugar**
- **2 sticks cinnamon**
- **8 whole cloves**
- **1 can (6 ounces) frozen lemonade concentrate**
- **1 can (6 ounces) frozen limeade concentrate**
- **½ cup light rum**

Combine all ingredients except rum in a 2-quart microproof casserole. Stir thoroughly. Cook on HI, 6 to 7 minutes, or until mixture boils. Set aside.

Place rum in a 1-cup glass measure and cook on HI, 30 seconds. Ignite rum and pour into casserole. Ladle into punch cups.

8 to 10 servings

CATALINA ISLAND OPEN-FACE

Cooking Time: 1 minute 45 seconds

- **1 can (6½ ounces) tuna, drained and flaked**
- **¼ cup mayonnaise**
- **½ teaspoon prepared mustard**
- **1 green onion, chopped**
- **2 slices whole wheat bread, toasted**
- **1 large tomato, sliced**
- **2 slices Swiss cheese**
- **½ cup alfalfa sprouts**

Combine tuna, mayonnaise, mustard and green onion. Spread evenly on toast. Place on microproof plate. Cover with waxed paper and cook on HI, 1 minute.

Arrange tomato and cheese on each sandwich. Cook on HI, 45 seconds, or until cheese begins to melt. Top with alfalfa sprouts.

2 sandwiches

IRISH COFFEE

Cooking Time: 1½ to 2 minutes

- **3 tablespoons Irish whiskey**
- **2 teaspoons sugar**
- **1 tablespoon instant coffee**
  Whipped cream

Measure whiskey into 8-ounce microproof glass or mug. Add sugar and coffee. Add water until container is three-fourths full. Mix well. Cook on HI, 1½ to 2 minutes, or until hot but not boiling. Stir to dissolve sugar.

Top with dollop of whipped cream. Do not stir. Coffee should be sipped through the layer of cream.

1 serving

AMERICAN BURGERS

Approximate Cooking Time: 10 minutes

- **1 pound lean ground beef**
- **1 small onion, chopped**
- **1 egg, beaten**
- **1 tablespoon ketchup**
- **½ cup shredded colby cheese**
- **4 slices cooked bacon**
- **4 hamburger buns, split**

Combine beef, onion, egg, and ketchup in medium bowl. Mix well. Shape into 4 patties.

Preheat browning dish according to manufacturer's directions. Place patties in browning dish and cook on HI, 1½ to 2 minutes. Turn patties over and cook on HI, 1½ to 2 minutes. Sprinkle cheese over patties and cook on HI, 45 seconds, or until cheese begins to melt.

Place patties in hamburger buns and top each with 1 slice bacon.

4 burgers

Burger fans, here's the secret to perfect doneness: if you prefer rare burgers, make thick patties. For well done, make thin patties. It's that easy.

REUBEN FOR ONE

Approximate Cooking Time: 6 minutes

> **2 ounces thinly sliced corned beef**
> **¼ cup sauerkraut, well drained**
> **2 pieces dark rye or pumpernickel bread**
> **2 tablespoons Thousand Island dressing**
> **1 slice (1 ounce) Swiss cheese**

Preheat browning dish according to manufacturer's directions. Meanwhile, place corned beef and sauerkraut on one slice of bread. Top with Thousand Island dressing, Swiss cheese, and second slice of bread. Butter both sides of bread well.

Place sandwich in browning dish and cook on HI, 30 seconds. Turn sandwich over, placing on unused part of browning dish, and cook on HI, 30 seconds.

1 serving

A crunchy deli pickle, please!

STATE FAIR HOT DOG

Cooking Time: 45 seconds to 1 minute

> **1 jumbo hot dog**
> **1 hot dog bun, split**
> **Mustard**
> **2 tablespoons sauerkraut, drained**
> **Relish, chili, grated cheese, or chopped onion**

Slash both sides of hot dog in several places with a sharp knife. Place on microproof plate and cook on HI, 30 to 45 seconds, or until hot.

Place hot dog in bun. Add mustard, sauerkraut, and selected garnish. Cook on HI, 15 seconds.

1 serving

Because the hot dog is large, it requires more cooking time than is needed to warm the bun. That's why the hot dog is cooked first, and then placed on the bun.

UN-SLOPPY JOES

Cooking Time: 5 to 7 minutes

> **1 pound lean ground beef**
> **1 medium onion, chopped**
> **1 stalk celery, chopped**
> **1 can (8 ounces) tomato sauce**
> **1 teaspoon prepared mustard**
> **1 teaspoon chili powder**
> **4 hamburger buns, split**
> **½ cup (2 ounces) shredded colby cheese**

Combine beef, onion, and celery in 1½-quart microproof casserole. Cover with casserole lid and cook on HI, 5 to 7 minutes, stirring once to break up beef. Drain.

Stir in tomato sauce, mustard, and chili powder. Spoon over bottom halves of buns. Sprinkle with cheese and cover with top halves of buns.

4 sandwiches

CALIFORNIA BURGERS

Approximate Cooking Time: 10 minutes

> **½ pound lean ground beef**
> **2 tablespoons wheat germ**
> **1 tablespoon chopped walnuts**
> **1 green onion, chopped**
> **¼ cup (1 ounce) shredded mozzarella cheese**
> **6 avocado slices**
> **4 hamburger buns, split**

Preheat browning dish according to manufacturer's directions.

Combine beef, wheat germ, walnuts, and green onion. Mix well. Shape into 2 patties.

Place patties on browning dish and cook on HI, 1½ to 2 minutes. Turn patties over and cook on HI, 1½ to 2 minutes. Sprinkle cheese over patties and cook on HI, 1 minute, or until cheese begins to melt.

Place patties in buns, top with avocado slices, and serve.

2 sandwiches

WHITE HOUSE CROISSANT

Cooking Time: 1 to 1½ minutes

- **1 croissant, cut in half lengthwise**
- **1 ounce deli-style sliced turkey**
- **1 ounce deli-style sliced boiled ham**
- **1 ounce Monterey jack cheese, thinly sliced**
- **¼ cup Basic White Sauce (page 144) or Creamy Dijon Sauce (page 148)**

Place croissant halves, cut-side up, on micro-proof plate. Layer turkey, ham, and cheese on each half. Cover with waxed paper and cook on 80, 1 to 1½ minutes, or until cheese melts.

Pour hot sauce over top.

1 serving

The classic White House sandwich with a flair — impossible without the microwave, which heats the sandwich so fast that the delicate croissant retains its texture and flavor.

JALAPENO BURGERS

Cooking Time: 10 minutes

- **1 pound lean ground beef**
- **1 small onion, chopped**
- **1 egg, beaten**
- **1 to 2 tablespoons chopped jalapeño peppers**
- **⅛ teaspoon ground coriander**
- **½ cup shredded Cheddar cheese**
- **¼ cup guacamole**
- **4 hamburger buns, split**

Combine beef, onion, egg, jalapeño peppers, and coriander in medium bowl. Mix well. Shape into 4 patties.

Preheat browning dish according to manufacturer's directions. Place patties in browning dish and cook on HI, 1½ to 2 minutes. Turn patties over and cook on HI, 1½ to 2 minutes. Sprinkle cheese over patties and cook on HI, 45 seconds, or until cheese is melted.

Place patties in hamburger buns and top each with 1 tablespoon guacamole.

4 burgers

White House Croissant

SPICED ALMOND COCOA

Cooking Time: 6 to 7 minutes

- ⅓ **cup cocoa**
- ¼ **cup sugar**
- 3 **cups milk**
- 2 **teaspoons grated orange rind**
- ¼ **teaspoon almond extract**
- 4 **cinnamon sticks**

Combine cocoa and sugar in 4-cup glass measure. Add ½ cup of the milk, and stir to make a smooth paste. Add remaining milk, orange rind, and almond extract. Stir until sugar dissolves. Cook on 70, 6 to 7 minutes, or until hot.

Pour into mugs. Place a cinnamon stick in each mug.

4 servings

WASSAIL PUNCH

Cooking Time: 7 minutes

- 2 **cups apple cider**
- 2 **cups cranberry juice**
- 1 **cup dry red wine**
- ½ **cup orange juice**
- ½ **cup lime juice**
- 2 **sticks cinnamon**
- 4 **whole cloves**
- 10 **red hot candies**

Combine all ingredients in 2-quart micro-proof bowl. Cook on 80, 7 minutes.

10 to 12 servings

If you wish, add a few raisins, slivered almonds, and an orange slice to each cup before adding the hot punch.

Beef Teriyaki (page 64) uses a special microwave stir-fry technique. The meat is cooked first and moved to the center when vegetables are added.

A special microwave browning dish is a useful addition to your cookware options. It becomes very hot, so always use tongs or hot pads.

Family Meat Loaf Ring (page 68) and Swedish Meat Loaf (page 66) show clearly that a good recipe will provide a well-browned appearance.

BEEF, LAMB, & PORK

Cooking meat in the microwave oven offers tremendous advantages over the conventional range. For juiciness and flavor, the microwave method excels. It also stretches your meat dollar by reducing shrinkage. And you can defrost, cook, or reheat in minutes while your kitchen remains cool and comfortable.

If some of your guests or family members prefer beef rare and others medium, the microwave solves the problem. After the roast is carved, just seconds bring slices of rare roast to medium or well done. In addition, meat for the barbecue is enhanced by precooking in the microwave. You get that wonderful charcoal flavor without the long watchful cooking that often results in burned or blackened meat. Microwave roasting methods are similar to dry roasting in your conventional oven. This means that the better, tender cuts of meat are recommended for best results. Less tender cuts should be marinated or tenderized and cooked at low power settings, such as 30 or 50. Easiest of all, the temperature probe can provide virtually automatic cooking and eliminates the need to calculate the cooking time. The best technique is to set the temperature probe at two (or more) temperatures, providing for a pause after the first temperature is reached. You can turn the meat over, baste, or add ingredients.

BROWNING MEAT

You can enhance the color and flavor of ground beef patties, steaks, meat loaf, and roasts by using one of the following: microwave browning sauces and powders, powdered brown gravy mix, a liquid browning agent, Worcestershire sauce, soy sauce, steak sauce, paprika, dehydrated onion soup mix, or a microwave browning dish, as used for the chops in the photograph (above left). (Several of our recipes recommend use of a browning dish. We think it is a very helpful item for occasional use. However, all browning dish recipes can be achieved in any microproof baking dish. If you are concerned about the color of your meat, simply add one of the suggested browning agents listed above.)

By trimming fat off roasts, and using only lean stewing meat for beef patties and meat loaf, you permit the microwave energy to go directly to the meat itself, rather than the fat. This will achieve more browning. Added fat is not required in microwave cooking.

ADAPTING YOUR RECIPES

Guides on the following pages outline microwave thawing and cooking times, and power settings, for most standard meat products. The temperature probe offers many cooking options as familiar as the use of a conventional meat thermometer. The bonus, of course, is that the temperature probe will automatically call you to the kitchen when the temperature you set has been reached. And if you are not ready to serve just then, no bother. The temperature probe automatically enters a "Hold" phase to keep your meat hot for an hour. You select and set your own desired temperatures and power levels prior to cooking.

Helpful Tips

Less tender cuts, such as chuck, bottom round, rump, or brisket are usually cooked by using 70 for the initial cooking sequence, then changing to 50. This provides the tenderization such cuts require by slower final cooking. The initial 70 power sequence aids browning and seals in the juices.

Lean ground beef should be used in microwave cooking because the extra fat is not required. If you use regular ground beef, be sure to drain the beef before adding other ingredients.

The temperature probe method is best for all tender cuts of meat, as well as meat loaf and pork.

Recipe times here presume meat is at refrigerator temperature. If your meat requires lengthy preparation, during which the meat may reach room temperature, reduce cooking times.

Baste, marinate, or season meat just as you would for conventional cooking.

You can use a microwave roasting rack to elevate meat from its drippings during cooking.

Check dishes that use relatively long cooking times to be sure liquid has not evaporated. Add liquid as necessary.

REHEATING GUIDE — MEAT*

Food	Power Control	Time	Probe Method	Special Notes
Barbecued beef, chili, stews, hash etc., 16 oz. can	80	4 to 6 min.	150°F	Place in microproof dish. Cover. Stir halfway through cooking time.
Entrées, frozen 5½ - 8 oz.		follow package directions		
Stuffed peppers, cabbage rolls, chow mein, etc., 16 - 32 oz.	80	6 to 9 min.	150°F	or follow package directions.
TV dinners 11½ - 14 oz.		follow package directions		
Meat pie, double crust, 8 oz.		follow package directions		

* Due to the tremendous variety in convenience food products available, times given here should be used only as guidelines. We suggest you cook food for the shortest recommended time and then check for doneness. Be sure to check the package for microwave instructions.

DEFROSTING MEAT

To prepare for defrosting, remove meat from its original paper or plastic wrappings. Place meat in a microproof dish.

Defrost in the microwave oven only as long as necessary, since standing time will complete the thawing process. Items like chops, bacon, and hot dogs should be separated as soon as possible. If some of the pieces are not thawed, distribute evenly in the oven and continue defrosting.

We recommend that you slightly increase the time for weights larger than on the chart. Do not double, for example. This conservative approach will help prevent the outside of meat from beginning to cook while the inside is still frozen.

If you do not plan immediate cooking, follow the guide for only one-half to three-fourths of the recommended time. Place meat in refrigerator until needed.

DEFROSTING GUIDE — MEAT

Meat	Amount	Power Control	Time (in minutes per pound)	Standing Time (minutes)	Special
Beef Ground beef	1 lb. 2 lbs. 1/4-lb. patty	30 (defrost) 30 (defrost) 30 (defrost	5 - 6 5 - 6 1 per patty	5 5 2	Turn over once. Remove thawed portions with fork. Return remainder. Freeze in doughnut shape. Depress center when freezing. Defrost on plate.
Pot roast, chuck	under 4 lbs. over 4 lbs.	30 (defrost) 70 (roast)	3 - 5 3 - 5	10 10	Turn over once. Turn over once.
Rib roast, rolled	2 to 4 lbs. 6 to 8 lbs.	30 (defrost) 70 (roast)	6 - 8 6 - 8	30 - 45 90	Turn over once. Turn over twice.
Rib roast, bone in		70 (roast)	5 - 6	45 - 90	Turn over twice.
Rump roast	3 to 4 lbs. 6 to 7 lbs.	30 (defrost) 70 (roast)	3 - 5 3 - 5	30 45	Turn over once. Turn over twice.
Round steak		30 (defrost)	4 - 5	5 - 10	Turn over once.
Flank steak		30 (defrost)	4 - 5	5 - 10	Turn over once.
Sirloin steak	1/2" thick	30 (defrost)	4 - 5	5 - 10	Turn over once.
Tenderloin steak	2 to 3 lbs.	30 (defrost)	4 - 5	8 - 10	Turn over once.
Stew beef	2 lbs.	30 (defrost)	3 - 5	8 - 10	Turn over once. Separate.
Lamb Cubed for stew		30 (defrost)	7 - 8	5	Turn over once. Separate.
Ground lamb	under 4 lbs. over 4 lbs.	30 (defrost) 70 (roast)	3 - 5 3 - 5	30 - 45 30 - 45	Turn over once. Turn over twice.
Chops	1" thick	30 (defrost)	5 - 8	15	Turn over twice.
Leg	5 - 8 lbs.	30 (defrost)	4 - 5	15 - 20	Turn over twice.
Pork Chops	1/2" thick 1" thick	30 (defrost) 30 (defrost)	4 - 6 5 - 7	5 - 10 10	Separate chops halfway through defrosting time.
Spareribs, country-style ribs		30 (defrost)	5 - 7	10	Turn over once.
Roast	under 4 lbs. over 4 lbs.	30 (defrost) 70 (roast)	4 - 5 4 - 5	30 - 45 30 - 45	Turn over once. Turn over twice.
Bacon	1 lb.	30 (defrost)	2 - 3	3 - 5	Defrost until strips separate.
Sausage, bulk	1 lb.	30 (defrost)	2 - 3	3 - 5	Turn over once. Remove thawed portions with fork. Return remainder.
Sausage links	1 lb.	30 (defrost)	3 - 5	4 - 6	Turn over once. Defrost until pieces can be separated.
Hot dogs		30 (defrost)	5 - 6	5	
Veal Roast	3 to 4 lbs. 6 to 7 lbs.	30 70	5 - 7 5 - 7	30 90	Turn over once. Turn over twice.
Chops	1/2" thick	30	4 - 6	20	Turn over once. Separate chops and continue defrosting.
Variety Meat Liver		30	5 - 6	10	Turn over once.
Tongue		30	7 - 8	10	Turn over once.

NOTE: If your oven is equipped with an Auto Defrost or Programmed Defrost feature, please consult your Use & Care Manual for assistance in defrosting with those methods. The timings in the chart here are for manual, or attended, defrosting techniques.

COOKING MEAT

There are no special secrets to cooking meat in the microwave oven. It's quite easy. Meat should be completely thawed before cooking, all fat should be trimmed, and most meat should be placed on a microwave roasting rack in a microproof baking dish.

If you wish, meat may be covered lightly with waxed paper to stop splatters.

We suggest that you use the temperature probe for the most accurate cooking of larger cuts. Insert temperature probe as horizontally as possible in the densest area, avoiding fat pockets or bone.

Unless otherwise noted, times given for steaks and patties will give medium doneness. Don't forget the trick of forming thinner patties for medium or well done, and thick patties for rare. Then, the cooking time is the same for each.

Ground meat to be used for casseroles should be cooked briefly first. Crumble it into a microproof dish and cook, covered with a paper towel. Then drain off any fat and add meat to the casserole.

During standing time, the internal temperature of roasts will rise between 5°F and 15°F. Hence, standing time is considered an essential part of the time required to complete cooking.

Cutlets and chops that are breaded are cooked with the same timing and at the same power control setting as shown in the guide for unbreaded.

Special Tips about Bacon

Cook bacon on a paper towel-lined plate, and cover with additional paper towels to prevent splatters and absorb drippings.

To reserve drippings, cook bacon on a microwave roasting rack in a microproof baking dish or on a microwave bacon rack. Bacon can also be cooked, in slices or cut up, in a casserole and removed, if necessary, with a slotted spoon.

For bacon that is soft rather than crisp, cook at the minimum timing.

Bacon varies in quality. The thickness and amount of sugar and salt used in curing will affect browning and timing. Thicker slices take a bit longer to cook.

Sugar in bacon causes brown spots to appear on the paper towels. If the bacon tends to stick a bit to the towel, it is due to an extra high amount of sugar. We recommend that only white paper towels be used because others may contain harmful dyes.

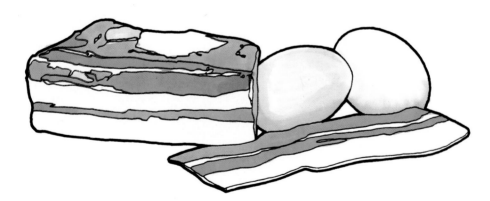

COOKING GUIDE — MEAT

Food	First Cook Time and Power Control	Second Cook Time and Power Control	Probe Method	Special Notes
Beef Ground beef, bulk	2 min. per lb. on HI	3 min. per lb. on HI		Crumble in microproof dish.
Ground beef* patties, 1 - 4 4 oz. each	1½ min. on HI turn over	1½ - 2 min. on HI		Preheat browning dish according to manufacturers directions.
Meatloaf, 1½ - 2 lbs.	12 - 14 min. on HI	None	160°F	Let stand 5 - 10 minutes.
Beef rib roast, boneless	4 - 5 min. per lb. on HI — turn over	3 - 4 min. per lb. on 70	Rare: 120°F Med: 130°F	Microproof dish with microwave roasting rack. Let stand 10 minutes.
Beef rib roast, bone-in	4 - 5 min. per lb. on HI — fat-side down — turn over	3 - 4 min. per lb. on 70	Rare: 120°F Med: 130°F Well: 140°F	Microproof dish with microwave roasting rack. Let stand 10 minutes.
Beef pot roast, boneless	5 min. per lb. on 70 — turn over	10 - 15 min. per lb. on 50	Med: 130°F Well: 140°F	Covered microproof casserole or cooking bag. Let stand 15 to 20 minutes.
Beef brisket, corned beef, flat cut, 2 - 3 lbs.	5 min. per lb. on 70 — check liquid add if necessary turn over	20 - 30 min. per lb. on 50		In 4-quart covered microproof casserole. Cover with water. Let stand 15 - 20 minutes after cooking.
Top round steak, 2 - 3 lbs.	4½ min. per lb. on HI — turn over check liquid	5 min. per lb. on 50		Microproof casserole with tight cover. Needs liquid. Let stand 10 - 15 minutes.
Sirloin steak ¾" thick	Rare: 3½ min. Med: 4 min. Well: 4½ - 5 min. on HI — turn over	2 min. 2 min. 2 min. on HI		Shallow microproof baking dish or preheated browning dish. Let stand 5 - 10 minutes.
Minute steak, cube steak, 4 - 6 oz.	1 - 2 min. on HI — turn over	1 - 2 min. on HI		Shallow microproof baking dish or preheated browning dish. Let stand 5 - 10 minutes.
Tenderloin steak, 4 - 8 oz. 1-inch thick	Rare: 5 min. Med: 6 min. Well: 8 min. on HI — turn over	1 - 2 min. 2 - 3 min. 2 - 3 min. on HI		Shallow microproof baking dish or preheated browning dish. Let stand 5 - 10 minutes.
Rib eye or strip steak, 1-inch thick	Rare: 4 min. Med: 5 min. Well: 6 min. on HI — turn over	½ - 1 min. 1 - 2 min. 2 - 3 min. on HI		Shallow microproof baking dish or preheated browning dish. Let stand 5 - 10 minutes.
Lamb Ground lamb* patties, 4 4 oz. each.	4 min. on HI turn over	4 - 5 min. on HI		Shallow microproof baking dish or preheated browning dish. Let stand 5 - 10 minutes.
Lamb chops ¾" thick	6 min. per lb. on HI	7 - 8 min. on 80		Shallow microproof baking dish or preheated browning dish. Let stand 5 - 10 minutes.
Lamb leg or shoulder roast, bone in, 6½ lbs.	4 - 5 min. per lb. fat side down on 70 — turn over	4 - 5 min. per lb. on 70 — (Cover end of bone with foil.)	Rare: 145°F Med: 155°F Well: 165°F	In microproof dish with microwave roasting rack. Let stand 5 - 10 minutes.
Lamb roast, boneless 3 - 4 lbs.	4 - 5 min. per lb. fat side down on 70 — turn over	4 - 5 min. per lb. on 70	150°F	In microproof dish with microwave roasting rack. Let stand 5 - 10 minutes.
Veal Shoulder or rump roast, boneless, 3 - 3½ lbs.	9 min. per lb. on 70 — turn over	9 - 10 min. per lb. on 70	155°F	In microproof dish with microwave roasting rack. Let stand 5 - 10 minutes.
Veal cutlets or chops ½" thick	2 min. on HI turn over	2 - 3½ min. on HI		Shallow microproof baking dish or preheated browning dish.

*For rare patties, form ¾ to 1-inch thick. For medium and well done, form thinner patties.

COOKING GUIDE — MEAT

Food	First Cook Time and Power Control	Second Cook Time and Power Control	Probe Method	Special Notes
Pork				
Pork chops, ½ - ¾" thick	6 min. per lb. on HI — turn over	5 - 6 min. on HI		Shallow microproof dish or preheated browning dish.
Spareribs, 3 - 4 lbs.	6 - 7 min. per lb. on 70 — turn over	6 - 7 min. per lb. on 70		Begin in liquid in 3 - 4 quart casserole and transfer to microproof baking dish to finish.
Pork loin roast, boneless, 4 - 5 lbs.	5 - 7 min. per lb. on HI — turn over	5 - 6 min. per lb. on 70	165°F	Microproof baking dish. Let stand 10 - 15 minutes.
Pork loin, center cut, 4 - 5 lbs.	5 - 7 min. per lb. on HI — turn over	4 - 5 min. per lb. on 70	165°F	Microproof baking dish. Let stand 10 - 15 minutes.
Ham, boneless precooked	5 - 6 min. per lb. on 70 — turn over	5 - 6 min. per lb. on 70	130°F	Microproof baking dish. Let stand 5 - 10 minutes.
Ham slice, center cut, precooked	4 - 5 min. per lb. on 70 — turn over	5 - 6 min. per lb. on 70		Shallow microproof baking dish. Let stand 5 minutes.
Ham, canned 3 - 5 lbs.	5 - 6 min. per lb. on 70 — turn over	5 - 6 min. per lb. on 70	130°F	Microproof baking dish.
Sausage pattie, ½ - ¾" thick	2 min. on HI turn over	1½ - 2 min. on HI		Shallow microproof dish or preheated browning dish.
Sausage, bulk 1 lb.	3 min. per lb. on HI — stir	1 - 2 min. per lb. on HI		Crumble in 1½-quart microproof dish, covered with paper towel.
Pork sausage links, ½ - 1 lb.	2 min. per lb. on HI — turn over	1 - 1½ min. on HI		Pierce casings. Shallow microproof dish or preheated browning dish. Cover with paper towel.
Precooked Polish sausage, knockwurst, ring bologna	2 - 2½ min. per lb. on 80 — rearrange	2 - 2½ min. per lb. on 80		Pierce casings. Shallow microproof dish or preheated browning dish. Cover with paper towel.
Hot dogs - 1 2 4	45 - 60 sec. 50 - 70 sec. 1½ - 2 min.			Shallow microproof dish.
Bacon 1 slice 2 slices 4 slices 8 slices	45 sec. - 1 min. 2 - 2½ min. 4 - 4½ min. 5 - 7 min. on HI			On paper towel-lined dish or microwave bacon rack covered with paper towel with edges tucked under rack or dish.

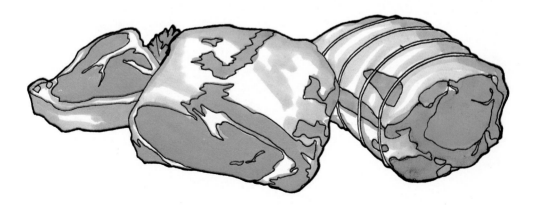

BEEF ROULADEN

Cooking Time: 18 minutes

- ½ **pound beef top round steak,
  ½ inch thick**
- 2 **teaspoons Dijon-style mustard**
- 2 **large dill pickles, cut into
  julienne strips**
- 1 **medium onion, diced**
- 2 **strips bacon, cooked and crumbled**
- 2 **tablespoons all-purpose flour,
  divided**
- ¼ **teaspoon pepper**
- 1 **cup hot beef broth**
- 4 **peppercorns**
- 1 **bay leaf**

Cut steak into 4 pieces. Pound with meat mallet until ¼ inch thick. Spread mustard evenly on one side of each steak. Place 4 strips dill pickle on each steak. Top each with onion and bacon. Roll steaks, securing with toothpick. Set aside. Combine flour and pepper. Coat steak rolls with flour mixture. Place in 1½-quart microproof casserole.

Stir any remaining flour mixture into beef broth. Pour around rouladen. Add peppercorns and bay leaf. Cover with casserole lid and cook on 50, 18 minutes. Turn rouladen over. Cover and let stand for 5 minutes.

2 to 4 servings

Traditional rouladen are rolled around pickles only. You may want to add julienne strips of carrot for color.

POT ROAST

Cooking Time: 65 to 70 minutes

- 1 **lean beef chuck roast (3 to
  4 pounds)**
- 4 **small whole red potatoes**
- 4 **carrots, peeled and cut into
  1½-inch chunks**
- ⅛ **teaspoon pepper**
- 1 **cup beef broth**

Cut a 1-inch strip from open end of cooking bag. Trim fat from roast. Place roast, potatoes, and carrots in bag; place in shallow microproof baking dish. Sprinkle with pepper. Add broth. Tie bag loosely with plastic strip. Cook on 70, 10 minutes.

Cook on 50, 30 minutes.

Turn bag to baste roast and vegetables with drippings. Cook on 30, 25 to 30 minutes, or until roast and vegetables are tender.

4 servings

SHORT RIBS OF BEEF

Cooking Time: 45 to 55 minutes

- 2 **pounds beef chuck short ribs**
- 3 **cups hot beef broth**
- 1 **large onion, quartered**

Arrange short ribs in 3-quart microproof casserole. Add just enough hot broth to cover ribs. Add onion. Cover with casserole lid and cook on HI, 10 minutes. Rearrange ribs.

Cook on 50, 35 to 45 minutes, or until meat is tender. Let stand 5 minutes.

4 servings

Short ribs are traditionally served with sharp-flavored accompaniments. Fresh horseradish is excellent. For barbecued ribs, cook as directed above. Remove ribs from broth. Place ribs on microwave roasting rack in shallow microproof dish. Baste with Barbecue Sauce (page 145) and cook on 50, 10 minutes.

TENDERLOIN OF BEEF SUPREME

Approximate Cooking Time: 20 minutes

- 1　**beef loin tenderloin roast (2 to 2½ pounds)**
- 3　**tablespoons dehydrated onion soup mix**
- ½　**pound mushrooms, sliced**

Place roast in shallow microproof baking dish. Pat soup mix evenly onto roast. Arrange mushrooms on top. Cover with paper towel and place in oven. Cook on HI, 10 minutes.

Turn roast over. Insert temperature probe into center of roast. Cover with paper towel and place in oven. Plug in probe. Cook on HI with probe set at 120°F for rare, or 130°F for medium-rare. Let stand 5 to 10 minutes before serving.

4 servings

BEEF TERIYAKI

Cooking Time: 10 to 12 minutes

- ½　**cup teriyaki sauce**
- ¼　**cup dry sherry**
- 1　**teaspoon sugar**
- 1　**clove garlic, minced**
- 2　**slices fresh ginger (⅛ inch thick), minced**
- 1　**to 1½ pounds beef loin top sirloin steak boneless, cut into thin strips**
- ½　**pound broccoli, cut into florets, stalks removed**
- 1　**package (6 ounces) frozen pea pods**
- 1　**can (5 ounces) sliced water chestnuts, drained**
- 1　**medium green pepper, cut into thin strips**
- 1　**medium red pepper, cut into thin strips**
- 6　**green onions, cut into 2-inch lengths**

Place teriyaki sauce, sherry, sugar, garlic, and ginger in shallow 2½-quart microproof casserole. Mix well. Add steak and stir until coated. Cover and marinate at room temperature 30 minutes, stirring occasionally. Push meat to center of casserole.

Arrange vegetables around steak. Cover with casserole lid and cook on 80, 10 to 12 minutes. Serve with unseasoned rice.

4 servings

Tenderloin of Beef Supreme

SAUERBRATEN

Cooking Time: 45 minutes

- 1 **beef round rump roast (2½ to 3 pounds)**
- 2 **medium onions, sliced**
- 8 **whole peppercorns**
- 4 **whole cloves**
- 1 **bay leaf**
- 1 **cup water**
- 1 **cup white vinegar**
- ½ **cup cider vinegar**
- 2 **cups beef broth**
- 1½ **tablespoons all-purpose flour**
- 8 **gingersnaps, finely crushed**

Place beef in 3-quart microproof casserole. Add onions, peppercorns, cloves, bay leaf, water, white vinegar, and cider vinegar. If meat is not covered by marinade, place in smaller casserole. Cover and refrigerate overnight.

Pour off marinade. Stir flour into broth. Add broth and gingersnaps. Cover with casserole lid and cook on 70, 10 minutes.

Cook on 50, 35 minutes, or until beef is tender.

4 to 6 servings

SWEDISH MEAT LOAF

Cooking Time: 13 to 15 minutes

- ¾ **pound lean ground beef**
- ¾ **pound ground pork**
- ½ **cup fresh bread crumbs**
- 1 **medium onion, minced**
- 2 **eggs**
- ¼ **cup milk**
- 1 **teaspoon prepared mustard**
- ¼ **teaspoon prepared horseradish**
- 1 **teaspoon salt**
- ¼ **teaspoon pepper**
- 1 **pork sausage link (4 ounces)**
- 1 **tablespoon browning sauce**
- 1 **tablespoon water**

In large mixing bowl, combine beef, pork, bread crumbs, onion, eggs, milk, mustard, horseradish, salt, and pepper. Mix well. Place half the meat mixture in a 9 × 5-inch microproof loaf pan. Place the sausage link in center of meat mixture. Cover with remaining meat mixture.

Stir together browning sauce and water. Pour over top of meat loaf. Cook on HI, 13 to 15 minutes.

4 servings

ROAST BEEF

Approximate Cooking Time: 30 minutes

- 1 **beef rib roast small end boneless (5 pounds)**
- 1 **pound mushrooms, sliced**

Place roast, fat-side down, on microwave roasting rack in shallow microproof baking dish. Sprinkle mushrooms over top and sides of roast. Cook on HI, 15 minutes.

Turn roast over. Spoon juices and mushrooms over top. Insert temperature probe horizontally into thickest part of roast without touching fat or bone. Place in oven. Plug in probe. Cover roast lightly with waxed paper. Cook on 70 with temperature probe set at 120°F for rare, or 130°F for medium. Let stand 10 minutes. Internal temperature of roast will rise to approximately 135°F during standing time for rare, to 145°F for medium.

6 to 8 servings

STUFFED GREEN PEPPERS

Cooking Time: 22 to 25 minutes

- 1 **pound lean ground beef**
- 1 **medium onion, finely chopped**
- 2 **tablespoons minced celery**
- 1 **clove garlic, minced**
- ½ **cup cooked rice**
- 1 **egg**
- 1 **cup tomato sauce, divided**
- 3 **tablespoons minced fresh parsley**
- 1 **tablespoon Worcestershire sauce**
- ½ **teaspoon salt**
- ¼ **teaspoon pepper**
- 4 **large green peppers, tops and seeds removed**

Place beef, onion, celery, and garlic in 2-quart microproof bowl. Cover. Cook on HI, 5 to 6 minutes, stirring once to break up beef.

Stir in rice, egg, ¾ cup of the tomato sauce, parsley, Worcestershire, salt, and pepper.

Fill green peppers with beef mixture, mounding top. Arrange peppers in a ring in round or oval microproof baking dish just large enough to hold peppers upright. Cover with casserole lid and cook on 80, 17 to 19 minutes.

Spread 1 tablespoon of the remaining tomato sauce on top of each pepper. Serve with crusty garlic bread, if desired.

4 servings

For a more highly seasoned pepper, stir 1 tablespoon dry red wine, ½ teaspoon basil, and ¼ teaspoon oregano into beef mixture. Sprinkle tomato sauce topping with grated Parmesan cheese.

STUFFED CABBAGE

Cooking Time: 27 to 28 minutes

- 1 **small cabbage (about 1½ pounds), cored, blemished leaves discarded**
- ¼ **cup water**
- 1 **pound lean ground beef**
- ½ **pound ground pork**
- ¾ **cup cooked rice**
- 1 **large egg, lightly beaten**
- 1 **tablespoon chopped fresh parsley**
- 1 **clove garlic, minced**
- ½ **teaspoon thyme**
- ½ **teaspoon salt**
- ¼ **teaspoon pepper**
- ¼ **cup butter or margarine**
- 1 **can (16 ounces) tomato sauce**

Place cabbage and water in 3-quart microproof casserole. Cover with casserole lid and cook on HI, 7 minutes.

Drain cabbage well; let cool slightly. Remove 6 to 8 large outside leaves, discarding tough centers. Combine beef, pork, rice, egg, parsley, garlic, thyme, salt, and pepper. Divide mixture evenly among large outside cabbage leaves, wrapping leaves tightly around mixture. Line bottom of 12 × 7-inch microproof baking dish with the remaining cabbage leaves. Top with stuffed cabbage rolls. Cover with remaining leaves. Dot with butter. Cover with tomato sauce. Cover with plastic wrap and cook on HI, 5 minutes.

Baste with pan juices. Cover and cook on 50, 15 to 17 minutes, or until cabbage is tender. Let stand, still covered, 5 minutes.

3 to 4 servings

SPECIAL SWISS STEAK

Cooking Time: 57 minutes

- **2 pounds beef top round steak,
  ½ inch thick**
- **2 tablespoons butter**
- **2 teaspoons cornstarch**
- **3 to 4 large tomatoes, seeded and
  coarsely chopped**
- **½ cup beef broth**
- **1 medium onion, minced**
- **1 tablespoon Worcestershire sauce**
- **½ teaspoon Italian herb seasoning**
- **2 cups (½ pint) whole cherry tomatoes**
- **1 package (10 ounces) frozen
  whole green beans**
- **1 package (10 ounces) frozen
  pearl onions**

Pound steak on both sides with a meat mallet or flat side of cleaver. Cut into 4 pieces and set aside.

Place butter in 2½-quart shallow microproof casserole. Cook on HI, 2 minutes. Add cornstarch and stir until well blended. Stir in tomatoes, broth, onion, Worcestershire and Italian seasoning. Add steak. Spoon sauce over steak. Cover with casserole lid. Cook on 50, 35 minutes.

Rearrange meat. Arrange cherry tomatoes, beans, and onions on top. Cover and cook on 50, 20 minutes.

4 servings

FAMILY MEAT LOAF RING

Cooking Time: 16 to 18 minutes

- **¼ cup firmly packed brown sugar**
- **1 can (8 ounces) tomato sauce, divided**
- **1 teaspoon prepared mustard**
- **2 pounds lean ground beef**
- **1 medium onion, minced**
- **¼ cup cracker crumbs**
- **2 eggs, lightly beaten**
- **1½ teaspoons salt**
- **¼ teaspoon pepper**

Combine brown sugar, tomato sauce, and mustard. Set aside. Combine beef, onion, cracker crumbs, eggs, salt, and pepper. Add ½ cup of the tomato sauce mixture and stir until well mixed. Place mixture in 8-cup microproof ring mold. Pour remaining tomato sauce over meat. Cook on HI, 16 to 18 minutes, or until done.

6 servings

Temperature probe may be used. Insert probe in center portion of meat loaf. Cook on HI with temperature probe set at 160°F. For a quick and easy variation, substitute 1 package dry onion soup mix for sugar, mustard, salt, and pepper.

Special Swiss Steak

YANKEE STEW

Cooking Time: 1 hour to 1 hour 30 minutes

2½ **to 3 pounds beef for stew**
¼ **cup all-purpose flour**
3 **medium onions, quartered**
3 **carrots, sliced**
3 **stalks celery, cut into**
  2-inch pieces
3 **medium red potatoes**
4 **ounces fresh mushrooms**
1 **can (16 ounces) stewed tomatoes**
2 **cups hot beef broth**

Dredge beef in flour and place in 3-quart microproof casserole. Add onions, carrots, celery, potatoes, and mushrooms. Stir any remaining flour into tomatoes. Add tomatoes and broth to beef and vegetables. Stir. Cover with casserole lid and cook on 70, 10 minutes.

Stir. Cover and cook on 70, 50 to 80 minutes, or until beef is tender. Let stand, covered, 5 minutes.

4 servings

For 2 servings, halve ingredients. Cook on 70, 30 to 40 minutes.

STROGANOFF

Cooking Time: 10 to 12 minutes

1½ **pounds beef loin top sirloin steak**
  boneless, cut into thin strips
2 **tablespoons all-purpose flour**
¼ **cup beef broth**
2 **teaspoons Worcestershire sauce**
⅛ **teaspoon pepper**
8 **ounces mushrooms**
1 **medium onion, sliced**
1 **cup dairy sour cream**

Dredge steak in flour. Combine steak, broth, Worcestershire, and pepper in 2½-quart microproof casserole. Push meat to center of casserole. Set aside.

Wipe mushrooms with damp towel. Cut into thick slices. Arrange mushrooms and onion around meat. Cover with casserole lid and cook on 80, 10 to 12 minutes, or until tender. Stir in sour cream.

4 servings

ITALIAN MEATBALLS

Cooking Time: 11½ to 14 minutes

½ **pound lean ground beef**
½ **pound bulk Italian sausage**
½ **cup fresh bread crumbs**
2 **tablespoons chopped fresh parsley**
2 **cloves garlic, chopped**
1 **green onion, chopped**
1 **egg**
1 **teaspoon Italian herb seasoning**
½ **teaspoon salt**
⅛ **teaspoon pepper**
1 **can (8 ounces) tomato sauce**

Combine beef, sausage, bread crumbs, parsley, garlic, green onion, egg, Italian seasoning, salt, and pepper. Mix well. Form into 12 2-inch balls. Arrange in a ring on microwave roasting rack. Cook on 80, 7 minutes.

Turn meatballs over. Cook on 80, 3 to 5 minutes.

Place meatballs on serving platter. Cover with aluminum foil and set aside. Pour drippings into 2-cup glass measure. Add tomato sauce. Cook on HI, 1½ to 2 minutes, or until hot. Pour over meatballs. Serve with garlic bread and your favorite pasta.

12 meatballs

For a hearty Italian sandwich, serve meatballs on a hard crusty roll. Serve with peperoncini.

HUNGARIAN GOULASH

Cooking Time: 60 to 70 minutes

- **2 pounds beef for stew**
- **4 large tomatoes, chopped**
- **1 onion, coarsely chopped**
- **1½ tablespoons paprika**
- **1 teaspoon salt**
- **½ teaspoon pepper**
- **1 cup dairy sour cream**

Place beef, tomatoes, onion, paprika, salt, and pepper in 3-quart microproof casserole. Stir. Cover with casserole lid and cook on 50, 60 to 70 minutes, or until beef is tender, stirring twice during cooking time. Gradually stir in sour cream. Cover and let stand 5 minutes.

4 servings

COUNTRY CHILI

Cooking Time: 38 to 50 minutes

- **1½ pounds lean ground beef**
- **2 medium onions, chopped**
- **1 clove garlic, minced**
- **1 can (16 ounces) stewed tomatoes**
- **1½ cups tomato juice**
- **1 can (6 ounces) tomato paste**
- **1 to 2 tablespoons chili powder**
- **1 teaspoon Worcestershire sauce**
- **1 can (16 ounces) red kidney beans**
  Salt and pepper to taste

Combine beef and onions in 3-quart microproof casserole. Cook on HI, 8 to 10 minutes, or just until beef loses its pink color, stirring once. Add remaining ingredients. Stir to mix. Cover and cook on 80, 30 to 40 minutes, or until hot, stirring once. Let stand covered, 5 minutes.

6 to 8 servings

IDAHO MEATBALLS

Cooking Time: 15 minutes

- 1 **pound lean ground beef**
- 1 **medium potato, peeled and coarsely grated**
- 2 **tablespoons onion soup mix**
- 1 **tablespoon parsley flakes**
- 1 **egg, lightly beaten**
- 2 **cups beef broth**
- 1 **tablespoon Worcestershire sauce**
- 2 **tablespoons cornstarch**
- 2 **tablespoons water**

Combine beef, potato, soup mix, parsley, and egg. Form into twelve 1½-inch balls. Combine broth and Worcestershire in 2-quart microproof casserole. Add meatballs. Cover with casserole lid and place in oven. Cook on 70, 10 minutes.

Dissolve cornstarch in water. Stir into casserole. Cover and cook on 70, 3 minutes. Stir. Cook on 70, 2 minutes. Let stand 5 minutes before serving.

4 servings

VEAL CORDON BLEU FOR TWO

Cooking Time: 5 minutes

- 4 **veal cutlets, ½ inch thick (about ½ pound)**
- 4 **slices (about 4 ounces) Swiss cheese**
- 2 **slices (2 ounces) boiled ham**
- 1½ **tablespoons all-purpose flour**
- ¼ **cup dry bread crumbs**
- 1 **egg**
- 1 **tablespoon water**
- 1½ **tablespoons butter or margarine**
- 1 **tablespoon chopped fresh parsley**
- 2 **tablespoons dry vermouth**

Place each piece of veal between 2 sheets waxed paper and pound with smooth-surfaced meat mallet until veal is ⅛ inch thick. Place 1 piece Swiss cheese on each slice ham, cutting to fit. Roll ham tightly around cheese. Place one ham and cheese roll on each piece of veal. Top each with another piece of veal.

Place flour on waxed paper. Place bread crumbs on another piece of waxed paper. Beat egg with water in shallow dish. Dip veal packets in flour, then in beaten egg, then in bread crumbs. Press edges of packets together lightly to seal. Set aside for 10 minutes for edges to set.

Place butter in 8-inch microproof baking dish. Cook on HI, 1 minute. Place veal in butter. Cook on HI, 2 minutes. Turn veal over. Cook on HI, 2 minutes.

Remove veal. Add parsley and wine to pan juices. Pour wine mixture over veal and serve.

2 servings

VEAL PARMIGIANA

Approximate Cooking Time:
19½ to 21½ minutes

- 1 **egg**
- ¼ **teaspoon salt**
- 3 **tablespoons cracker crumbs**
- ⅓ **cup grated Parmesan cheese**
- 4 **veal cutlets (about 1 pound)**
- 2 **tablespoons vegetable oil**
- ¼ **cup Chianti**
- 1 **medium onion, minced**
- 1 **cup (4 ounces) shredded mozzarella cheese**
- 1 **can (8 ounces) tomato sauce**
- ⅛ **teaspoon oregano**
- ⅛ **teaspoon pepper**

Beat eggs and salt together in shallow dish. Combine cracker crumbs and Parmesan cheese on waxed paper. Place each veal cutlet between 2 pieces of waxed paper and pound with smooth-surfaced meat mallet until ¼ inch thick. Dip each piece of veal in egg and then roll in cracker crumbs. Set aside.

Preheat microwave browning dish according to manufacturer's directions. Place oil in browning dish. Add cutlets and cook on HI, 1½ minutes. Turn cutlets over and cook on HI, 1 to 2 minutes, or until meat loses its pink color. Pour wine over cutlets. Sprinkle with onion and cheese. Spoon tomato sauce over cheese. Sprinkle with oregano and pepper. Cook on 60, 10 to 11 minutes, or until cheese begins to melt and sauce is hot.

4 servings

Alternate method: If you do not have a browning dish, brown cutlets in skillet on top of stove. When brown, transfer to an 8- or 9-inch microproof baking dish and add remaining ingredients as above. Cover and cook on 60, 10 minutes.

VEAL SHOULDER ROAST

Approximate Cooking Time: 36 minutes

1 veal shoulder roast, boneless (2 pounds)

Place roast, fat-side down, on microwave roasting rack in 12 × 7-inch microproof baking dish. Cover roast lightly with waxed paper. Cook on 70, 15 minutes.

Turn roast over. Insert temperature probe horizontally into thickest part of roast without touching fat. Place in oven. Cover. Plug in probe. Cook on 70 with temperature probe set at 145°F.

Cover roast with aluminum foil and let stand 10 minutes. During standing time, internal temperature of roast will rise to 160°F.

4 servings

TRADITIONAL IRISH STEW

Cooking Time: 1 hour 30 minutes to 1 hour 40 minutes

2 pounds lamb for stew
1 package (1½ ounces) brown gravy mix with mushrooms
1 cup water
4 medium potatoes, peeled and cut into eighths
4 medium onions, quartered

Place lamb in 3-quart microproof casserole. Stir gravy mix into water. Pour over lamb. Cover with casserole lid and cook on 70, 50 minutes, stirring once during cooking time.

Stir in vegetables until well coated with gravy. Cover and cook on 50, 40 to 50 minutes, or until vegetables and lamb are tender. Let stand 5 minutes before serving.

4 to 6 servings

Irish stew freezes very well. You might like to serve half and freeze the remainder. Thaw a whole recipe on 30, 10 minutes, or until stew can be removed from container. Carefully stir during thawing to distribute heat. Finish heating on 70, 20 minutes. To thaw half the recipe, thaw as above, 6 to 7 minutes. Reheat 10 to 12 minutes. You can also prepare half of the recipe by cutting the ingredients in half. Cook on 70, 40 minutes. Add vegetables and cook on 50, 30 to 35 minutes, or until tender.

CALIFORNIA LAMB CHOPS

Approximate Cooking Time: 22½ to
24½ minutes

- **4 lamb shoulder arm chops (4 ounces each)**
- **½ cup butter or margarine**
- **1 cup white wine or chicken broth**
- **2 teaspoons chopped chives**
- **½ teaspoon Dijon-style mustard**
- **½ teaspoon tarragon**
- **½ teaspoon rosemary**
- **⅛ teaspoon pepper**
- **2 eggs, beaten**

Trim all fat from lamb chops. Set aside.

Combine remaining ingredients, except eggs, in a 2-cup glass measure. Cook on HI, 2½ minutes. Slowly beat hot liquid into eggs. Set aside.

Preheat browning dish according to manufacturer's directions. Place lamb chops on dish and cook on HI, 5 minutes.

Turn chops and cook on 80, 6 to 7 minutes, or until done.

Reheat sauce on 50, 2 to 3 minutes, stirring once. Pour sauce evenly onto 4 serving plates. Set meat on sauce.

2 servings

LAMB RAGOUT

Cooking Time: 40 to 45 minutes

- **1 pound lamb for stew**
- **1 package (⅝ ounce) brown gravy mix**
- **1 tablespoon paprika**
  Salt and pepper to taste
- **1 clove garlic, minced**
- **1 teaspoon tomato paste**
- **¼ cup dry red wine**
- **3 medium carrots, cut into chunks**
- **2 stalks celery, cut into chunks**
- **2 potatoes, peeled and cubed**
- **1 cup hot beef broth**

In 3-quart microproof casserole, combine lamb and gravy mix. Cook, uncovered, on 70, 10 minutes, stirring once during cooking time. Add remaining ingredients. Stir well. Cover with casserole lid and cook on 50, 30 to 35 minutes, or until lamb and vegetables are tender. Stir once during cooking time. Let stand 3 to 4 minutes before serving.

4 servings

The ingredients in this lamb stew may easily be cut in half for two servings. For best results, use 2 thin carrots. Cook lamb and gravy mix 10 minutes as above. After remaining ingredients are added, cook on 50, 18 to 20 minutes.

California Lamb Chops

HERBED LEG OF LAMB
Approximate Cooking Time: 50 minutes

  2 **cloves garlic**
  1 **lamb leg roast boneless (4 pounds), butterflied**
1½ **tablespoons soy sauce**
  1 **teaspoon dry mustard**
  1 **teaspoon salt**
  ½ **teaspoon thyme**
  ¼ **teaspoon rosemary**
  ⅛ **teaspoon pepper**
  1 **teaspoon lemon juice**

Cut 1 clove garlic in half and rub over lamb. Cut both cloves garlic into slivers. Slit outside of lamb at intervals and insert garlic slivers. Combine remaining ingredients. Spread over lamb. Roll roast up and tie at intervals with string. Place on microwave roasting rack in shallow microproof baking dish. Cover lamb lightly with waxed paper. Cook on 70, 30 minutes.

Turn lamb over. Insert temperature probe horizontally into densest part of meat. Place in oven. Plug in probe. Cover and cook on 70 with temperature probe set at 145°F. Let stand 5 minutes before serving.

6 to 8 servings

This recipe provides medium doneness. If you prefer your lamb well done, set temperature probe at 165°F for the second cook time.

SWEET AND SOUR PORK
Cooking Time: 24 minutes

  4 **medium carrots, thinly sliced**
  ¼ **cup vegetable oil**
  1 **medium onion, sliced**
  2 **green peppers, sliced**
  2 **pounds lean boneless pork, cut in ¾-inch cubes**
  1 **can (16 ounces) pineapple chunks, syrup reserved**
  ¼ **cup cornstarch**
  ½ **cup firmly packed brown sugar**
  ½ **cup soy sauce**
  ¼ **cup wine vinegar**
  1 **tablespoon Worcestershire sauce**
  ¼ **teaspoon hot-pepper sauce**
  ½ **teaspoon pepper**

Place carrots and oil in 3-quart microproof casserole. Stir. Cover with casserole lid and cook on HI, 4 minutes. Add onion, green peppers, and pork. Stir. Cover and cook on HI, 5 minutes.

Combine reserved pineapple syrup and cornstarch. Stir in remaining ingredients. Add to pork, along with pineapple chunks. Stir. Cover and cook on HI, 15 minutes, or until sauce has thickened and pork is done. Serve with rice or chow mein noodles.

8 servings

APRICOT-GLAZED HAM SLICE
Cooking Time: 4½ to 6 minutes

  1 **smoked ham center slice, ½ inch thick (about 8 ounces)**
  3 **tablespoons apricot marmalade**
  2 **tablespoons golden raisins**
  ¼ **teaspoon paprika**
  ⅛ **teaspoon nutmeg**

Place ham on microproof serving dish. Set aside. Combine marmalade, raisins, paprika, and nutmeg in 1-cup glass measure. Cook on HI, 1 minute. Spoon sauce over ham slice and cook on 70, 3½ to 5 minutes, depending on thickness of ham slice.

1 to 2 servings

STUFFED PORK CHOPS

Approximate Cooking Time: 16 to 20
minutes

- 1 **large orange, peeled and chopped**
- 2 **tablespoons raisins**
- ½ **cup fresh bread crumbs**
- 2 **tablespoons minced celery**
- 1 **egg**
- 1 **tablespoon butter or margarine**
- ⅛ **teaspoon poultry seasoning**
- 2 **loin pork chops, 1 inch thick,
  with pockets**

Combine all ingredients except pork chops. Stir until well mixed. Stuff pork chops. Pre-heat browning dish according to manufacturer's directions. Set chops in browning dish. Cook on HI, 4 to 6 minutes.

Turn and cook on HI, 4 to 6 minutes, or until meat is done.

2 servings

HAM DIVAN FOR TWO

Cooking Time: 8½ to 10 minutes

- 1 **teaspoon butter, melted**
- 1 **teaspoon flour**
- ½ **cup milk**
- ¼ **cup dairy sour cream**
- 1 **egg yolk, lightly beaten**
- ¼ **cup (1 ounce) grated
  Parmesan cheese**
- 1 **package (10 ounces) frozen broccoli
  spears, cooked and drained**
- ¼ **pound thinly sliced ham**
- 1 **teaspoon chopped fresh parsley**
- ½ **teaspoon rosemary**

Place butter in 2-cup glass measure and cook on 50, 1 minute. Add flour and stir to blend. Gradually blend in milk.

Cook on HI, 1 to 1½ minutes.

Stir in sour cream, egg yolk, and Parmesan cheese. Set aside. Arrange broccoli in 2 buttered individual microproof baking dishes. Place ham over broccoli. Top with sauce. Sprinkle with parsley and rosemary.

Cook on 60, 4 minutes.

Rotate dishes and cook on 60, 2½ to 3½ minutes, or until hot. Serve directly from baking dishes or over hot toast points.

2 servings

SPICY SPARERIBS

Cooking Time: 33 to 39 minutes

- 1 **can (15 ounces) tomato sauce**
- 3 **green onions, chopped**
- ⅛ **teaspoon cumin**
- ⅛ **teaspoon pepper**
- 1 **tablespoon Worcestershire sauce**
- 2 **tablespoons molasses**
- ½ **teaspoon Italian herb seasoning**
- 2 **pounds pork loin country-style ribs**
- 5 **cups hot beef broth**

Combine tomato sauce, onions, cumin, pepper, Worcestershire, molasses, and Italian seasoning in 4-cup glass measure. Cook on HI, 3 to 4 minutes, or until mixture boils. Set aside.

Arrange ribs in 3-quart microproof casserole. Cover with hot broth. Add more broth to cover, if needed. Cover with casserole lid and cook on HI, 15 minutes. Drain.

Baste with sauce. Cover and cook on 50, 15 to 20 minutes, or until tender.

4 servings

BAKED HAM WITH PINEAPPLE

Cooking Time: 29 to 31 minutes

- 1 **smoked ham butt portion (about 3
  pounds)**
- 1 **can (8 ounces) pineapple slices**
- ¼ **cup firmly packed brown sugar
  Whole cloves**

Place ham, fat-side down, in shallow microproof baking dish. Cook on 70, 21 minutes. Turn ham over.

Drain pineapple, reserving juice. Combine 2 teaspoons of juice with brown sugar to make a paste. Spread over top of ham. Place pineapple slices on top and stud with cloves. Attach pineapple with toothpicks if necessary.

Cook on 70, 8 to 10 minutes. Let stand, covered with aluminum foil, about 10 minutes before serving.

8 to 10 servings

Hunter's Pork Stew

HUNTER'S PORK STEW

Cooking Time: 21½ to 31½ minutes

- 2 **tablespoons brown sugar**
- 1 **tablespoon butter or margarine**
- ½ **cup apple cider**
- 1 **pork tenderloin (about 1 pound), cut into 8 pieces**
- 2 **tablespoons flour**
- 2 **cooking apples, cut into 8 pieces each**
- ½ **pound butternut squash, peeled and cut into 6 pieces**
- 1 **sweet potato or yam (about 6 ounces), peeled and cut into pieces**
- 1 **medium onion, sliced**

Mix together brown sugar, butter, and cider in a 1-cup glass measure. Cook on HI, 1½ minutes. Set aside.

Dredge tenderloin in flour. Place in 2-quart microproof casserole, placing the thickest portions toward the outside of casserole. Arrange apples and vegetables over and around meat. Pour cider mixture over vegetables and meat. Cover with casserole lid and cook on 50, 20 to 30 minutes, or until meat is tender. Remove from broth and arrange on serving platter.

2 servings

For a delightful serving surprise, choose a large butternut squash. Peel one half, cut and add to stew as above. Cook second half on HI, 6 minutes. Set aside. Serve stew in squash half.

PLUM PORK ROAST

Approximate Cooking Time: 30 minutes

- 2 **tablespoons all-purpose flour**
- 1 **onion, thinly sliced**
- 1 **2-pound pork top loin roast boneless**
- ¼ **cup plum wine**
- 1 **tablespoon soy sauce**
- 1 **tablespoon brown sugar**
- ¼ **teaspoon black pepper**
- 1 **teaspoon chopped fresh ginger**

Cut a 1-inch strip from the open end of cooking bag. Place flour and onion slices in bag. Place roast on top of onion. Place bag in shallow microproof baking dish. Combine remaining ingredients in small bowl and stir to blend. Pour over meat. Tie end of bag loosely with strip cut from cooking bag. Cook on 50, 15 minutes.

Carefully turn bag over. Open bag and insert temperature probe horizontally into center of roast. Re-tie bag. Place dish in oven and plug in temperature probe. Cook on 50 with probe set at 165°F.

Let stand 10 to 15 minutes.

4 servings

Serve with hot plum sauce, if you wish, or hot cooked plums.

Chicken Breasts Miyako

An uncoated chicken breast (left center) and a few of the possible coatings: seasoned bread crumbs, barbecue sauce, cornflake crumbs, and honey-soy glaze.

Chicken Breasts Miyako (page 85) are rolled and placed along outside edge of a microproof baking dish for even cooking. Delicious, too.

A cut up broiler-fryer chicken is ready for microwave cooking with thickest portions set along outside edge of dish for even cooking.

POULTRY

Chicken, turkey, duck, and Cornish hen are especially juicy, tender, and flavorful when cooked in a microwave oven. Because they require less attention than other entrées, they are great favorites for microwave cooks on those days when too many things seem to be happening at once. Poultry turns out golden brown but not crisp. If you have crisp-skin lovers at your table, you can satisfy them by crisping the skin in a conventional oven at 450°F, after the microwave cooking. You can also avoid the frustrations of long barbecue cooking by partially cooking poultry in the microwave oven, then finishing it off on the charcoal grill. Try the tasty recipes suggested here and then adapt your own. You'll even want to experiment with new recipes when you discover how much easier it is to cook poultry in your microwave oven than in the conventional oven. The nicest thing of all is that most poultry recipes cook with little or no attention from the cook. What's more, many of them can be cooked with the temperature probe, eliminating the need for you to calculate the cooking time.

ADAPTING YOUR RECIPES

Conventional one-dish poultry recipes that call for cut-up pieces are easy to adapt to the microwave oven. The temperature probe can help achieve accurate doneness in whole chicken recipes as well as in casseroles. Refer to the comparative chicken recipes on pages 32 and 33 to guide you in converting your favorite dishes.

Helpful Tips

To obtain uniform doneness and flavor, cook poultry weighing no more than 10 pounds in the microwave oven. Poultry over 10 pounds should be cooked conventionally.

Butter- or oil-injected turkeys often have uneven concentrations of fat and thus cook unevenly. For best results, use uninjected turkeys.

Conventional pop-up indicators for doneness do not work correctly in the microwave oven.

The temperature probe may be used in cooking whole poultry. Insert the probe in the fleshy part of the inside thigh muscle without touching the bone.

Poultry pieces prepared in a cream sauce should be cooked on 70 to prevent the cream from separating or curdling.

Chicken coated with a crumb mixture cooks to crispness more easily if left uncovered.

Less tender game birds should be cooked on a microwave roasting rack, placed in a microproof baking dish. Cook on 70 to provide tenderizing. Pour off fat as necessary. For best results, marinate game birds before cooking.

Standing time is essential to complete cooking. Allow up to 15 minutes standing time for whole poultry, depending upon size. The internal temperature will rise approximately 15°F during 15 minutes standing time. Chicken pieces and casseroles need only 5 minutes standing time.

REHEATING GUIDE — POULTRY*

Food	Power Control	Time	Special Notes
Chicken, frozen fried, 1½-2 lbs.	follow package directions		Shallow microproof baking dish.
Chicken Kiev 1 - 2 pieces	follow package directions		Microproof baking dish.
Chicken à la King, frozen, 8 oz.	HI	4 - 6 min.	Place on microproof plate.
Creamed chicken, 10½ oz. can	80	4 - 5 min.	Stir once.
Chicken chow mein, 14-24 oz. can	80	5 - 7 min.	Stir halfway through cooking time.
Turkey tetrazzini, frozen, 12 oz.	HI	5 - 7 min.	Place on microproof plate. Cover with waxed paper.
Turkey, sliced in gravy, frozen, 5 oz.	HI	4 - 6 min.	Slit pouch. Place in microproof dish.

* Due to the tremendous variety in convenience food products available, times given here should be used only as guidelines. We suggest you cook food for the shortest recommended time and then check for doneness. Be sure to check the package for microwave instructions.

DEFROSTING POULTRY

To prepare for defrosting, remove poultry from original paper or plastic wrappings. Metal leg clamps of frozen turkey need not be removed until after thawing. Keep metal at least 1 inch from oven walls.

Defrost only as long as necessary. Poultry should be cool in the center, in fact still a bit icy. Standing time completes the thawing.

If you wish to use the oven, remove poultry during standing time. You can also choose to immerse poultry in cold water during the standing time.

Separate cut-up chicken pieces as soon as partially thawed. Remove those that feel even slightly warm.

Wing and leg tips and area near breast bone may need to be shielded to prevent cooking. As soon as they appear thawed, cover with small strips of foil, keeping foil at least 1 inch from oven walls.

Turn all poultry over between the first and second stage of defrosting. (At the pause signal, if you use the PAUSE touch pad and set both defrosting sequences before touching START.)

COOKING POULTRY

There are just a few basic recommendations in cooking poultry, and many of them would apply just as well to conventional cooking. Defrost frozen poultry completely before cooking, remove the giblets, rinse poultry in cool water, and pat dry. If you wish to do so, brush poultry with a microwave browning sauce before cooking.

When cooking whole birds, place on a microwave roasting rack in a glass baking dish large enough to catch drippings.

Turn poultry over, as directed in the cooking guide or recipe, usually about halfway through the cooking time. Baste if you wish.

We recommend that you cook whole poultry covered loosely with a waxed paper tent to prevent splattering. Toward end of cooking time, small pieces of aluminum foil may be used for shielding to cover legs, wing tips, or breast bone area to prevent overcooking. Foil should be at least 1 inch from oven walls.

We also suggest that you cover poultry pieces with either the lid of the microproof casserole or plastic wrap during cooking and standing time.

Use the temperature probe inserted in thickest part of thigh, set at 180°F for whole poultry, and at 170°F for parts, including turkey breasts. Standing time completes the cooking of poultry.

DEFROSTING GUIDE — POULTRY

Food	Amount	Minutes (per pound)	Power Control	Standing Time (in minutes)	Special Notes
Capon	6 - 8 lbs.	2	70	60	Turn over once. Immerse in cold water for standing time.
Chicken, cut up	2 - 3 lbs.	5 - 6	30	10 - 15	Turn every 5 minutes. Separate pieces when partially thawed.
Chicken, whole	2 - 3 lbs.	6 - 8	30	25 - 30	Turn over once. Immerse in cold water for standing time.
Cornish hen	1 - 1½ lbs.	12 - 13	30	20	Turn over once.
Duckling	4 - 5 lbs.	6 - 8	30	30 - 40	Turn over once. Immerse in cold water for standing time.
Turkey	8 - 10 lbs.	3 - 5 / 3 - 5	70 / 30	60	Turn over once. Change setting. Shield warm areas. Immerse in cold water for standing time.
Turkey breast	Under 4 lbs. / Over 4 lbs.	3 - 5 / 1 / 2	30 / 70 / 30	20 / 20	Turn over once. Start at 70, turn over, continue on 30.
Turkey parts	1 - 2 lbs.	4 - 6	30	15 - 20	Turn every 5 minutes. Separate pieces when partially thawed.
Turkey roast, boneless	2 - 4	3 - 4	30	10	Remove from foil pan. Cover with waxed paper.
Turkey fillets	1 - 2 lbs.	5 - 6	30	5	Turn over once. Separate fillets when partially thawed.
Ground turkey, bulk	1 lb.	4 - 5	30	5	Turn over once. Slit package.

NOTE: If your oven is equipped with an Auto Defrost or Programmed Defrost feature, please consult your Use & Care Manual for assistance in defrosting with those methods. The timing in the chart here is for manual, or attended, defrosting.

COOKING GUIDE — POULTRY

Food	First Cook Time and Power Control	Second Cook Time and Power Control	Probe Method	Special Notes
Chicken, whole, 3½ - 5 lbs.	3 - 4 min. per lb. breast down on HI - turn over	4 - 5 min. per lb. on HI	180°F	Microproof dish with microwave rack. Let stand 5 minutes, covered with foil.
Chicken, pieces, 2½ - 4 lbs.	10 min. skin down on HI - turn over	4 - 5 min. per lb. on HI	170°	Microproof baking dish. Let stand 5 minutes.
Cornish hens, 1 - 1½ lbs.	4 min. per lb. breast up on HI - turn over	3 min. per lb. on HI	180°F	Microproof baking dish with microwave rack. Let stand 5 minutes.
Duckling 4 - 5 lbs.	4 min. per lb. breast down on 70 - turn over	4 min. per lb. on 70	170°	Microproof dish with microwave rack. Drain excess fat. Let stand 8 - 10 minutes.
Turkey, whole 8 - 10 lbs.	5 - 6 min. per lb. breast up on HI - turn over	4 min. per lb. on 70	170°	Microproof dish with microwave rack. Let stand 10 - 15 minutes, covered with foil.
Turkey breast, 3 - 4 lb.	7 min. per lb. skin down on HI - turn over	5 min. per lb. on HI	170°F	Microproof baking dish.
Turkey roast, boneless, 2 - 4 lbs.	10 min. per lb. on 70 - turn over	9 min. per lb. on 70	170°F	Microproof baking dish.
Turkey parts, 2 - 3 lbs.	7 - 8 min. per lb. on 70	7 - 8 min. per lb. on 70		Microproof baking dish. Start skin down. Let stand 5 minutes.
Turkey fillets, 1 - 2 lbs.	3 min. per lb. on 70	3 - 4 min. per lb. on 70		Microproof baking dish. Cover with waxed paper.
Ground turkey, bulk	2 min. per lb. on HI	3 - 4 min. per lb. on HI		Crumble in microproof dish.

ITALIAN-STYLE CHICKEN BREASTS

Cooking Time: 11 minutes

> 1 **tablespoon margarine**
> 1 **teaspoon cornstarch**
> ½ **teaspoon Italian herb seasoning**
> ¼ **cup chicken broth**
> 1 **whole chicken breast (about 1 pound), skinned, boned, and split**
> 1 **medium tomato, coarsely chopped**
> 1 **tablespoon chopped fresh parsley**

Combine margarine, cornstarch, Italian seasoning, and chicken broth in 1-cup glass measure. Stir well. Cook on HI, 1 minute. Set aside.

Roll up chicken breasts and place, seam-side down, in 1-quart microproof casserole. Cover with tomatoes and sprinkle with parsley. Pour broth mixture over chicken. Cover with casserole lid and cook on 50, 4 minutes.

Baste. Cover and cook on 70, 6 minutes.

2 servings

CHICKEN BREASTS A LA SUISSE

Cooking Time: 4½ to 5 minutes

> 1 **whole chicken breast (1 pound) skinned, boned, and split**
> 1 **teaspoon cornstarch**
> ¼ **teaspoon paprika**
> ¼ **teaspoon white pepper**
> ⅓ **cup light cream**
> 2 **tablespoons apple juice**
> ½ **cup shredded Swiss cheese**
> 1 **tablespoon chopped fresh parsley**

Place chicken in shallow microproof baking dish. Combine cornstarch, paprika, white pepper, cream, and apple juice. Stir thoroughly. Pour over chicken. Cover with plastic wrap and cook on HI, 1 minute.

Stir sauce and turn chicken over. Cover and cook on HI, 2 minutes. Stir. Sprinkle cheese over chicken. Remove cover and cook on HI, 1½ to 2 minutes, or until cheese is melted and chicken is fork-tender. Sprinkle with parsley before serving.

2 servings

ORANGE-GLAZED CHICKEN FOR TWO

Cooking Time: 11½ minutes

> 1 **whole chicken breast (1 pound), split, rinsed, and patted dry**
> **Paprika**
> 1 **tablespoon brown sugar**
> 2 **tablespoons orange juice**
> 2 **tablespoons vinegar**
> ½ **teaspoon grated orange peel**
> ½ **teaspoon cornstarch**

Place chicken in 9-inch round microproof baking dish, thick edges toward rim. Sprinkle lightly with paprika. Cover with waxed paper and cook on HI, 3 minutes. Pour off fat and set aside.

Combine brown sugar, orange juice, vinegar, orange peel, and cornstarch in 2-cup glass measure. Cook on HI, 2½ minutes. Stir. Pour over chicken. Cook on HI, 3 minutes.

Rotate dish. Baste with pan juices and sprinkle with paprika. Cover with plastic wrap and cook on HI, 3 minutes.

2 servings

HOT CHICKEN SALAD FOR ONE

Cooking Time: 4 minutes

> 1 **cup cubed cooked chicken**
> ½ **cup diced celery**
> ¼ **cup toasted slivered almonds**
> 1 **green onion, chopped**
> 4 **tablespoons grated Monterey jack cheese**
> ½ **teaspoon dillweed**
> 1 **teaspoon lemon juice**
> ½ **cup mayonnaise**
> 1 **tablespoon dry bread crumbs**
> **Paprika**

Combine all ingredients except bread crumbs and paprika and mix thoroughly. Spoon salad into 1-quart microproof casserole. Cook on HI, 2 minutes.

Sprinkle bread crumbs and paprika over salad. Cook on HI, 2 minutes.

1 serving

BROWNING DISH CHICKEN

Approximate Cooking Time: 17 minutes

- ½ **cup all-purpose flour**
- ½ **teaspoon salt**
- ¼ **teaspoon pepper**
- ⅛ **teaspoon dry mustard**
- 1 **broiler-fryer chicken (3 to 3½ pounds), cut up, backbone and wing tips removed**
- 2 **tablespoons lemon juice**
- 2 **tablespoons vegetable oil**
- 2 **tablespoons butter**
  Paprika

Combine flour, salt, pepper, and mustard in paper bag. Brush chicken with lemon juice. Add chicken to seasoned flour in batches and shake to coat well. Shake off excess flour. Preheat microwave browning dish according to manufacturer's directions. Add oil and butter to dish. Arrange chicken, skin-side down, on browning dish; do not crowd. Cover lightly with waxed paper. Cook on HI, 4 minutes.

Turn chicken over. Sprinkle with paprika. Cover and cook on HI, 5 minutes.

4 servings

CHICKEN BREASTS MIYAKO

Cooking Time: 7 to 9 minutes

- 2 **whole chicken breasts (1 pound each), skinned, boned, and split**
- 2 **teaspoons Dijon-style mustard**
- 8 **fresh Chinese pea pods**
- 1 **small sweet red pepper, cut into julienne strips**
- 4 **ounces Brie cheese**
- 1 **teaspoon cornstarch**
- ¼ **cup chicken broth**
- 1 **tablespoon lemon juice**
- 1 **green onion, chopped**

Lightly pound each chicken breast with meat mallet. Spread one side with mustard, and top with two pea pods and one-fourth the pepper strips. Cut Brie into 4 pieces. Place over red pepper strips. Roll up each chicken breast and place in 1-quart micro-proof casserole. Set aside.

Combine cornstarch, broth, and lemon juice in 1-cup glass measure. Stir until cornstarch dissolves. Cook on HI, 1 minute. Stir. Pour hot broth mixture over chicken. Sprinkle onion over chicken. Cover with casserole lid and cook on 70, 6 to 8 minutes, or until chicken is tender.

4 servings

CHICKEN CACCIATORE

Cooking Time: 34 to 40 minutes

- 1 **medium onion, chopped**
- 1 **medium green pepper, seeded and thinly sliced**
- 1 **tablespoon butter or margarine**
- 1 **can (28 ounces) whole tomatoes**
- ½ **cup dry red wine or water**
- ¼ **cup all-purpose flour**
- 1 **bay leaf**
- 3 **tablespoons fresh chopped parsley**
- 1 **teaspoon paprika**
- ½ **teaspoon salt**
- 1 **clove garlic, minced**
- ½ **teaspoon oregano**
- ¼ **teaspoon pepper**
- ¼ **teaspoon basil**
- 1 **frying chicken, 2½ to 3 pounds, cut up**

In a 3-quart microproof casserole, combine onion, green pepper, and butter. Cover with casserole lid and cook on HI, 4 to 5 minutes, or until onion is transparent. Add tomatoes and flour, and stir until smooth. Stir in remaining ingredients except chicken.

Cook, covered, on HI, 5 minutes. Add chicken pieces, immersing in sauce.

Cook, covered, on HI, 20 to 25 minutes, or until chicken is tender. Stir once during cooking. Let stand 5 minutes. Remove bay leaf before serving.

4 to 6 servings

CHICKEN PAPRIKASH

Cooking Time: 26½ to 31½ minutes

- 1 **broiler-fryer chicken (2½ to 3 pounds), cut up**
- 1 **tablespoon paprika**
- 1 **cup milk**
- 1 **tablespoon flour**
- ¼ **cup sour cream**

Rinse chicken and pat dry. Arrange chicken in 2½-quart microproof casserole, placing thicker portions around outside of dish and chicken wings in center. Sprinkle with paprika. Set aside.

Pour milk into 2-cup glass measure and cook on HI, 1½ minutes. Pour hot milk around chicken. Cover and cook on 80, 25 to 30 minutes, or until chicken is tender.

Stir flour into sour cream. Remove chicken pieces and stir sour cream into milk. Pour around chicken to serve.

4 servings

Imported Hungarian paprika gives this dish subtle flavor as well as authenticity. Look for it in spice shops or ethnic grocery stores.

CHICKEN LIVERS WITH MUSHROOMS

Cooking Time: 12 to 14 minutes

- 1 **large onion, sliced**
- 2 **tablespoons butter or margarine**
- 1 **pound chicken livers, halved**
- ½ **pound fresh mushrooms, sliced**
- 2 **tablespoons dry white wine**
- ½ **teaspoon Worcestershire sauce**
- ¼ **teaspoon Italian herb seasoning**
- ⅛ **teaspooon pepper**

Place onion and butter in 2-quart microproof casserole. Cover with casserole lid and cook on HI, 4 minutes, or until onion is transparent. Remove onions with slotted spoon and set aside.

Place liver in casserole. Stir. Cover and cook on 50, 5 to 7 minutes. Add mushrooms, onion, wine, Worcestershire, Italian seasoning, and pepper. Cover and cook on 50, 3 minutes, or until hot, stirring once.

2 to 4 servings

CHICKEN MILANO

Cooking Time: 12 minutes

- 1 **teaspoon salt**
- ½ **teaspoon pepper**
- ¼ **teaspoon oregano**
- ¼ **teaspoon basil**
- 3 **tablespoons olive oil**
- 4 **large chicken thighs**
- 1 **cup fine bread crumbs**
- 2 **medium potatoes, peeled and quartered**
  Paprika

Combine salt, pepper, oregano, basil, and olive oil. Coat chicken thighs with marinade. Cover and let stand in refrigerator for 2 hours.

Drain chicken, reserving marinade. Roll chicken in bread crumbs. Place in shallow 9-inch square microproof baking dish, skin-side down, with thickest portions near edge of dish.

Roll potatoes in marinade, adding more oil, if needed. Place in dish with chicken. Cover with waxed paper and cook on HI, 5 minutes.

Turn chicken skin-side up and turn potatoes over. Sprinkle chicken and potatoes with paprika. Cook on HI, 7 minutes. Cover with aluminum foil and let stand 5 minutes before serving.

4 servings

Chicken Paprikash

CHICKEN BREASTS WITH VEGETABLES

Cooking Time: 20 to 21 minutes

- 2 **small parsnips, peeled and cut into julienne strips**
- 2 **carrots, cut into julienne strips**
- 2 **stalks celery, cut into julienne strips**
- 2 **small potatoes, peeled and cut into julienne strips**
- 1 **medium onion, thinly sliced**
- 2 **tablespoons butter or margarine**
- ½ **teaspoon salt**
  Dash ground pepper
- 2 **tablespoons minced fresh parsley**
- 2 **whole chicken breasts (about 1 pound each) skinned, boned, and split**
  Paprika

Place vegetables in shallow 1½-quart micro-proof dish. Dot with butter and sprinkle with salt, pepper, and parsley. Cover with plastic wrap and cook on HI, 10 minutes, stirring halfway through cooking time.

Stir vegetables again. Arrange chicken breasts on vegetables around outside of dish. Sprinkle chicken with paprika. Cover with plastic wrap and cook on HI, 10 to 11 minutes, or until chicken is fork-tender.

4 servings

GINGER CHICKEN

Approximate Cooking Time: 27 minutes

- 1 **small onion, halved**
- 1 **broiler-fryer chicken (2½ to 3 pounds)**
- ¼ **cup soy sauce**
- ¼ **cup dry sherry**
- 3 **slices fresh ginger**

Place onion in cavity of chicken. Brush skin all over with soy sauce. Cut small strip from end of cooking bag. Place chicken, breast-side up, in cooking bag. Add sherry, remaining soy sauce, and ginger to bag. Insert temperature probe into fleshy part of inside of thigh, being careful not to touch bone. Tie bag loosely with plastic strip. Place in shallow microproof baking dish.

Place dish in oven and plug in probe. Cook on 80 with probe set at 180°F. Let stand 10 minutes before serving.

4 servings

If not using the probe, cook in bag on 80, 8 to 10 minutes per pound, or until done. If you want to reduce calories, substitute chicken bouillon for sherry.

MAUI CHICKEN

Cooking Time: 10 to 11 minutes

- ½ **cup chicken broth**
- 1 **tablespoon dry white wine**
- 1 **tablespoon dry sherry**
- 1 **teaspoon sugar**
- 1 **teaspoon cornstarch**
- 1 **whole chicken breast (about 1 pound), skinned, boned, and cubed**
- 1 **small green pepper, cut into strips**
- 1 **small sweet red pepper, cut into strips**
- 3 **green onions, cut into 1-inch pieces**
- ½ **cup sliced bamboo shoots**
- 1 **to 2 slices fresh ginger**
- 1 **cup fresh pineapple chunks**
- ½ **cup whole cashews**

Combine broth, white wine, sherry, sugar, and cornstarch in 2-cup glass measure. Stir thoroughly. Cook on HI, 1½ minutes, or until sauce is clear, stirring once. Set aside.

Combine chicken, green and red peppers, green onions, bamboo shoots, and ginger in 2-quart casserole. Cover and cook on HI, 6 to 7 minutes.

Add pineapple, cashews, and sauce mixture. Cover and cook on HI, 2½ minutes, or until hot.

4 servings

If fresh pineapple is not available, substitute 1 can (8 ounces) pineapple chunks, drained.

CHICKEN WITH HERBS

Approximate Cooking Time: 34 minutes

- 1 **whole broiler-fryer chicken (3 to 3½ pounds)**
- 2 **tablespoons vegetable oil**
- 2 **tablespoons browning sauce**
- 1 **clove garlic, minced**
- ½ **teaspoon rosemary**
- ½ **teaspoon sage**
- ½ **teaspoon thyme**

Rinse chicken and pat dry. Place chicken, breast-side up, on microwave roasting rack in shallow microproof baking dish. Fold wings under back of chicken. Set aside.

Combine oil, browning sauce, garlic, and herbs. Stir to mix well. Brush ½ of the herb mixture over chicken.

Insert temperature probe into fleshy part of inside of thigh without touching bone. Cover with tent of waxed paper. Place in oven and plug in probe. Cook on HI with probe set at 120°F.

At signal, turn chicken over, being careful not to dislodge temperature probe. Brush with remaining herb mixture. Cook on HI with probe set at 180°F. Let stand 10 minutes before carving.

4 servings

Baked chicken offers yet another opportunity to explore international cuisine and the world of herbs and spices. For an Italian flavor, use basil and oregano for the herbs. For Indian flavor, use curry powder or your own mixture of cumin, turmeric, chili, and cayenne. Choose your favorites — but remember — herbs and spices should enhance, not dominate, your dish.

BARBECUED CHICKEN

Cooking Time: 18 to 20 minutes

- 1 **broiler-fryer chicken (3 to 3½ pounds), quartered**
- ½ **cup Barbecue Sauce (page 145)**
- 1 **tablespoon chopped fresh parsley**
- 1 **tablespoon onion flakes**

Arrange chicken pieces, skin-side down, placing thick edges toward outside of 12 × 7 × 2-inch microproof baking dish. Combine remaining ingredients. Brush half the sauce over chicken. Cover with waxed paper and cook on HI, 10 minutes.

Turn chicken over and brush with remaining sauce. Cover and cook on HI, 8 to 10 minutes, or until chicken is fork-tender. Let stand, covered, 5 minutes before serving.

4 servings

CORNISH HENS WITH CITRUS GLAZE

Cooking Time: 25 to 27 minutes

> 2 **Cornish hens (1½ pounds each)**
> 1 **onion, quartered**
> 1 **stalk celery, cut into pieces**
> ¼ **cup butter or margarine**
> 1 **slice lemon**
> **Paprika**
> **Citrus Sauce (page 148)**

Rinse Cornish hens in cool water and pat dry. Place onion, celery, and lemon in hen cavities.

Place hens, breast-side up, in oval microproof baking dish with thickest parts toward outside of dish. Sprinkle with paprika. Cook on HI, 15 minutes.

Turn hens breast-side down and baste with pan juices. Cook on HI, 6 to 7 minutes.

Turn hens breast-side up and brush with Citrus Sauce. Cook on 50, 4 to 5 minutes, or until glaze is set.

4 servings

CORNISH HENS WITH WILD RICE

Approximate Cooking Time: 42 minutes

> 2 **Cornish hens (1½ pounds each)**
> 1 **package (10 ounces) frozen wild rice**
> 2 **tablespoons butter or margarine**
> ½ **cup current jelly**
> 2 **teaspoons dry sherry**

Rinse Cornish hens in cool water and pat dry; set aside. Place rice and butter in 3-quart microproof casserole. Cover with casserole lid and cook on 80, 4 minutes.

Stir and continue to cook on 80, 3 minutes.

Remove rice from oven and let stand until cool. Combine jelly and sherry; set aside. Spoon cooled rice into hen cavities and secure with wooden toothpicks; set any extra rice aside. Place hens, breast-side down, in oval microproof baking dish with thickest parts toward outside of dish. Insert temperature probe horizontally into fleshy part of inside thigh of one hen without touching bone. Brush hens evenly with half the sherry glaze. Place in oven. Plug in probe. Cook on HI with temperature probe set at 120°F.

At signal, turn hens breast-side up, being careful not to remove temperature probe. Brush with remaining sherry glaze. Arrange reserved rice around hens. Cook on HI with temperature probe set at 170°F. Let stand 10 minutes before serving.

4 servings

TURKEY PATTIES

Approximate Cooking Time: 12 minutes

> ½ **pound ground turkey**
> ¼ **cup chopped mushrooms**
> 1 **green onion, finely chopped**
> ¼ **cup seasoned bread crumbs**
> 1 **egg, lightly beaten**
> 2 **tablespoons butter or margarine**
> **Basic White Sauce (page 144)**

Combine turkey and mushrooms in medium bowl. Shape into 2 patties. Set aside.

Preheat browning dish according to manufacturer's directions. Combine green onion and bread crumbs. Dip patties into egg, then into bread crumbs and onion mixture. Place butter in preheated browning dish. Add patties and cook on HI, 2 minutes.

Turn patties over and cook another 2 to 3 minutes on HI, or until patties are tender and lightly browned. Place on serving platter and top with Basic White Sauce. Garnish with parsley or other fresh herbs, if desired.

2 servings

For a quick luncheon surprise, simply serve these patties on fresh poppy seed hard rolls with lettuce and mayonnaise. Eliminate the Basic White Sauce, or serve open-face on toasted English muffins topped with the sauce.

Cornish Hens with Citrus Glaze

TURKEY FLORENTINE

Cooking Time: 11 to 13 minutes

- 1 **package (10 ounces) frozen chopped spinach or 8 ounces fresh spinach, cooked and chopped**
- ¼ **cup chopped water chestnuts**
- ¼ **teaspoon nutmeg**
- 2 **tablespoons chopped pimiento**
- 1 **green onion, chopped**
  Basic White Sauce (page 144)
- 4 **slices turkey breast (2 ounces each)**
- ¼ **cup grated Parmesan cheese**

Place unopened package of spinach on microproof plate. (If spinach is wrapped in foil, remove foil.) Cook on HI, 6 minutes. Let stand 5 minutes. Squeeze dry.

Combine spinach, water chestnuts, onion, pimiento, nutmeg, and Basic White Sauce. Mix well.

Place turkey slices in 8-inch round microproof baking dish with thick portions toward outside of dish. Pour sauce evenly over turkey. Sprinkle with Parmesan cheese. Cover with waxed paper and cook on HI, 5 to 7 minutes, or until meat is done and sauce is hot.

2 to 4 servings

QUICK TURKEY DIVAN

Cooking Time: 11 to 12 minutes

- 1 **package (10 ounces) frozen broccoli spears**
- 4 **fresh turkey breast slices (about 2 ounces each)**
- 1 **cup Basic White Sauce (page 144)**
- ¼ **cup grated Parmesan cheese**

Place unopened package of broccoli on microproof plate and cook on HI, 3 minutes. (If broccoli is in foil-wrapped package, remove foil.) Let stand 3 minutes. Separate spears and pat dry. Arrange in 1-quart microproof casserole. Fold each slice of turkey breast in half and arrange on broccoli.

Pour sauce over turkey. Sprinkle with Parmesan cheese. Cover and cook on HI, 5 minutes.

Uncover and cook on 50, 3 to 4 minutes.

2 servings

TURKEY WITH CORNBREAD STUFFING

Approximate Cooking Time: 1½ hours

- ½ **pound bulk pork sausage**
- 1 **small onion, chopped**
- 1 **stalk celery, chopped**
- 1 **cup diced mushrooms**
- 1 **cup hot chicken stock**
- 2 **cups cornbread stuffing mix**
- 1 **10 pound turkey, rinsed and patted dry**
  Vegetable oil
  Paprika

Combine sausage, onion, and celery in 3-quart microproof bowl. Cook on HI, 5 minutes, stirring once during cooking time to break up sausage.

Stir in mushrooms. Cook on HI, 2 minutes. Add stock and stir to mix. Add stuffing mix and stir gently until well mixed, adding more liquid if mixture seems too dry.

Spoon stuffing into turkey cavities. Tuck in wings. Rub turkey with oil and sprinkle with paprika. Place turkey, breast-side up, on microwave roasting rack in shallow microproof baking dish. Cook on HI, 20 minutes.

Turn turkey over and insert temperature probe into fleshy part of inside of thigh, being careful not to touch bone. Baste with pan juices. Place in oven and plug in probe. Cook on 70 with probe set at 180°F.

At signal, baste and cook on 30, 15 minutes.

8 to 10 servings

If you like an extra-crisp skin, remove probe and place turkey in conventional oven, preheated to 450°F. Cook 10 to 15 minutes, or until desired crispness.

Turkey Florentine

TURKEY BREAST JARDINIERE

Cooking Time: 37 to 55 minutes

- 1 **medium carrot, cut into julienne strips**
- 1 **celery stalk, cut into julienne strips**
- 1 **small onion, thinly sliced and separated into rings**
- 1 **small potato, cut into julienne strips**
- 1 **tablespoon chopped fresh parsley**
- 2 **tablespoons butter**
  Salt and freshly ground pepper
- ½ **turkey breast (3 to 4 pounds) Paprika**

Place carrot, celery, onion, potato, and parsley in center of an oval microproof baking dish large enough to accommodate all ingredients. Dot with butter. Season lightly with salt and pepper. Cover with waxed paper and cook on HI, 7 minutes, stirring once during cooking time.

Place turkey breast on vegetables and sprinkle with paprika. Cover with waxed paper and cook on HI, 10 to 12 minutes per pound.

1 to 2 servings

RASPBERRY DUCKLING

Approximate Cooking Time: 55 minutes

- 1 **duckling (4 pounds), giblets removed**
- 1 **carrot, peeled and cut into chunks**
- 1 **medium onion, cut into quarters**
- 1 **jar (10 ounces) raspberry jelly**
- ¼ **cup raspberry liqueur**
- 2 **tablespoons fresh lemon juice**

Rinse duckling in cool water and pat dry. Place carrot and onion pieces in body cavity. Secure neck skin with wooden toothpicks or skewers. Tie legs together with string; tie wings to body. Pierce skin all over to allow fat to drain. Place duckling, breast-side up, on microwave roasting rack in microproof baking dish.

Place duckling in oven and cook on HI, 20 minutes.

Meanwhile, combine remaining ingredients in small bowl and stir until smooth.

Turn duckling over and drain excess fat. Insert temperature probe. Plug in probe. Brush duck with glaze. Cook on 70 with temperature probe set at 160°F.

Turn duckling over and baste without removing probe. Cook on HI with temperature probe set at 170°F. Let stand 10 minutes before serving.

2 servings

For a "the boss is coming" special dinner, add 1 pint fresh whole raspberries, or 1½ cups thawed frozen whole raspberries to juices after duckling is cooked. Toss lightly and cook on 80, 2 to 2½ minutes, or until warmed through. Spoon over duckling and serve.

DUCKLING A L'ORANGE

Approximate Cooking Time: 45 minutes

- 1 **4- to 5-pound duckling**
- 1 **teaspoon salt**
- ¼ **teaspoon pepper**
- 1 **small onion, quartered**
  Leaves from 2 to 3 celery stalks
  Orange Sauce (page 146)

Rinse duckling thoroughly in cool water; pat dry. Sprinkle cavity with salt and pepper. Set onion and celery leaves inside cavity. Tie legs and wings together with string. Pierce skin around leg and wing joints with fork. Arrange duckling, breast-side down, on microwave roasting rack in microproof baking dish.

Place in oven and cook on HI, 20 minutes.

Remove from oven. Pour off excess fat. Turn duckling over and pierce entire surface with fork to allow fat to drain. Insert probe in breast close to leg without touching bone. Plug in probe. Cook on 70 with temperature probe set at 170°F. Serve with Orange Sauce.

2 to 4 servings

Your duckling will be nicely browned at the end of the microwave cooking time. However, if you prefer a crisp skin, preheat conventional oven to 450°F. Brush duckling with Orange Sauce, and crisp in conventional oven for 10 to 20 minutes, or until done to your preference.

Lake Country Stuffed Trout (page 101) cooks best in a microproof au gratin dish. Notice the foil covering to prevent overcooking.

Fish fillets brown nicely in a browning dish. A metal trivet is useful to place the hot browning dish on when removed from the oven.

For microwave cooking, shrimp are arranged with the tails toward the center of a microproof baking dish. They cook unbelievably fast.

FISH & SHELLFISH

Poaching and steaming have always been the most classic methods of cooking fish. Now, discover the newest "classic" — fish and shellfish microwave-style! So moist, tender, and delicious that you'll never want to cook seafood any other way. And all this with no elaborate procedures: No need to tie the fish in cheesecloth or use a special fish poacher. Shellfish steam to a succulent tenderness with very little water. If you think your microwave oven cooks chicken and meat fast, you'll be amazed at its speed with fish! For best results, fish should be prepared at the last minute. Even standing time is short. In fact, formal standing time isn't required in microwave fish cookery. By the time you bring the fish to the table, and take your seat, your fish or shellfish dinner will be at its perfectly-done moment and ready to eat. So, when planning a fish dinner, have everything ready. Then start to cook. Seafood cooks so quickly because it has no muscle or connective tissue that needs tenderizing by a lengthy cooking process. The microwave oven provides the delicate cooking required, preserving moisture. Little or no evaporation occurs because no hot air is present to dry the surface. Shrimp and other shellfish should be cooked until they just turn pink (no water is needed). Fish needs just enough cooking time for it to turn opaque and flake easily. It will toughen if overcooked.

ADAPTING YOUR RECIPES

If your family likes seafood only when it is fried crackly-crisp, surprise them with a new taste delight when you try traditional fish recipes cooked in the microwave oven. They'll swear fish has become pampered and poached by the most famous French chef. Use the cooking guides and the recipes as references for adapting your own dishes. If you don't find a recipe that matches or comes close to the conventional recipe you want to adapt, follow this general rule of thumb: Begin cooking at 70 or at HI for one-fifth of the time that the conventional recipe recommends. Observe, and if it appears to be done earlier, open the door and check. If the dish is not done, continue cooking 30 seconds at a time. As in conventional cooking, the secret to seafood is to watch it carefully, since fish can overcook in seconds. It's best to remove seafood when barely done and allow it to finish cooking on its way to the table.

Helpful Tips

Most recipes that specify a particular variety of fish will work when any white fish is substituted. When a recipe calls for fresh or thawed frozen fish fillets, use sole, flounder, bluefish, cod, scrod, or any similar fish.

Cook fish covered unless it is coated with crumbs, which seal in the juices.

When cooking whole fish, the dish should be rotated one-quarter turn twice during the cooking process to help provide even cooking. The odd shape of the fish requires this procedure.

Fish is done when the flesh becomes opaque and barely flakes with a fork.

Shellfish is done when flesh is opaque and just firm.

Shellfish come in their own cooking containers which respond well to microwaves. Clam and mussel shells open before your eyes. Shrimp, crab, and lobster shells turn pink.

You can use the browning dish for fillets or fish patties. Preheat, add butter or oil, and brown on one side for best results.

To remove seafood odors from the oven, combine 1 cup water with lemon juice and a few cloves in a small bowl. Cook on HI, 3 to 5 minutes.

DEFROSTING FISH AND SHELLFISH

To prepare for defrosting, remove seafood from its original wrapper and place in a microproof dish.

To prevent the outer edges from drying out or beginning to cook, it is best to remove seafood from the oven before it has completely thawed. Even if it is a bit icy,

REHEATING GUIDE — SEAFOOD*

Food	Power Control	Time	Special Notes
Fish sticks frozen, (12)	follow package directions		Microproof baking dish.
Shrimp or crab newburg, frozen 6½ oz.	HI	4 - 6	Slit pouch, place on plate. Flex pouch to mix halfway through cooking time.
Scallops or fish kabobs, 7 oz.	follow package directions		Microproof baking dish.
Tuna casserole, frozen, 16 oz.	HI	5 - 7	Remove from package to 1-quart microproof casserole. Stir once during cooking.

* Due to the tremendous variety in convenience foods products available, times given here should be used only as guidelines. We suggest you cook food for the shortest recommended time and then check for doneness. Be sure to check the package for microwave instructions.

that's fine. Standing time will complete the thawing process. Seafood is so delicate that you must be the final judge.

Finish defrosting under cold running water, separating fillets.

All seafood profits from approximately 5 minutes standing time. However, if you are adding the seafood to a chowder or seafood casserole, standing time can be eliminated.

Cover the head of whole fish with aluminum foil during thawing. There is so little flesh in that area that it will begin to cook unless shielded.

We recommend turning seafood over or rearranging during defrosting. Remove any pieces that are nearly thawed.

COOKING FISH AND SHELLFISH

Place seafood in a microproof baking dish with thick edges of fillets and steaks and thick ends of shellfish toward the outer edge of the dish.

Cover the dish with plastic wrap or waxed paper. Test often during the cooking period to avoid overcooking. The timing is the same for seafood in the shell or without the shell.

DEFROSTING GUIDE — SEAFOOD

Food	Amount	Power Control	Time (in minutes)	Standing Time (in minutes)	Special Notes
Fish fillets	1 lb.	30	4 - 6	4 - 5	Carefully separate fillets under cold water.
	2 lbs.	30	5 - 7	5	
Fish steaks	1 lb.	30	4 - 6	5	Carefully separate steaks under cold running water.
Whole fish	8 - 10 oz.	30	4 - 6	5	Shallow dish, shape of fish determines size. Should be icy when removed. Finish at room temperature. Cover head with aluminum foil.
	1½ - 2 lbs.	30	5 - 7	5	
Lobster tails	8 oz.	30	5 - 7	5	Remove from package to baking dish.
Crab legs	8 - 10 oz.	30	3 - 4	5	Break apart.
Crab meat	6 oz.	30	4 - 5	5	Defrost in package on dish. Break apart.
Shrimp	1 lb.	30	3 - 4	5	Remove from package to dish. Spread loosely in baking dish and rearrange during thawing as necessary.
Scallops	1 lb.	30	6 - 8	5	Defrost in package if in block; spread out on baking dish if in pieces. Turn over and rearrange during thawing as necessary.
Oysters, shucked	12 oz.	30	3 - 4	5	Remove from package to dish. Turn over or stir gently during thawing as necessary.

NOTE: If your oven is equipped with an Auto Defrost or Programmed Defrost feature, please consult your Use & Care Manual for assistance in defrosting with those methods. The timing in the chart here is for manual, or attended, defrosting.

COOKING GUIDE — SEAFOOD AND FISH

Food	Power Control	Time (in minutes)	Probe Method	Special Notes
Fish fillets, 1 lb. ½ inch thick,	HI	4 - 5	140°F	Shallow microproof dish, covered.
2 lbs.	HI	7 - 8	140°F	
Fish steaks, 1 inch thick, 1 lb.	HI	5 - 6	140°F	Shallow microproof dish, covered.
Whole fish				
8 - 10 oz.	HI	3½ - 4	170°F	Appropriate shallow microproof dish.
1½ - 2 lbs.	HI	5 - 7	170°F	
Crab legs				
8 - 10 oz.	HI	3 - 4		Appropriate shallow microproof dish, covered. Turn once.
16 - 20 oz.	HI	5 - 6		
Shrimp, scallops				
8 oz.	70	3 - 4		Appropriate shallow microproof dish, covered. Rearrange halfway.
1 lb.	70	5 - 7		
Snails, clams, oysters, 12 oz.	70	3 - 4		Shallow microproof dish, covered. Rearrange halfway.
Lobster tails				
1: 8 oz.	HI	3 - 4		Shallow microproof dish. Split shell to reduce curling.
2: 8 oz. each	HI	5 - 6		
3: 8 oz. each	HI	9 - 11		

Poached Halibut

POACHED HALIBUT

Cooking Time: 7 to 9 minutes

  1 **lemon, thinly sliced**
  1 **teaspoon instant minced onion**
  1 **teaspoon salt**
  1 **bay leaf**
  2 **peppercorns**
  1½ **cups hot water**
  ⅓ **cup dry white wine**
  4 **small halibut steaks or**
    2 large steaks

Place lemon, onion, salt, bay leaf, pepper-corns, water, and wine in oval microproof baking dish. Stir. Cook on HI, 5 minutes, or until mixture boils.

Carefully place halibut steaks in hot liquid. Cover with plastic wrap and cook on HI, 2 to 4 minutes, or until fish flakes easily when tested with a fork. Let stand 1 minute before serving.

4 servings

Poaching is also an excellent way to cook salmon, cod, swordfish, or red snapper. Serve garnished with lemon wedges and fresh parsley. Or make a sauce, using the poaching liquid as a base.

ORANGE ROUGHY

Cooking Time: 6 to 7 minutes

  2 **orange roughy or haddock fillets**
    (4 ounces each)
    Paprika
  1 **small tomato, diced**
  1 **green onion, sliced**
  2 **tablespoons chopped green pepper**
  2 **tablespoons chopped celery**
  2 **tablespoons chopped parsley**
  1 **tablespoon butter**
  1 **tablespoon dry white wine**
    Juice of 1 lime
    Dash salt and pepper

Place fish fillets in 10 × 6-inch microproof baking dish. Sprinkle with paprika. Combine tomato, onion, green pepper, celery, and parsley. Spoon vegetables over fillets. Set aside.

Place butter in 1-cup glass measure. Cook on HI, 1 minute. Add wine and lime juice to melted butter, and pour over vegetables and fish. Sprinkle with salt and pepper. Cover with waxed paper. Cook on HI, 3 minutes. Rotate dish and continue to cook on HI, 2 to 3 minutes.

2 servings

FISH FILLETS WITH MUSHROOMS

Cooking Time: 8 minutes

- 1 **pound fish fillets**
- 2 **tablespoons butter or margarine**
- 2 **tablespoons dry white wine**
- ½ **teaspoon lemon juice**
- ½ **cup sliced mushrooms**
- 2 **green onions, finely chopped**
- 1 **tomato, peeled and diced**
- ½ **teaspoon salt**

Arrange fish fillets so that thick edges are toward the outside of a 12 × 7 × 2-inch microproof baking dish. Dot with butter. Combine wine and lemon juice, and pour over fish. Sprinkle with mushrooms, green onions, and tomato. Cover with waxed paper and cook on HI, 8 minutes, or until fish flakes easily when tested with a fork.

Remove from oven and let stand, covered, 2 minutes.

3 to 4 servings

This recipe may be halved. Halve all ingredients and use one small tomato. Cook on HI, 3 to 3½ minutes.

GRILLED HALIBUT STEAKS

Approximate Cooking Time: 12 to 13 minutes

- 2 **tablespoons lemon juice**
- 1 **tablespoon olive oil**
- ¼ **teaspoon tarragon**
- 2 **halibut steaks (6 to 8 ounces), 1 inch thick**
- ¼ **teaspoon paprika**

Combine lemon juice, olive oil, and tarragon. Brush over steaks and set aside to marinate at room temperature, 15 minutes. Sprinkle with paprika.

Preheat browning dish according to manufacturer's directions. Place steaks in browning dish and cook on HI, 5 to 6 minutes, or until fish flakes easily when tested with a fork. Turn fish over and serve grilled-side up. Garnish with lemon slices.

2 servings

FILLET OF FISH AMANDINE

Cooking Time: 10 to 10½ minutes

- ½ **cup slivered almonds**
- ½ **cup butter or margarine**
- 1 **pound fish fillets**
- 1 **teaspoon lemon juice**
- ½ **teaspoon salt**
- ¼ **teaspoon dill**
- ⅛ **teaspoon pepper**
- 1 **teaspoon chopped fresh parsley**

Place almonds and butter in 8-inch microproof baking dish. Cook, uncovered, on HI, 5 minutes, or until almonds and butter are golden brown. Remove almonds and set aside.

Place fish in baking dish, turning fish to coat both sides with butter. Sprinkle with lemon juice, salt, dill, and pepper. Top with parsley. Cover with waxed paper and cook on HI, 4 minutes.

Sprinkle almonds over fish. Cover with paper towel and cook on HI, 1 to 1½ minutes, or until fish flakes easily when tested with a fork. Let stand 1 minute before serving.

3 to 4 servings

LIME-POACHED FISH FILLETS

Cooking Time: 4 to 5 minutes

- ¾ **pound fish fillets**
- 1 **tablespoon butter or margarine**
- 1 **green onion, chopped**
- 1 **teaspoon chopped fresh parsley**
- ½ **teaspoon grated orange peel**
- 2 **tablespoons lime juice**

Arrange fillets in 8-inch microproof baking dish with thickest portions toward outside. Place butter in 1-cup glass measure and cook on HI, 30 seconds, or until butter melts.

Stir in green onion, parsley, orange peel, and lime juice. Pour butter mixture over fillets. Cover with waxed paper and cook on HI, 3½ to 4½ minutes.

2 servings

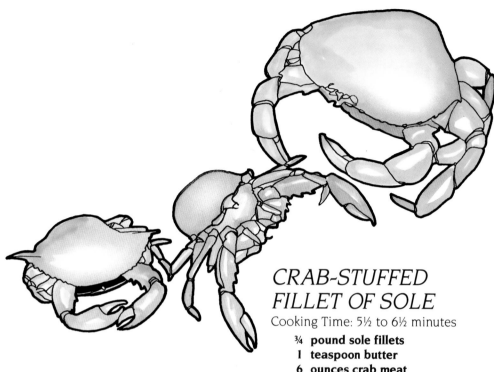

CRAB-STUFFED FILLET OF SOLE

Cooking Time: 5½ to 6½ minutes

- ¾ **pound sole fillets**
- 1 **teaspoon butter**
- 6 **ounces crab meat**
- ¼ **cup celery, finely chopped**
- 1 **tablespoon dry bread crumbs**
- 1 **tablespoon grated Parmesan cheese**
  Lemony Dill Sauce (page 149)

Rinse fillets with cold water and pat dry. Set aside. Place butter in 1-cup glass measure and cook on HI, 30 seconds, or until butter melts.

Stir in crab meat, celery, bread crumbs, and cheese. Mix well. Spread crab meat mixture evenly over fillets. Roll each fillet and place seam-side down in a ring along the outside edge of a 9-inch round microproof baking dish. Cover with waxed paper and cook on HI, 5 to 6 minutes.

Serve with Lemony Dill Sauce.

2 servings

LAKE COUNTRY STUFFED TROUT

Cooking Time: 7 minutes

- 2 **trout (5 ounces each), cleaned**
- 2 **tablespoons butter or margarine**
- ½ **cup chopped fresh mushrooms**
- ¼ **cup grated carrots**
- ¼ **cup seasoned dry bread crumbs**
- ½ **teaspoon tarragon**
- ⅛ **teaspoon pepper**
  Juice of 1/2 lemon
  (about 2 tablespoons)

Rinse trout and pat dry. Place in 12 × 7 × 2-inch microproof baking dish. Place butter in 2-cup glass measure. Cook on HI, 1 minute.

Add mushrooms, carrots, bread crumbs, tarragon, and pepper. Stir until well mixed. Stuff mushroom mixture into trout cavities. Sprinkle lemon juice over trout. Cover with waxed paper and cook on HI, 6 minutes.

2 servings

SALMON IN PARCHMENT

Cooking Time: 3 to 4 minutes

- 1 **piece parchment, 12 inches square**
- 1 **salmon fillet (5 to 6 ounces)**
- 1 **carrot, cut into 2-inch long
      julienne strips**
- ½ **stalk celery, cut into 2-inch
      long julienne strips**
- 2 **tablespoons butter, melted**
- 1 **tablespoon lemon juice**
- 1 **sprig fresh dill or ¼ teaspoon
      dillweed**

Place salmon in center of parchment. Arrange carrots and celery around salmon. Pour butter over fish and vegetables. Sprinkle with lemon juice and top with dill. Seal parchment, butcher-wrap style. Place on microproof plate. Cook on HI, 3 to 4 minutes, or until parchment is steaming, but not dry.

1 serving

This is a wonderful way to serve any fish. Vary the vegetable combination and herbs to suit your moods. The parchment remains sealed until you tear it open at the table.

SALMON IN COQUILLES

Cooking Time: 4 minutes

- 1 **can (7½ ounces) salmon,
      drained and flaked**
- 1 **stalk celery, finely chopped**
- 1 **green onion, finely chopped**
- 1 **teaspoon chopped parsley**
- ½ **teaspoon dill
      Juice of ½ lemon**
- ¼ **cup mayonnaise**
- 2 **lettuce leaves**
- 1 **tablespoon melted butter**
- ¼ **cup soft bread crumbs
      Paprika**

Combine salmon, celery, green onion, parsley, dill, lemon juice, and mayonnaise. Place each lettuce leaf in an individual microproof baking dish. Spoon salmon mixture onto lettuce leaves. Stir melted butter into bread crumbs until well mixed. Sprinkle buttered crumbs over salmon. Sprinkle lightly with paprika. Cook on HI, 2 minutes. Rotate dishes and continue to cook on HI, 2 minutes.

Garnish with parsley sprigs and lemon wedges.

2 servings

Salmon in Parchment

SCALLOPS AU VIN
Approximate Cooking Time: 13 minutes

- **2 tablespoons butter**
- **2 large cloves garlic, minced**
- **2 green onions, chopped**
- **⅛ teaspoon paprika**
- **2 tablespoons dry white wine**
- **¾ pound large sea scallops**
- **1 tablespoon lemon juice**

Combine butter, garlic, onions, paprika, and wine in 1-cup glass measure. Cook on HI, 2 minutes. Cover with plastic wrap and set aside.

Preheat browning dish according to manufacturer's instructions. Place scallops in dish and cook on HI, 4 to 5 minutes. Transfer to serving dish. Pour hot butter sauce over scallops, and sprinkle with lemon juice.

2 servings

SHRIMP TEX-MEX STYLE
Cooking Time: 11 to 13 minutes

- **1 can (16 ounces) stewed tomatoes**
- **2 teaspoons cornstarch**
- **2 green onions, chopped**
- **1 clove garlic, minced**
- **1 teaspoon chopped fresh parsley**
- **1 to 2 teaspoons chili powder**
- **¼ teaspoon cayenne**
- **1 pound medium shrimp, cleaned and deveined**

Combine tomatoes and cornstarch in 2-quart microproof casserole. Stir until cornstarch is blended. Add onions, garlic, parsley, chili powder, and cayenne. Cover with casserole lid and cook on HI, 6 to 7 minutes, or until mixture boils. Set aside.

Place shrimp in 1-quart casserole. Cover with casserole lid and cook on HI, 4 minutes. Drain and stir into tomato mixture. Cover and cook on HI, 1 to 2 minutes, or until hot.

4 servings

SEAFOOD JAMBALAYA
Cooking Time: 20 to 23 minutes

- **½ cup ground smoked ham**
- **½ cup ground smoked pork sausage**
- **1 large onion, chopped**
- **2 stalks celery, chopped**
- **1 medium green pepper, chopped**
- **1 cup cooked rice**
- **4 large tomatoes, peeled and coarsely chopped**
- **1 cup chicken broth**
- **½ cup tomato sauce**
- **½ cup cubed cooked chicken**
- **2 green onions, chopped**
- **2 bay leaves**
- **1 to 2 teaspoons cayenne**
- **3 teaspoons Italian herb seasoning**
- **½ pound medium shrimp, cleaned and deveined**
- **½ pound medium oysters**

Combine ham, sausage, onion, celery, and green pepper in 3-quart microproof casserole. Cover and cook on HI, 5 to 6 minutes, or until vegetables are tender.

Stir in rice, tomatoes, broth, tomato sauce, chicken, green onions, bay leaves, cayenne, and Italian seasoning. Cover and cook on HI, 10 to 12 minutes, or until hot, stirring once.

Stir in shrimp and oysters. Cover and cook on HI, 5 minutes.

4 servings

Like bouillabaise and cioppino, jambalaya is one of those dishes that adapt easily to the preferences of the cook. So, substitute freely to suit your family's tastes.

Scallops au Vin

SHRIMP CHOW MEIN

Cooking Time: 9 to 13 minutes

- ¾ **pound medium shrimp,
    shelled and deveined**
- 1 **package (10 ounces) frozen
    snow peas**
- 1 **can (10 ounces) sliced
    water chestnuts**
- 1 **cup (4 ounces) fresh bean sprouts**
- 2 **green onions, chopped**
- 2 **tablespoons sliced pimiento**
- 1 **tablespoon cornstarch**
- ¼ **cup soy sauce**
- 1 **clove garlic, minced**
- 1 **tablespoon sesame seed**
- 1 **cup chicken broth**

Combine shrimp, snow peas, water chestnuts, bean sprouts, onions, and pimiento in 2½-quart shallow microproof casserole. Cover with casserole lid and cook on HI, 5 to 6 minutes, stirring once.

In a 2-cup glass measure, stir cornstarch into soy sauce until blended. Add garlic, sesame seed, and chicken broth. Cook on HI, 2 to 3 minutes, or until thick, stirring once.

Stir sauce into shrimp and vegetables. Cover and cook on HI, 2 to 4 minutes, or until hot.

4 servings

EASY SALMON LOAF

Approximate Cooking Time: 25 to 30 minutes

- 2 **cans (16 ounces each) red salmon,
    drained, with bone and
    skin removed**
- 3 **slices soft bread, cubed**
- ½ **cup milk**
- 1 **egg, lightly beaten**
- ¼ **cup melted butter**
- ½ **teaspoon salt**

Combine all ingredients, and mix well. Pack mixture firmly into greased 8 × 4 × 3-inch microproof loaf pan. Insert temperature probe into center of loaf. Place loaf in oven and plug in probe. Cook on 70 with probe set at 150°F.

4 to 6 servings

You can serve Easy Salmon Loaf with Lemon Butter Sauce (page 148) or Lemony Dill Sauce (page 149).

This recipe may be cut in half by halving all ingredients except the egg. Form the loaf in an oval or round microproof dish. Cook, covered, on 70, 15 to 20 minutes.

EGGS & CHEESE

Sunny-Side-Up Eggs (page 114) are a browning dish treat. A gang for brunch? Eggs poach neatly in a microproof muffin ring.

Microwave omelets are unusually easy, especially with a special microproof omelet dish. Add your favorite fillings.

Scrambled eggs are fluffier when prepared in the microwave oven and they only need to be stirred once during cooking, and once before serving.

Eggs and cheese are great microwave partners, but they can stand by themselves, too. There's nothing quite like plain scrambled eggs or cheese fondue made in the microwave oven. From the most simple omelets to fancy quiches, the microwave oven can enliven an ordinary breakfast, Sunday brunch, or any meal. The recipes in this chapter are perfect for unexpected guests any time of day. Just remember to have on hand a carton of fresh eggs and some cheeses, like Cheddar or Swiss, that keep well. Then, a little onion and seasonings are all you need to make a quick, easy, and delicious meal. As a special treat, we have included in this chapter a special recipe for Classic Quiche Lorraine (page 112). One reminder: Do not hard-boil eggs in the microwave oven. Pressure builds up inside the shell, which causes the egg to burst. Eggs must be removed from their shells and egg yolks should always be carefully pierced before cooking to prevent them from popping. Keep in mind that eggs and cheese are delicate ingredients. Handle them with care and you will have delectable results.

ADAPTING YOUR RECIPES

The best advice for adapting recipes that use eggs and cheese as primary ingredients is "better to undercook than overcook." Cheese and eggs cook so quickly that a few seconds can make the difference between airy excellence and a rubbery disaster. That's why we sometimes call egg cookery "eye cookery." Eggs and cheese are such delicate ingredients and must be handled with care for delectable results. That's not to make you shy away from developing your own recipes. You will be able to make countless variations on the recipes here, substituting vegetables and cooked meat, and adding your own spices and sauces. Conventional soufflé recipes do not adapt well to microwave cooking. Microwave soufflé recipes require a special form of stablization because they cook so quickly; therefore, evaporated milk is used for the cream sauce base. The tips below will guide you to microwave success with all your egg and cheese recipes.

Helpful Tips

We recommend that you undercook eggs slightly and allow standing time to complete cooking. Eggs become tough when overcooked. Always check doneness to avoid overcooking.

Cover poaching or baking eggs to trap steam and ensure even cooking. Eggs are usually cooked at 60 or 70.

If you want a soft yolk, remove the egg from oven before whites are completely cooked. A brief standing time allows whites to set without overcooking yolks.

Add ⅛ to ¼ teaspoon vinegar to the water when poaching eggs to help the white coagulate.

Cook bacon and egg combinations on HI, since most of the microwaves are attracted to the bacon because of its high fat content.

Omelets and scrambled eggs should be stirred at least once during cooking. Fondues and sauces profit from occasional stirring during the cooking time.

Cheese melts quickly and makes an attractive topping for casseroles and sandwiches.

Cook cheese on 70 or a lower setting for short periods of time to avoid separation and toughening.

COOKING EGGS

Eggs should be at refrigerator temperature before cooking. If they are at room temperature, somewhat less cooking time will be required.

To scramble: Break eggs into a 4-cup glass measure. Add milk or cream and beat with a fork. Add butter, cover with waxed paper, and cook on 60, according to the guide. Stir once during cooking, and just before serving. Let stand 1 minute before serving.

To poach: Bring water and ¼ teaspoon vinegar to a boil in a 1-cup glass measure or appropriate microproof dish. Break egg carefully into hot water and pierce yolk lightly with a toothpick. Cover with waxed paper and cook on 50, according to the guide. Let stand 1 minute.

COOKING GUIDE — SCRAMBLED EGGS
Uses Power Control 60

Number of Eggs	Liquid (Milk or Cream)	Butter	Minutes to Cook
1	1 tablespoon	1 teaspoon	1 to 1½
2	2 tablespoons	2 teaspoons	2 to 2½
4	3 tablespoons	3 teaspoons	4½ to 5½
6	4 tablespoons	4 teaspoons	7 to 8

COOKING GUIDE — POACHED EGGS
Uses Power Control HI for water, 50 after adding egg.

Number of Eggs	Water	Container	Minutes to Boil Water	Minutes to Cook
1	¼ cup	6-ounce microproof custard cup	1½ to 2	1
2	¼ cup	6-ounce microproof custard cups	2	1½ to 2
3	¼ cup	6-ounce microproof custard cups	2 to 2½	2 to 2½
4	1 cup	1-quart microproof dish	2½ to 3	2½ to 3

EASY SWISS FONDUE

Cooking Time: 8 to 10 minutes

   3 **cups (¾ pound) diced Swiss cheese**
   1 **cup (4 ounces) diced Gruyère**
      cheese
   2 **tablespoons all-purpose flour**
   1 **clove garlic, minced**
   ⅛ **teaspoon nutmeg**
   2 **cups dry white wine**

Combine cheeses, flour, garlic, and nutmeg. Stir until well mixed. Set aside. Pour wine into 2-quart microproof casserole. Cook on HI, 4 to 5 minutes, or until hot.

   Stir in cheese mixture. Cook on 70, 4 to 5 minutes, or until cheese melts.

4 to 6 servings

Fondue is flexible. You can use any white cheeses that melt well, such as havarti, Monterey jack, or mild gouda. For an authentic touch, add 2 tablespoons kirchwasser, a cherry brandy, after adding cheeses to heated wine.

CHILI CHEESE STRATA

Cooking Time: 22 to 24 minutes

   1 **pound lean ground beef**
   1 **green onion, chopped**
   ⅛ **teaspoon pepper**
   1 **can (8 ounces) kidney beans,**
      drained
   2 **tablespoons chopped green chilies,**
      optional
   1 **teaspoon chili powder**
   1 **tablespoon butter or margarine**
   2 **tablespoons flour**
   1 **cup milk**
   3 **eggs, lightly beaten**
   1 **cup (4 ounces) shredded**
      colby cheese
   1 **cup (4 ounces) shredded**
      Monterey jack cheese
   1 **teaspoon paprika**

Combine beef, green onion, and pepper in 1-quart microproof casserole. Cook on HI, 5 minutes. Stir in kidney beans, chilies, and chili powder. Set aside.

   Place butter in 2-cup glass measure. Cook on HI, 30 to 45 seconds. Stir in flour. Cook on HI, 1 minute. Gradually add milk and eggs. Cook on 80, 2 to 4 minutes, or until mixture thickens, stirring once. Set aside.

   Place half the meat mixture in 2-quart microproof casserole. Cover with half the cheese. Repeat layers of meat and cheese. Pour white sauce over top layer, and sprinkle with paprika. Cook on 70, 14 to 15 minutes, rotating dish once during cooking time.

   Remove from oven. Let stand 15 minutes before serving.

4 servings

Many supermarkets now carry Colby-Jack cheese, sometimes sold as "marbled cheese." It's a mixture of colby and Monterey jack cheeses. If you can find it, use it in this recipe.

OMELET FOR TWO

Cooking Time: 5 minutes

> 1 **tablespoon butter or margarine**
> 4 **eggs**
> 4 **tablespoons water**
> ½ **teaspoon salt**
> ⅛ **teaspoon pepper**

Place butter in 9-inch microproof pie plate. Cook on HI, 1 minute, or until melted.

Combine eggs, water, salt, and pepper. Beat lightly with a fork. Pour into pie plate. Cover with waxed paper and cook on 60, 4 minutes, or until center is nearly set.

Let stand, covered, 1 to 2 minutes. Fold in half and serve immediately.

2 servings

Before folding omelet, top with crumbled cooked bacon, grated Cheddar cheese, chopped cooked ham, or chopped tomato, if you wish.

PUFFY CHEDDAR OMELET

Cooking Time: 8 to 10 minutes

> 4 **eggs, separated**
> ⅓ **cup mayonnaise**
> 1 **tablespoon butter or margarine**
> ½ **cup grated Cheddar cheese**
> 1 **tablespoon minced fresh parsley**

Beat egg whites in large bowl until soft peaks form. Beat egg yolks with mayonnaise and 2 tablespoons water in separate bowl. Place butter in 9-inch microproof pie plate. Cook on HI, 1 minute, or until butter melts.

Tilt pie plate to coat evenly with butter. Pour egg mixture into pie plate. Cook on 60, 6 to 8 minutes. Rotate dish if eggs seem to be rising unevenly.

When eggs are set but still moist, sprinkle with cheese. Cook on 60, 1 minute, or until cheese melts.

Fold omelet in half and slide onto serving plate. Sprinkle with parsley.

2 servings

MUSHROOM OMELET FOR ONE

Cooking Time: 4½ to 7 minutes

> ½ **cup sliced fresh mushrooms**
> 1 **green onion, chopped**
> 1 **teaspoon butter**
> 2 **teaspoons chopped fresh parsley**
> **Dash salt and pepper**
> 2 **eggs**
> 2 **tablespoons milk**
> 1½ **teaspoons butter**
> 1 **tablespoon shredded Cheddar cheese**
> **Paprika**

Combine mushrooms, green onion, butter, parsley, salt, and pepper in 2-cup glass measure. Cook on HI, 1½ to 2½ minutes, or until mushrooms are tender. Beat eggs with milk in 1-quart mixing bowl. Set aside.

Remove mushroom mixture, cover, and set aside. Place 1 tablespoon butter in 9-inch microproof pie plate and cook on HI, ½ minute.

Pour egg mixture into pie plate and cover tightly with plastic wrap. Cook on 60, 1½ to 2 minutes.

Stir egg mixture toward center. Cover and cook on 60, 1 to 2 minutes, or until set.

Let stand, covered, 2 minutes. Spread mushroom filling over half of omelet. Loosen omelet and fold in half over filling. Sprinkle with shredded Cheddar cheese and paprika. Cut omelet in half. Slide each half onto serving plate.

2 servings

Omelet for Two

EGGS BENEDICT

Cooking Time: 4 to 4½ minutes

> **2 English muffins, split and
>   toasted**
> **4 slices boiled ham, ¼ inch thick**
> **4 poached eggs (Guide, page 108)**
> **¾ cup Hollandaise Sauce (page 146)**

Place muffin halves on a paper towel-lined microproof plate. Top each muffin half with 1 slice ham. Cook uncovered, two at a time, on 60, 4 to 4½ minutes, or until ham is hot.

Top each with poached egg. Cover with Hollandaise sauce, and serve immediately.

4 servings

CRAB AND SPINACH QUICHE

Cooking Time: 25 to 30 minutes

> **4 eggs**
> **1 can (12 ounces) evaporated milk**
> **1 teaspoon prepared mustard**
> **¾ teaspoon salt**
> **⅛ teaspoon nutmeg**
> **2 tablespoons dry sherry**
> **6 ounces crab meat,
>   cartilage removed**
> **5 ounces (½ package) frozen chopped
>   spinach, thawed and drained**
> **¾ cup (3 ounces) shredded
>   Swiss cheese**
> **1 prebaked 9-inch Homemade
>   Pie Shell (page 165)**

Beat eggs in large bowl. Add milk, mustard, salt, nutmeg, and sherry. Stir until well blended. Add crab meat, spinach, and cheese to egg mixture. Stir well.

Pour into prepared pastry shell. Cook on 60, 25 to 30 minutes, or until nearly set in center. Rotate dish one-quarter turn at 10-minute intervals during cooking time.

Remove from oven and let stand 5 minutes before serving.

6 servings

CLASSIC QUICHE LORRAINE

Cooking Time: 18 minutes

> **1 baked 9-inch Homemade Pie Shell
>   (page 165)**
> **6 slices bacon, cooked and crumbled**
> **3 green onions, chopped**
> **2 cups (8 ounces) shredded
>   Swiss cheese**
> **1 can (12 ounces) evaporated milk
>   or evaporated skim milk**
> **1 teaspoon prepared mustard**
> **¼ teaspoon nutmeg**
> **¼ teaspoon salt
>   Dash cayenne**
> **4 eggs, beaten**

Reserve about 1 tablespoon each of bacon and onions for topping. Sprinkle remaining bacon, remaining onions, and cheese evenly into pie shell. Set aside.

Place milk in 2-cup glass measure. Cook on HI, 3 minutes, or just until milk boils. Stir mustard, nutmeg, salt, and cayenne into eggs. Gradually pour hot milk into egg mixture while continuing to stir. Carefully pour into pie shell.

Sprinkle reserved bacon and onions over top. Cook on 50, 15 minutes, or until center is nearly set.

Remove from oven and let stand 10 minutes before serving.

6 servings

HUEVOS RANCHEROS

Cooking Time: 9 to 10 minutes

- **2 tablespoons butter or margarine**
- **1 can (4 ounces) diced green chilies**
- **1 large tomato, peeled, coarsely chopped, and drained**
- **2 tablespoons minced onion flakes**
- **6 eggs**
- **6 tablespoons milk**
- **⅛ teaspoon garlic powder**
- **Salt and pepper to taste**
- **1 cup (4 ounces) shredded Cheddar cheese**
- **Chopped fresh parsley**

Place butter in oval microproof dish or pie plate and cook on HI, 1 minute. Swirl butter to coat bottom. Add chilies, tomato, and onion and cook on HI, 2 minutes.

Beat eggs, milk, garlic powder, salt, and pepper in medium bowl. Pour over tomato mixture. Cook on HI, 5 minutes, or until eggs are barely set, stirring outer edge of egg mixture toward center several times. Sprinkle with cheese and continue to cook on HI, 1 to 2 minutes, or until cheese is melted. Sprinkle with parsley.

3 to 4 servings

You may wish to substitute ½ cup diced green pepper for chilies. Cook on HI, 1 minute before adding to butter.

ENCHILADAS FOR TWO

Cooking Time: 9½ minutes

- **1½ cups (6 ounces) shredded Longhorn cheese**
- **1 carton (8 ounces) dairy sour cream**
- **¼ cup chopped green onions**
- **½ teaspoon prepared mustard**
- **¼ teaspoon white pepper**
- **1½ teaspoons butter**
- **1½ teaspoons all-purpose flour**
- **½ cup milk**
- **1 cup (4 ounces) shredded Cheddar cheese**
- **4 flour tortillas**
- **½ cup enchilada sauce**

Combine Longhorn cheese and sour cream in 1-quart glass measure. Cook on 50, 1 minute.

Stir. Add green onions, mustard, and pepper; mix well. Set aside.

Place butter in 2-cup glass measure and cook on HI, ½ minute. Stir in flour and milk. Cook on 80, 2 minutes.

Stir in Cheddar cheese; set aside. Spread one-fourth of the cheese and sour cream mixture on each tortilla. Roll tightly; place in 1½-quart shallow microproof casserole. Pour enchilada sauce evenly over tortillas. Top with Cheddar cheese sauce. Cook on 80, 6 minutes.

2 servings

Top enchiladas with your choice of sliced avocado, diced tomato, shredded lettuce, chopped .jalapeño peppers, or additional enchilada sauce.

SHIRRED EGGS

Cooking Time: 3 to 3½ minutes

- 1 **teaspoon butter or margarine**
- 2 **eggs**
- 1 **tablespoon cream**
   Salt and pepper

Place butter in microproof ramekin or small cereal bowl. Cook on 70, 1 minute, or until melted.

Break eggs into ramekin. Pierce yolks carefully with toothpick. Add cream. Cover tightly with plastic wrap. Cook on 60, 2 to 2½ minutes. Let stand 1 minute before serving. Season to taste with salt and pepper.

1 serving

SUNNY-SIDE-UP EGGS

Approximate Cooking Time: 2½ to 3 minutes

- 1 **tablespoon butter or margarine**
- 2 **eggs**
   Salt and pepper to taste

Preheat browning dish according to manufacturer's directions. Place butter in browning dish. Using hot pads, tilt dish to coat surface.

Break eggs into dish and pierce yolks. Sprinkle lightly with salt and pepper. Cook on HI, 30 to 60 seconds, or until done to your taste.

Remove from oven and let stand 1 minute before serving.

1 to 2 servings

WELSH RABBIT AND TOMATOES

Cooking Time: 14 to 15 minutes

- 4 **cups (1 pound) shredded sharp Cheddar cheese**
- 4 **teaspoons butter or margarine**
- 1 **tablespoon Worcestershire sauce**
- ½ **teaspoon salt**
- ½ **teaspoon paprika**
- ¼ **teaspoon dry mustard**
- ¼ **teaspoon cayenne**
- 2 **eggs, lightly beaten**
- 1 **cup flat beer or ale, at room temperature**
   Toasted English muffin halves or Dutch rusks
- 1 **medium tomato, sliced**
- 8 **slices bacon, cooked**

Combine cheese, butter, Worcestershire, salt, paprika, mustard, and cayenne in 2-quart microproof casserole and mix well. Cook on 50, 8 minutes, stirring once, just until cheese melts. Stir a little cheese mixture into beaten eggs. Slowly stir eggs back into remaining cheese; blend well. Gradually blend in beer.

Cover and cook on 50, 3 minutes. Stir through several times. Cover and cook on 50, 3 to 4 minutes, or until heated through. Stir thoroughly.

Place each muffin half in individual shallow bowl. Top with tomato slice. Ladle cheese mixture into bowls. Top each with 2 slices bacon.

4 servings

Shirred Eggs

DENVER OMELET

Cooking Time: 7 minutes

>   2 **tablespoons butter or margarine**
>   4 **eggs**
>   3 **tablespoons milk**
>   2 **tablespoons grated Cheddar cheese**
>   2 **tablespoons diced ham**
>   1 **tablespoon chopped green pepper**
>   1 **tablespoon chopped green onion**
> ¼ **teaspoon dry mustard**
>   **Salt and pepper to taste**

Place butter in 9-inch microproof pie plate. Cook on HI, 1 minute.

Add eggs and beat with fork until frothy. Stir remaining ingredients into eggs. Cover with waxed paper. Cook on 60, 3 minutes.

Gently stir cooked portion of egg mixture toward center of pie plate. Cover and cook on 60, 3 minutes.

2 servings

EGG AND ASPARAGUS BAKE

Cooking Time: 17 to 19 minutes

>   1 **can (10¾ ounces) cream of celery soup**
> ½ **cup milk**
> ½ **cup (2 ounces) shredded Colby cheese**
> ½ **cup (2 ounces) grated Parmesan cheese**
>   5 **hard-cooked eggs, sliced**
>   6 **slices bacon, cooked**
>   1 **package (10 ounces) frozen cut asparagus, thawed and drained**
>   **Paprika**

Combine soup, milk, and cheeses. Stir until well mixed. Layer half of the eggs, bacon, and asparagus in 1½-quart microproof casserole. Spread half of the cheese mixture over asparagus layer. Repeat layers. Top with remaining cheese mixture. Sprinkle with paprika. Cover with waxed paper.

Cook on 60, 17 to 19 minutes, or until hot and bubbly. Rotate casserole one-half turn halfway through cooking time.

4 servings

You may substitute different frozen, cut vegetables for the asparagus each time you prepare this complete meal-in-one casserole.

One-Step Lasagna (page 125) and Vegetarian Lasagna (page 122) cook in a microproof baking dish, covered tightly with plastic wrap.

It is inconvenient to cook pasta separately in the microwave oven. Rice, however, cooks easily and well in a tightly-covered microproof bowl.

Leftover pasta dishes no longer mean difficult reheating or scorched casserole bottoms. Reheat right on a serving platter with no added moisture.

RICE & PASTA

The microwave oven provides no significant saving of time when cooking pasta and rice. It takes just as long to rehydrate these products in the microwave oven as it does conventionally. While the oven can cook pasta separately, there is no advantage. Once the pasta is prepared and added to the rest of the ingredients according to the recipe, casseroles and similar dishes cook in speedy microwave time. And there are some wonderful recipes in this chapter that don't require advance preparation of the pasta before adding into the casserole or baking dish.

Rice does much better on its own in the microwave oven than pasta, because rice does not usually require as great a volume of water as pasta. It also reconstitutes more quickly.

Another great advantage the microwave oven offers is its ability to reheat pasta, rice, and cereal without adding water or having to stir. No worry about soggy noodles or starchy rice. And you'll find that pasta and rice taste as good reheated as when freshly cooked!

ADAPTING YOUR RECIPES

You will discover that your conventional rice or noodle-based casseroles can be easily adjusted to microwave cooking. When you find a similar recipe here, adapt your ingredients to the microwave method, but follow only about three-quarters of the recommended microwave cooking times in the similar recipe. Then check, and extend the cooking time at 1-minute intervals until done. Make a note of the final cooking time for a repeat of the dish. By "trial" and trying to avoid "error," you'll soon be able to add to our collection of pasta and rice dishes.

Helpful Tips

Cooked pasta or rice to be used in a casserole should be slightly firmer than if it is to be eaten at once. Simply cook a bit less.

Quick-cooking rice may be substituted in converting from conventional recipes that call for uncooked rice, in order to make sure the rice will cook in the same short time as the rest of the ingredients. Otherwise, precook regular rice to a firm stage and add to the casserole.

To reheat pasta, rice, and cereals in the microwave without drying them out, cover tightly with plastic wrap. Set the power control at 80 and cook for just a few minutes, depending upon amount.

Pasta and rice are best when added to other ingredients, as in casseroles. However, the oven can cook them separately.

To cook pasta: Place spaghetti in 13 × 9-inch baking dish. Add 2½ cups hot water for 2 ounces of uncooked spaghetti; 4 cups for 4 ounces of spaghetti. Cover with plastic wrap. Cook on HI, 5 to 8 minutes, or until water boils. Stir. Finish cooking on 50 (6 minutes for 2 ounces; 8 minutes for 4 ounces).

Do not add oil to water when cooking pasta products in the microwave oven. An oil/water mixture can overheat.

To cook rice: Follow directions in guide (below) and cook, covered with casserole lid.

To cook grits or other hot cereals: Cook on HI, 6 to 7 minutes for ⅓ cup grits (uncooked). Follow package directions for liquid.

COOKING GUIDE — RICE

Food	Amount Uncooked	Water	Power Control	Time (minutes)	Standing Time (minutes)	Special Notes
Short-grain	1 cup	2 cups	HI	12 - 15	5	3-quart casserole
Long-grain	1 cup	2 cups	HI	14 - 17	5	3-quart casserole
Wild rice	1 cup	3 cups	50	40 - 45	5	3-quart casserole
Brown rice	1 cup	3 cups	50	45 - 50	5	3-quart casserole
Quick-cooking	1 cup	1 cup	HI	3 - 4	5	1-quart casserole

SPINACH AND RICE

Cooking Time: 19 to 20 minutes

- **1 package (10 ounces) frozen chopped spinach**
- **1¼ cups quick-cooking rice**
- **¼ cup grated Parmesan cheese**
- **1 stalk celery, chopped**
- **1 green onion, chopped**
- **½ teaspoon dillweed**
- **2 cups milk**
- **3 eggs, beaten**

Place unopened package of spinach on microproof plate (if spinach is in foil-wrapped package, remove foil). Cook on HI, 5 minutes.

Remove from oven and let stand 5 minutes; squeeze dry. Combine spinach with rice, Parmesan cheese, celery, green onion, dill, milk, and eggs in 2-quart microproof casserole. Cover with casserole lid and cook on HI, 14 to 15 minutes, or until knife inserted in center comes out clean.

Remove from oven and let stand, covered, 5 minutes before serving.

4 to 6 servings

ARTICHOKE PILAF

Cooking Time: 5½ minutes

- **2 jars (6 ounces each) marinated artichoke hearts**
- **1 cup chopped onion**
- **1 clove garlic, minced**
- **½ cup thinly sliced celery**
- **1 cup chicken broth**
- **1 cup cooked rice**
- **⅓ cup minced fresh parsley**
- **½ teaspoon salt**
- **⅛ teaspoon pepper**

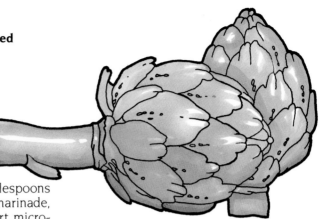

Drain artichokes, reserving 3 tablespoons marinade. Place the reserved marinade, onion, garlic, and celery in 2-quart microproof dish. Cook on HI, 2½ minutes, or until onion is transparent.

Stir in artichokes, broth, rice, parsley, salt, and pepper. Cover and cook on HI, 3 minutes, stirring once during cooking time.

Remove from oven and let stand 5 minutes before serving.

4 to 6 servings

Team this unusual pilaf with a roast for a distinctive dinner. The artichoke marinade provides the intriguing seasoning.

SIMPLE HERBED RICE

Cooking Time: 12 to 14 minutes

- **2 cups chicken or beef broth**
- **1 cup long grain rice**
- **¼ cup minced onion**
- **2 tablespoons minced fresh parsley**

Combine broth, rice, onion, and parsley in 2-quart microproof casserole. Cover and cook on HI, 12 to 14 minutes.

Remove from oven and let stand, covered, 10 minutes, or until all broth is absorbed.

4 servings

Vary rice to suit your taste and complement the other dishes on the menu. Substitute vegetable or onion bouillon for the chicken broth, or substitue any fresh herbs you prefer.

CHEESY VEGETABLES AND RICE

Cooking Time: 17 to 20 minutes

- **1 cup long grain rice**
- **2 cups hot water**
- **2 cups (8 ounces) shredded Monterey jack cheese, divided**
- **1 large zucchini, sliced**
- **1 medium tomato, chopped**
- **1 green onion, chopped**
- **1 teaspoon Italian herb seasoning**
- **1 container (8 ounces) dairy sour cream**

Place rice and water in 1½-quart microproof casserole. Cover with casserole lid and cook on HI, 8 to 10 minutes.

In layers over rice, place half the cheese, zucchini, tomato, green onion, Italian seasoning, and remaining cheese. Cover and cook on 80, 8 to 9 minutes.

Spread sour cream evenly over top. Cover and continue to cook on 80, 1 minute.

Remove from oven and let stand, covered, 5 minutes.

4 servings

This protein-rich dish can be the focus of a meatless meal, or it can be a side dish. A green salad and crusty bread round out the meal.

Oriental Rice Medley

ORIENTAL RICE MEDLEY
Cooking Time: 19 to 21 minutes

- 1 **cup long grain white rice**
- 2 **cups chicken broth**
- 1 **package (10 ounces) oriental-style frozen vegetables, thawed**
- 1 **can (4 ounces) sliced mushrooms, drained**
- 2 **green onions, chopped**
- ¼ **cup butter or margarine**
- 2 **tablespoons soy sauce**

Combine rice and broth in 3-quart microproof casserole. Cover with casserole lid and cook on HI, 12 minutes.

Stir in oriental vegetables, mushrooms, onions, butter, and soy sauce. Cover and cook on HI, 7 to 9 minutes, or until hot, stirring once.

4 servings

WILD RICE WITH TURKEY
Cooking Time: 14 to 15 minutes

- 1 **box (6 ounces) long grain and wild rice mix**
- 1 **can (10½ ounces) condensed cream of mushroom soup, undiluted**
- 1 **cup hot chicken broth**
- 2 **cups cubed cooked turkey**
- 1 **can (4 ounces) sliced mushrooms**
- ¼ **teaspoon celery seed**

Combine rice mix, soup, and broth in 2-quart microproof casserole. Cover with casserole lid. Cook on HI, 12 minutes.

Stir in turkey, mushrooms, and celery seed. Cover and cook on HI, 2 to 3 minutes, or until rice is cooked. Remove from oven and let stand, covered, 5 minutes before serving.

4 servings

MACARONI AND CHEESE
Cooking Time: 14 to 16 minutes

- 1½ **cups uncooked elbow macaroni**
- 3 **cups hot water**
- 2 **cups (10 ounces) diced process American cheese**
- 2 **tablespoons butter or margarine**
- ¼ **cup milk**
  Salt and pepper to taste

Combine macaroni and water in 9-inch microproof baking dish. Double-wrap tightly with plastic wrap and cook on HI, 9 to 10 minutes, or until noodles are cooked but still firm.

Pour off any remaining water. Stir in cheese, butter, milk, salt, and pepper. Cover and cook on HI, 5 to 6 minutes, stirring once.

4 servings

An American classic, and easier than ever! Cooking macaroni in the casserole saves clean-up time as well as cooking time.

VEGETARIAN LASAGNA

Cooking Time: 38½ to 43½ minutes

- 1 **large onion, chopped**
- ½ **pound carrots, shredded**
- ½ **pound mushrooms, coarsely chopped**
- 2 **containers (15 ounces each) ricotta cheese**
- 4 **eggs**
- ½ **cup (2 ounces) grated Parmesan cheese**
- 1 **cup spaghetti sauce**
- 9 **uncooked lasagna noodles**
- 1 **package (20 ounces) frozen chopped spinach, thawed and drained**
- ½ **pound tomatoes, peeled and coarsely chopped**
- 2 **cups (8 ounces) shredded mozzarella cheese**

Place onion in 1-quart microproof casserole. Cover with casserole lid and cook on HI, 2½ minutes. Spread out on paper towel to absorb excess moisture. Place carrots in same casserole. Cover and cook on HI, 3 minutes. Spread out on paper towel. Repeat with mushrooms, cooking on HI, 3 minutes.

In the same casserole, stir together ricotta, eggs, and Parmesan cheese. Set aside.

Spoon spaghetti sauce into shallow 2½-quart microproof casserole. Add remaining ingredients in layers as follows.

Form the first layer with 3 lasagna noodles, spinach, onions, and one-third the ricotta mixture.

Form the second layer with 3 lasagna noodles, carrots, mushrooms, and one-third the ricotta mixture.

Form the third layer with the remaining ricotta mixture, tomatoes, and mozzarella. Double-wrap casserole tightly with plastic wrap. Refrigerate 6 to 12 hours.

Remove casserole from refrigerator and let stand 1 hour. Cook on HI, 10 minutes.

Rotate dish one-half turn. Cook on 50, 20 to 25 minutes, or until hot and bubbly.

Remove from oven and let stand 10 minutes before serving.

8 servings

This is a truly original dish — a delight to the eye as well as the palate. While it does require some effort on your part, we're sure you'll think the results are well worth it. The advance preparation enables flavors to blend and the pasta to soften somewhat before cooking.

Vegetarian Lasagna

CHICKEN NOODLE CASSEROLE

Cooking Time: 13 to 15 minutes

- 1½ **cups uncooked thin egg noodles, broken up**
- 2 **to 3 cups cubed cooked chicken or turkey**
- 1 **cup chicken broth**
- ½ **cup milk**
- ½ **teaspoon salt**
- ⅛ **teaspoon pepper**
- 1 **cup shredded Cheddar cheese**
- ¼ **cup sliced stuffed green olives**

Combine noodles, chicken, milk, broth, salt and pepper in 2-quart microproof casserole. Stir. Cover with casserole lid and cook on 70, 8 to 10 minutes, or until noodles are cooked but still firm, stirring once.

Stir in cheese and olives. Cook, uncovered, on 20, 5 minutes, or until cheese melts.

4 to 6 servings

For 2 to 3 servings, cut ingredients in half. Cook, covered, on 70, 6 to 8 minutes, or until noodles are done, stirring once. Continue as directed for full recipe.

SOUTHERN CHEDDAR GRITS

Cooking Time: 23 to 25 minutes

- 4 **cups hot water**
- 1 **cup uncooked quick grits**
- 1 **teaspoon salt**
- 1 **cup grated sharp Cheddar cheese**
- ½ **cup butter or margarine**
- 2 **eggs, beaten**
- ¼ **teaspoon garlic powder**
- ¼ **teaspoon hot pepper sauce**

Combine water, grits, and salt in 3-quart microproof casserole. Cook on HI, 12 minutes, stirring halfway through cooking time. Add cheese and butter, and stir thoroughly. Cook on HI, 1 minute, or until cheese melts.

Combine eggs, garlic, and hot pepper sauce. Stir into grits. Cook on 70, 10 to 12 minutes, or until center is nearly set. Let stand 5 minutes before serving.

8 servings

ROTINI WITH HAM AND TOMATOES

Cooking Time: 28 to 30 minutes

- 2 **cans (16 ounces each) stewed tomatoes**
- 8 **ounces rotini noodles**
- ¼ **cup butter**
- 1 **teaspoon Italian herb seasoning**
- 1½ **cups tomato juice**
- 1 **pound cubed cooked ham**
- ¼ **cup grated Parmesan cheese**

Combine tomatoes, rotini, butter, Italian herb seasoning, and tomato juice in 3-quart microproof casserole. Mix well. Cover with casserole lid and cook on HI, 10 minutes, stirring once during cooking time.

Stir in ham. Sprinkle with cheese. Cover and cook on 50, 18 to 20 minutes.

Remove from oven and let stand, covered, 5 minutes.

4 servings

ONE-STEP LASAGNA
Cooking Time: 42 to 47 minutes

- **1 pound lean ground beef**
- **1 jar (15 ounces) spaghetti sauce**
- **½ cup hot water**
- **1 package (7 ounces) lasagna noodles, trimmed to fit 12 × 7-inch baking dish**
- **1 container (15 ounces) ricotta cheese, drained**
- **3 cups (12 ounces) shredded mozzarella cheese, divided**
- **½ cup grated Parmesan cheese**
  Chopped fresh parsley

Crumble beef in a 2-quart microproof casserole. Cover with casserole lid and cook on HI, 5 minutes, stirring once during cooking time.

Pour off fat. Add spaghetti sauce and water. Mix well.

Spread one-third of the meat sauce in 12 × 7-inch microproof baking dish. Arrange half the uncooked noodles over sauce. Spread with half of the ricotta. Top with one-third of the meat sauce. Sprinkle with 1 cup of the mozzarella. Repeat layers with remaining noodles, ricotta, and meat sauce. Top with Parmesan cheese. Double-wrap tightly with plastic wrap. Cook on HI, 20 minutes.

Cook on 50, 15 to 20 minutes.

Sprinkle with remaining mozzarella. Cook on HI, 2 to 2½ minutes, or until cheese melts. Sprinkle with parsley and serve with additional Parmesan cheese if desired.

6 servings

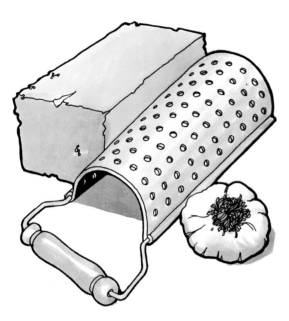

SPAGHETTI CASSEROLE
Cooking Time: 28 minutes

- **1 pound lean ground beef**
- **1 medium onion, chopped**
- **1 stalk celery, chopped**
- **1 package (7 ounces) thin spaghetti, broken up**
- **1 can (28 ounces) stewed tomatoes**
- **1½ cups tomato juice**
- **1 tablespoon lemon juice**
- **2 tablespoons brown sugar**
- **1 teaspoon Italian herb seasoning**
- **½ teaspoon basil**
- **½ teaspoon salt**
- **¼ teaspoon thyme**
- **¼ cup grated Parmesan cheese**

Combine beef, onion, and celery in 3-quart microproof casserole. Cover with paper towel and cook on HI, 5 minutes. Pour off fat. Stir in spaghetti. Add remaining ingredients except the Parmesan cheese. Cover with casserole lid and cook on HI, 5 minutes.

Cook on 90, 18 minutes, or until noodles are cooked but still firm. Top with Parmesan cheese before serving.

6 servings

Microwave Vegetable Variety

When preparing vegetables for microwave cooking, cut pieces as uniform in size as possible for more even cooking.

Most vegetables are covered when cooked in the microwave oven. A whole head of cauliflower cooks in 8 to 9 minutes on HI.

Broccoli used to be a challenge for the microwave cook until someone suggested splitting the stalks to expose more area and arranging with florets toward the center of the dish.

VEGETABLES

Your microwave oven enables you to enter one of the most exciting areas of the culinary arts: The world of succulent tender-crisp cooked vegetables. Because very little water is used, sometimes none at all, vegetables emerge from the microwave oven with bright, fresh color, full of flavor, tender and nutritious. Even reheated, fresh vegetables retain their original flavor and color. They do not dry out, because the steam that heats them is primarily generated within the vegetables themselves. Canned vegetables heat well too, because they can be drained before cooking so that they retain their full fresh taste after cooking.

You'll truly be amazed at how easy it is to cook whole vegetables, like acorn squash or cauliflower. Try Cauliflower au Gratin (page 132) for an exciting introduction to microwave vegetable cookery. Believe it or not, the cauliflower is cooked *whole* with no more water than clings to it when it is washed! Like just about all of our vegetable recipes, it uses the maximum power control setting, HI.

ADAPTING YOUR RECIPES

Vegetables are best when eaten at the crisp stage — tender, yet resilient to the bite. If you prefer a softer texture, simply cook a bit longer. Because of the importance of vegetable cookery and the personal preferences involved, we have provided you with complete timing information plus instructions for cooking a wide variety of popular vegetables in chart form, as well as quite an array of recipes. We hope you enjoy our collection.

To adapt a conventional recipe, find a similar recipe in this chapter and also check the cooking guides. The following tips offer additional thoughts for you as you go about creating your own recipes and adapting your new and old favorites.

Helpful Tips

Celery, onions, green peppers, and carrots are usually precooked before being added to other vegetable casserole ingredients.

The temperature probe can also be used for cooking vegetables. Insert temperature probe in center of dish and cook on HI with temperature set at 150°F.

Freeze small portions of your favorite vegetable dishes in boilable plastic pouches. Tie with string or rubber bands, not wire twist ties, for defrosting/reheating in the microwave.

To defrost/reheat packaged frozen vegetables in pouches, snip off one top corner. Place bag on plate. Cook on 70, 5 minutes. Shake down contents and place bag upright on plate and cook another 5 minutes.

Frozen vegetables in foil-wrapped or lined cartons must be removed from their original packaging. Cook others in their original packages.

REHEATING GUIDE
VEGETABLES*

Food	Power Control	Time (in minutes)	Special Notes
Au gratin vegetables, frozen, 11½ oz.	70	10 - 12 min.	Microproof dish, covered.
Onion Rings, 9 oz.	follow package directions		
Potatoes, Country-cut fries, 1 lb.	follow package directions		
French fries, 1 lb.	follow package directions		
Instant mashed, 4 servings	HI	5 - 7 min.	Follow package directions. Reduce liquid by 1 tablespoon.
Tater tots, 1 lb.	follow package directions		
Vegetable crêpes, 6½ oz.	follow package directions		
Vegetable soufflé, 12 oz.	HI	12 - 15 min.	Transfer to microproof paper tray.
Vegetables, frozen in pouch, 10 - 12 oz.	HI	6 - 9 min.	Slit pouch. Place on microproof plate. Flex halfway through cooking time to mix.

* Due to the tremendous variety in convenience food products available, times given here should be used only as guidelines. We suggest you cook food for the shortest recommended time and then check for doneness. Be sure to check the package for microwave instructions.

COOKING VEGETABLES

It is not difficult to remember microwave cooking instructions for vegetables. *All vegetables are cooked on HI.* That's just about all there is to it. Choose a microproof casserole or baking dish and use a microwave roasting rack when appropriate. Cover all vegetables during cooking except whole vegetables (potatoes, squash, etc.).

Most vegetables profit from 2 to 3 minutes standing time before serving. That's it.

BLANCHING VEGETABLES

The microwave oven can be a valuable and appreciated aid in preparing fresh vegetables for the freezer. (The oven is not recommended for canning.) Some vegetables don't require any water at all and, of course, the less water used the better. You'll have that "fresh picked" color and flavor for your produce. Here are some tips in preparing vegetables for blanching.

Choose young, tender vegetables. Clean and prepare for cooking according to cooking guide.

Measure amounts to be blanched, and place by batches in a microproof casserole. Add water according to the blanching guide.

Cover and cook on HI, according to the guide on page 131.

Stir vegetables halfway through cooking. Let vegetables stand, covered, 1 minute after blanching.

Place vegetables in ice water at once to stop cooking. When vegetables feel cool, spread on towel to absorb excess moisture.

Package in freezer containers or pouches. Seal, label, date, and freeze quickly.

COOKING GUIDE — VEGETABLES
Uses Power Control HI

Food	Amount	Fresh Vegetable Preparation	Time (in minutes)	Water	Standing Time (in minutes)	Special Notes
Artichokes 3½" in diameter	Fresh: 1 2	Wash thoroughly. Cut tops off each leaf.	7 - 8 11 - 12	¼ cup ½ cup	2 - 3 2 - 3	When done, a leaf peeled from whole comes off easily.
	Frozen: 10 oz.	Slit pouch	5 - 6			
Asparagus spears and cut pieces	Fresh: 1 lb.	Wash thoroughly. Snap off tough base and discard.	2 - 3	¼ cup	None	Stir or rearrange once during cooking time.
	Frozen: 10 oz.		7 - 8	None	2 - 3	
Beans: green, wax, French-cut	Fresh: 1 lb.	Remove ends. Wash well. Leave whole or break in pieces.	12 - 14	¼ cup	2 - 3	Stir once or rearrange as necessary.
	Frozen: 6 oz.		7 - 8	None	None	
Beets	4 medium	Scrub beets. Leave 1" of top on beet.	16 - 18	¼ cup	None	After cooking, peel. Cut or leave whole.
Broccoli	Fresh, whole 1 - 2½ lbs.	Remove outer leaves. Slit stalks.	9 - 10	¼ cup	3	Stir or rearrange during cooking time.
	Frozen, whole		8 - 10	¼ cup	3	
	Fresh, chopped 1 - 1½ lbs.		9 - 10	¼ cup	2	
	Frozen, chopped 10 oz.		8 - 9	None	2	
Brussels sprouts	Fresh: 1 lb.	Remove outside leaves if wilted. Cut off Stems. Wash.	8 - 9	¼ cup	2 - 3	Stir or rearrange once during cooking time.
	Frozen: 10 oz.		6 - 7	None	None	
Cabbage	½ medium head, shredded	Remove outside wilted leaves.	5 - 6	¼ cup	2 - 3	
	1 medium head, wedges		13 - 15	¼ cup	2 - 3	Rearrange wedges after 7 minutes.
Carrots	4: sliced or diced	Peel and cut off tops.	7 - 9	1 Tb.	2 - 3	Stir once during cooking time.
	6: sliced or diced	Fresh young carrots cook best.	9 - 10	2 Tbs.	2 - 3	
	8: tiny, whole		8 - 10	2 Tbs.	2 - 3	
	Frozen: 10 oz.		8 - 9	None	None	
Cauliflower	1 medium, in flowerets	Cut tough stem. Wash. Remove outside leaves.	7 - 8	¼ cup	2 - 3	Stir after 5 minutes.
	1 medium, whole	Remove core.	8 - 9	½ cup	3	Turn over once.
	Frozen: 10 oz.		8 - 9	½ cup	3	Stir after 5 minutes.
Celery	2½ cups, 1" slices	Clean stalks thoroughly.	8 - 9	¼ cup	2	
Corn: kernel	Frozen: 10 oz.		5 - 6	¼ cup	2	Stir halfway through cooking time.
On the cob	1 ear 2 ears 3 ears 4 ears	Husk. Cook no more than 4 at a time.	3 - 4 6 - 7 9 - 10 11 - 12	None None None None	2 2 2 2	Place in microproof dish. Add ¼ cup water. Cover with plastic wrap. After cooking, let stand, covered, 2 minutes.
Eggplant	1 medium, sliced	Wash and peel. Cut into slices or cubes.	5 - 6	2 Tbs.	3	
	1 medium, whole	Pierce skin.	6 - 7			Place on microproof rack.
Greens: collard, kale, etc.	Fresh: 1 lb.	Wash. Remove wilted leaves or tough stem.	6 - 7	None	2	
	Frozen: 10 oz.		7 - 8	None	2	

COOKING GUIDE — VEGETABLES
Uses Power Control HI

Food	Amount	Fresh Vegetable Preparation	Time (in minutes)	Water	Standing Time (in minutes)	Special Notes
Mushrooms	Fresh: ½ lb. sliced	Add butter.	2 - 4		2	Stir halfway through cooking time.
Okra	Fresh: ½ lb.	Wash thoroughly. Leave whole or cut in thick slices.	3 - 5	¼ cup	2	
	Frozen: 10 oz.		7 - 8	None	2	
Onions	1 lb., tiny whole	Peel. Add 1 Tb. butter.	6 - 7	None	3	Stir once during cooking time.
	1 lb., medium to large	Peel and quarter. Add 1 Tb. butter.	7 - 9	None	3	
Parsnips	4 medium, quartered.	Peel and cut.	8 - 9	¼ cup	2	Stir once during cooking time.
Peas: green	Fresh: 1 lb. Fresh: 2 lbs. Frozen: 6 oz.	Shell peas. Rinse well.	7 - 8 8 - 9 5 - 6	¼ cup ½ cup None	2 2 - 3 None	Stir once during cooking time.
Peas and onions	Frozen: 10 oz.		6 - 8	2 Tbs.	2	
Pea pods	Frozen: 6 oz.		3 - 4	2 Tbs.	3	
Potatoes, sweet 5 - 6 oz. ea.	1 2 4 6	Wash and scrub well. Pierce with fork. Place on rack or paper towel in circle, 1" apart.	4 - 4½ 6 - 7 8 - 10 10 - 11	None None None None	3 3 3 3	
Potatoes, white baking 6 - 8 oz. ea.	1 2 3 4 5	Wash and scrub well. Pierce with fork. Place on rack or paper towel in circle, 1" apart.	4 - 6 6 - 8 8 - 12 12 - 16 16 - 20	None None None None	3 3 3 3	
boiling	3	Peel potatoes, cut in quarters.	12 - 16	½ cup	None	Stir once during cooking time.
Rutabaga	Fresh: 1 lb. Frozen: 10 oz.	Wash well. Remove tough stems or any wilted leaves.	6 - 7 7 - 8	None None	2 2	Stir once during cooking time.
Spinach	Fresh: 1 lb. Frozen: 10 oz.	Wash well. Remove tough stems. Drain.	6 - 7 7 - 8	None None	2 2	Stir once during cooking time.
Squash, acorn or butternut	1 - 1½ lbs. whole	Scrub. Pierce with fork.	10 - 12	None		Cut and remove seeds to serve.
Spaghetti squash	2 - 3 lbs.	Scrub, pierce with fork. Place on rack.	6 per lb.	None	5	Serve with butter. Parmesan cheese, or spaghetti sauce.
Turnips	4 cups cubed	Peel, wash.	9 - 11	¼ cup	3	Stir after 5 minutes.
Zucchini	3 cups sliced	Wash; do not peel. Add butter.	7 - 8		2	Stir after 4 minutes.

COOKING GUIDE
CANNED VEGETABLES
Uses Power Control 80

Size	Minutes Drained	Minutes Undrained	Special Notes
8 ounces	1½ - 2	2 - 2½	Regardless of quantity: use a 4-cup microproof casserole, covered. Stir once. Let stand, covered, 2 - 3 minutes before serving.
15 ounces	2½ - 3	3 - 4	
17 ounces	3½ - 4	4 - 5	

Note: Temperature probe may be used. Set Power Control on 80, temperature control at 150°F. Place probe in center of dish. Stir halfway through cooking time.

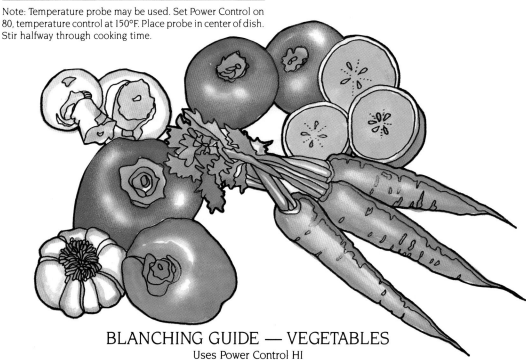

BLANCHING GUIDE — VEGETABLES
Uses Power Control HI

Food	Amount	Water	Approximate Time (in minutes)	Casserole Size
Asparagus (cut in 1-inch pieces)	4 cups	¼ cup	4½	1½ quart
Beans, green or wax (cut in 1-inch pieces)	1 pound	½ cup	5	1½ quart
Broccoli (cut in 1-inch pieces)	1 pound	⅓ cup	6	1½ quart
Carrots (sliced)	1 pound	⅓ cup	6	1½ quart
Cauliflower (cut in florets)	1 head	⅓ cup	6	2 quart
Corn (cut from cob)	4 cups	none	4	1½ quart
Corn-on-the-cob (husked)	6 ears	none	5½	1½ quart
Onions (quartered)	4 medium	½ cup	3 - 4½	1 quart
Parsnips (cubed)	1 pound	¼ cup	2½ - 4	1½ quart
Peas (shelled)	4 cups	¼ cup	4½	1½ quart
Snow peas	4 cups	¼ cup	3½	1½ quart
Spinach (washed)	1 pound	none	4	2 quart
Turnips (cubed)	1 pound	¼ cup	3 - 4½	1½ quart
Zucchini (sliced or cubed)	1 pound	¼ cup	4	1½ quart

NEAPOLITAN GREEN BEANS

Cooking Time: 13 to 15 minutes

- **2 packages (10 ounces each) frozen green beans**
- **¼ cup water**
- **1 small onion, thickly sliced**
- **¾ cup Italian dressing**
- **3 slices bacon, cooked**

Place green beans and water in 1½-quart microproof casserole. Cover and cook on HI, 9 to 10 minutes, or until tender-crisp, stirring once during cooking time. Add onion and Italian dressing. Cover and cook on HI, 4 to 5 minutes, or until beans are tender and onion is transparent. Sprinkle with crumbled cooked bacon.

6 servings

CAULIFLOWER AU GRATIN

Cooking Time: 9 to 11 minutes

- **1 medium head cauliflower, cored**
- **¼ cup water**
- **½ cup shredded mild Cheddar cheese**
- **¼ cup Italian seasoned bread crumbs**

Place cauliflower upside-down in 2-quart microproof casserole. Add water. Cover with casserole lid and cook on HI, 4 minutes. Turn cauliflower over. Cover and cook on HI, 4 to 5 minutes, or until cauliflower is tender. Drain cauliflower, reserving liquid.

Mix liquid with cheese and bread crumbs. Pat mixture gently onto cauliflower. Cover and cook on HI, 1 to 2 minutes, or until cheese begins to melt. Let stand, still covered, 3 minutes before serving.

5 to 6 servings

CARROT AND BASIL BAKE

Cooking Time: 15 to 17 minutes

- **1 pound carrots, peeled and shredded**
- **1 small onion, minced**
- **2 tablespoons butter or margarine**
- **2 tablespoons water**
- **1 teaspoon parsley flakes**
- **½ teaspoon basil**
- **½ teaspoon salt**

Combine all ingredients in 1¾-quart microproof casserole. Cover with casserole lid and cook on HI, 15 to 17 minutes, stirring twice during cooking time. Let stand 3 minutes before serving.

6 servings

JELLIED CARROTS

Cooking Time: 13 to 15 minutes

- **1 pound carrots, thinly sliced**
- **2 tablespoons water**
- **¼ cup butter or margarine**
- **¼ cup jellied cranberry sauce**
  Salt to taste

Place carrots and water in 1½ to 2-quart microproof casserole. Cover with casserole lid and cook on HI, 10 to 12 minutes, or until carrots are tender-crisp. Remove carrots from casserole, drain, and set aside.

Place butter and cranberry sauce in casserole. Cover and cook on HI, 1 minute. Stir in carrots. Season with salt. Cover and cook on HI, 2 minutes.

4 servings

ASPARAGUS WITH MUSTARD SAUCE

Cooking Time: 7 to 8½ minutes

**1½ pounds asparagus, cleaned and
     cut into pieces**
¼   cup water
⅓   cup mayonnaise
1   tablespoon minced fresh parsley
**1   teaspoon prepared Dijon-style
     mustard**
½   teaspoon onion salt
⅛   teaspoon white pepper

Combine asparagus and water in 2-quart microproof casserole. Cover with casserole lid and cook on HI, 6 to 7 minutes, or until tender, stirring once during cooking time. Drain. Set aside. Combine remaining ingredients in small bowl. Pour over asparagus and toss lightly to coat asparagus. Cook on HI, 1 to 1½ minutes, or until heated through.

6 servings

Two packages (9 ounces each) frozen cut asparagus can be substituted for fresh asparagus; omit water.

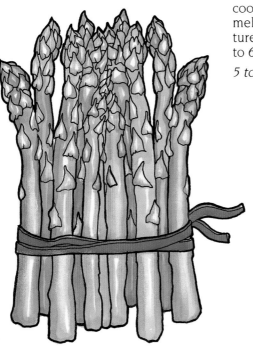

BROCCOLI CARROT CASSEROLE

Cooking Time: 11¾ to 13 minutes

**1   package (10 ounces) frozen
     broccoli spears**
1   cup finely shredded carrots
1   tablespoon all-purpose flour
1   tablespoon minced onion
¼   teaspoon salt
⅛   teaspoon pepper
**1   can (10¾ ounces) cream of chicken
     soup, undiluted**
½   cup dairy sour cream
2   tablespoons butter or margarine
¾   cup herb-seasoned stuffing cubes

Place package of unopened broccoli on microproof plate. (If broccoli is in foil-wrapped package, remove foil.) Cook on HI, 3 minutes. Set aside.

Combine carrots, flour, onion, salt, pepper, soup, and sour cream in 1½-quart microproof casserole. Cut broccoli into one-inch pieces and stir into carrot mixture. Cover with casserole lid and cook on HI, 3 minutes. Stir gently.

Place butter in 2-cup glass measure and cook on HI, 45 to 60 seconds, or until melted. Stir in stuffing. Spoon stuffing mixture over broccoli. Cook, uncovered, on HI, 5 to 6 minutes, or until hot.

5 to 6 servings

FAR EAST CELERY

Cooking Time: 10 to 12½ minutes

- **4 cups (8 to 10 stalks) celery, cut into 1-inch pieces**
- **¼ cup water**
- **½ teaspoon salt**
- **1 can (10 ounces) sliced water chestnuts, drained**
- **½ cup sliced almonds**
- **2 tablespoons diced pimiento**
- **1 green onion, sliced**
- **2 teaspoons cornstarch**
- **½ cup chicken broth**
- **1 teaspoon soy sauce**

Place celery, water, and salt in 1½-quart microproof casserole. Cover with casserole lid and cook on HI, 8 to 10 minutes, or until celery is tender.

Pour off water. Stir in water chestnuts, almonds, pimiento, and green onion. Set aside.

Combine cornstarch with broth and soy sauce, stirring until cornstarch is dissolved. Stir into vegetable mixture. Cover and cook on HI, 2 to 2½ minutes.

4 to 6 servings

Cut celery diagonally, french-style, for a more attractive dish.

CHEESED BROCCOLI FOR TWO

Cooking Time: 8¾ minutes

- **1 package (10 ounces) frozen broccoli spears**
- **¼ cup shredded Monterey jack cheese**

Unwrap broccoli; place in shallow microproof dish. Cover with plastic wrap. Cook on HI, 8 minutes. Drain.

Sprinkle cheese over broccoli. Cook, uncovered, on HI, 45 seconds.

2 servings

DILLED ZUCCHINI AND CORN

Cooking Time: 6 to 7 minutes

- **1 medium zucchini (1½ cups), sliced**
- **1½ cups fresh or 1 can (12 ounces) kernel corn, drained**
- **1 teaspoon dillweed**
- **2 tablespoons butter or margarine**

Combine zucchini, corn, and dillweed in 1½-quart microproof casserole. Dot with butter. Stir to mix. Cover and cook on HI, 6 to 7 minutes, or until hot, stirring once.

4 servings

BRUSSELS SPROUTS WITH ALMOND BUTTER

Cooking Time: 16 to 20 minutes

- **1 pound fresh Brussels sprouts**
- **3 tablespoons butter or margarine**
- **¼ cup sliced almonds**
- **¼ cup water**
- **⅛ teaspoon pepper**

Wash and trim Brussels sprouts. Soak in salted cold water 10 minutes. Drain.

Place butter in shallow microproof baking dish. Cover with waxed paper. Cook on HI, 6 to 8 minutes, or until butter is browned. Stir in almonds and set aside.

Combine water and Brussels sprouts in 2-quart microproof casserole. Cover and cook on HI, 10 to 12 minutes, or until tender. Drain. Place in serving dish. Pour almond butter over Brussels sprouts. Season with pepper.

4 to 6 servings

STUFFED EGGPLANT PARMIGIANA

Cooking Time: 13 to 13½ minutes

- **1 eggplant (1 pound)**
- **3 medium tomatoes, peeled, seeded, and chopped**
- **1 stalk celery, finely chopped**
- **1 green onion, chopped**
- **1 clove garlic, minced**
- **½ cup grated Parmesan cheese**
- **1 teaspoon Italian herb seasoning**
- **1½ cups (6 ounces) shredded mozzarella cheese, divided**
- **Paprika**

Cut eggplant in half lengthwise. Scoop out pulp, leaving ¼-inch shells. Chop the pulp coarsely. In a 2-quart microproof casserole, combine eggplant pulp, tomatoes, celery, green onion, and garlic. Cover with casserole lid. Cook on HI, 6 minutes.

Pour off liquid. Add Parmesan cheese, Italian seasoning, and 1 cup of the mozzarella cheese. Mix well.

Place eggplant shells in 8 × 8-inch microproof baking dish. Spoon half of the tomato mixture into each shell. Cover with waxed paper. Cook on HI, 3 minutes. Rotate dish. Continue to cook on HI, 3 minutes.

Top with remaining mozzarella cheese and sprinkle with paprika. Cook on HI, 1 to 1½ minutes, or until cheese begins to melt.

2 servings

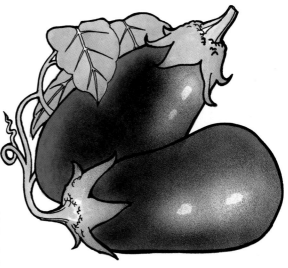

RATATOUILLE

Cooking Time: 19 to 21 minutes

- **1 small eggplant (1 pound)**
- **2 tablespoons olive oil**
- **1 medium onion, sliced**
- **2 cloves garlic, minced**
- **4 medium tomatoes**
- **1½ cups sliced zucchini**
- **1 green pepper, cut into strips**
- **1 tablespoon lemon juice**
- **1 teaspoon basil**
- **⅛ teaspoon thyme**
- **⅛ teaspoon pepper**
- **¼ cup minced fresh parsley**
- **2 tablespoons grated Parmesan cheese**

Pierce eggplant deeply in several places with long-tined fork. Place on microwave roasting rack in microproof baking dish. Cook on HI, 6 minutes. Set aside.

Combine oil, onion, and garlic in 2¼-quart microproof casserole. Cover with casserole lid and cook on HI, 4 minutes.

Peel eggplant, if desired, and cut into 1½-inch cubes. Add to onion mixture. Add tomatoes, zucchini, green pepper, lemon juice, basil, thyme, and pepper. Blend well. Cover and cook on HI, 5 minutes. Stir. Cook uncovered on HI, 4 to 6 minutes.

Stir in parsley and sprinkle with cheese.

4 to 6 servings

SPAGHETTI SQUASH PRIMAVERA

Cooking Time: 25 to 27 minutes

- 1 **spaghetti squash
  (1½ to 2 pounds)**
- 1 **large zucchini (about 8 ounces)
  cut into ½-inch slices**
- 1 **large green pepper, cut into
  1-inch pieces**
- 1 **stalk celery, sliced**
- ½ **teaspoon dill**
- ½ **teaspoon basil**
- ½ **teaspoon Italian herb seasoning**
- ¼ **cup butter or margarine**
- 2 **large tomatoes, coarsely chopped**
- ¼ **cup grated Parmesan cheese
  Parsley**

Pierce squash deeply several times with long-tined fork. Place in oven on microwave roasting rack and cook on HI, 7 minutes. Turn squash over and continue to cook another 3 to 5 minutes, or until done. Set aside.

Combine zucchini, green pepper, celery, dill, basil, and Italian seasoning in a 1½-quart microproof casserole. Dot vegetables with butter. Cover with casserole lid and cook on HI, 10 minutes. Stir in tomatoes. Cover and cook on HI, 5 minutes.

Cut squash in half and remove seeds. With two forks, carefully transfer squash strands to serving platter. Spoon vegetables over top. Sprinkle with Parmesan cheese. Garnish with parsley, if desired.

4 servings

APPLE-STUFFED ACORN SQUASH

Cooking Time: 17 to 21 minutes

- 2 **medium acorn squash
  (1 to 1½ pounds each)**
- 2 **tablespoons butter**
- 3 **medium cooking apples,
  cored and diced**
- ¼ **cup pecan halves, coarsely chopped**
- ¼ **cup honey**
- ½ **teaspoon cinnamon**

Pierce acorn squash deeply in several places with long-tined fork. Cook on HI, 10 to 12 minutes. Cut each squash in half and remove seeds. Set aside.

Place butter in 2-quart glass measure and cook on HI, 1 minute. Stir in apples, nuts, honey, and cinnamon. Fill squash cavities with apple mixture. Arrange on microwave roasting rack in shallow microproof baking dish. Cover with plastic wrap and cook on HI, 3 minutes. Rotate dish one-half turn. Cook on HI, 3 to 5 minutes or until apples are tender.

4 servings

Acorn squash halves are beautiful containers for other stuffings. Peas and onions are especially colorful. Herb bread stuffings are delicious and satisfying. Or, fill with a vegetable medley for a meatless meal.

Spaghetti Squash Primavera

CALEXICO BEAN BAKE

Cooking Time: 10 to 12 minutes

- 1 **medium onion, sliced**
- 1 **medium green pepper, cut into 1-inch pieces**
- 1 **medium sweet red pepper, cut into 1-inch pieces**
- 1 **clove garlic, minced**
- 2 **tablespoons butter or margarine**
- 1 **can (16 ounces) red kidney beans, drained**
- 1 **can (16 ounces) garbanzo beans, drained**
- 1 **can (16 ounces) pinto beans, drained**
- 1 **can (16 ounces) stewed tomatoes**
- ¼ **teaspoon chili powder**
- 1 **teaspoon Italian herb seasoning**

Combine onion, green pepper, red pepper, garlic, and butter in 3-quart microproof casserole. Cover with casserole lid and cook on HI, 3 to 4 minutes. Stir in remaining ingredients. Cover and cook on HI, 7 to 8 minutes, or until hot, stirring once.

4 servings

Vary the beans according to your own taste and what's available. Italian canelli beans are a very nice change. You may also use lima beans, black-eyed peas, or frozen beans. Amounts are flexible too — some beans are available in 15-ounce cans or 10-ounce frozen packages. Just try to retain the overall proportions recommended here. Of course, there's no reason you can't make it a "six-bean" bake!

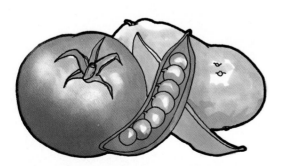

HARVARD BEETS

Cooking Time: 8½ to 9½ minutes

- 1 **can (16 ounces) diced or sliced beets**
- ¼ **cup sugar**
- 1 **tablespoon cornstarch**
- ¼ **cup wine vinegar**
- ½ **teaspoon salt**
- ⅛ **teaspoon pepper**

Drain beets, reserving liquid. Pour liquid into 1-cup glass measure. Add water to make 1 cup liquid.

Combine sugar, cornstarch, vinegar, salt, and pepper in 1-quart microproof casserole. Cook on HI, 3½ to 4 minutes, or until mixture thickens and is clear. Add beets and stir lightly. Cover with casserole lid and cook on HI, 5 to 5½ minutes, or until beets are hot.

4 servings

VEGETABLE TRIO

Cooking Time: 6½ to 9 minutes

- 1 **cup (4 ounces) fresh whole green beans**
- ½ **cup sliced yellow summer squash**
- ¼ **teaspoon thyme**
- ¼ **teaspoon sage**
- ⅛ **teaspoon pepper**
- 1 **large tomato, cut into 6 wedges**
- 2 **tablespoons butter**

Rinse green beans and squash. Place squash in center of 1-quart casserole. Arrange beans around outside edge. Stir in thyme, sage, and pepper. Cover with casserole lid and cook on HI, 5 to 7 minutes, or until vegetables are tender-crisp, stirring once.

Arrange tomato wedges over vegetables. Dot with butter. Cover and cook on HI, 1½ to 2 minutes, or just until butter melts.

2 servings

SWEET-SOUR RED CABBAGE

Cooking Time: 23 to 27 minutes

- 1½ **pounds red cabbage**
- 1 **tart apple, peeled, cored, and diced**
- 1 **tablespoon butter or margarine**
- 5 **tablespoons red wine or cider vinegar**
- 3 **to 5 tablespoons sugar**
- ½ **teaspoon salt**

Shred cabbage into 3-quart microproof casserole. Add apple, butter, and vinegar. Stir. Cover with casserole lid and cook on HI, 18 to 22 minutes, or until apples and cabbage are tender. Stir twice during cooking time. Stir in sugar and salt. Cover and cook on HI, 5 minutes, or until liquid comes to a boil.

6 servings

PEAS FRANCINE

Cooking Time: 9 to 10 minutes

- 2 **cups fresh shelled peas or**
  - 1 **package (10 ounces) frozen peas**
- 1 **teaspoon sugar**
- ¼ **cup water**
- 3 **or 4 large lettuce leaves**
  - **Dash salt and pepper**

Place peas, sugar, and water in 1½-quart microproof casserole. Stir. Cover with casserole lid and cook on HI, 4 minutes. Stir. Place lettuce leaves over peas. Cover and cook on HI, 5 to 6 minutes, or until peas are tender. Discard lettuce leaves. Drain peas. Stir in salt and pepper. Cover and let stand 2 to 3 minutes before serving.

4 servings

Have some fun! Substitute red cabbage leaves, radiccio, or kale for the lettuce.

SAUTEED MUSHROOMS

Cooking Time: 3 to 3½ minutes

- ½ **pound mushrooms, cleaned and sliced**
- ¼ **cup butter or margarine**
- 1 **clove garlic, minced**

Combine all ingredients in shallow microproof baking dish. Cover with paper towel and cook on HI, 3 to 3½ minutes, or until tender.

Stir through several times before serving.

2 to 4 servings

Serve with roast beef or steak, or as a "surprise" side dish with any meal. Sautéed Mushrooms are also a delicious main dish when served on toast and sprinkled with Parmesan cheese.

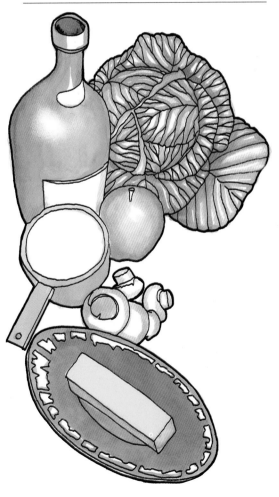

PARSLEY NEW POTATOES

Cooking Time: 10 to 12 minutes

12 small new potatoes (1 pound)
¼ cup water
1 tablespoon minced fresh parsley
2 tablespoons butter
    Dash salt and pepper

Cut a ½-inch strip of peel from around the middle of each potato. Place potatoes in 2-quart microproof casserole. Add water. Cover with casserole lid and cook on HI, 10 to 12 minutes, or until tender, stirring once during cooking time.

Drain potatoes and stir in parsley, butter, salt, and pepper.

4 servings

PAN-BAKED POTATOES

Cooking Time: 10¾ to 12¾ minutes

2 tablespoons butter or margarine
¼ cup grated Parmesan cheese
½ teaspoon salt
¼ teaspoon white pepper
4 medium potatoes (4 to 5 ounces each)
    Paprika

Place butter in 1-cup glass measure and cook on HI, 45 seconds. Set aside. Stir together cheese, salt, and pepper in a separate bowl.

Cut potatoes in half lengthwise. Dip cut side in butter, then in cheese mixture. Place potatoes, cut-side up, in shallow microproof baking dish. Cook on HI, 10 to 12 minutes, or until tender. Let stand 5 minutes. Sprinkle with paprika before serving.

8 servings

Italian bread crumbs or cornflake crumbs may be substituted for Parmesan cheese.

TWICE-BAKED POTATOES

Cooking Time: 18 minutes

4 baking potatoes
    (4 to 5 ounces each)
½ cup butter or margarine
½ cup dairy sour cream
½ teaspoon salt
    Dash pepper
    Paprika

Pierce potatoes with a fork several times. Place in oven end-to-end in a ring on a paper towel, spacing about 1 inch apart. Cook on HI, 8 minutes. Turn potatoes over and cook on HI, 6 minutes. Remove from oven. Let stand several minutes.

When potatoes can be handled, remove ¼-inch horizontal slice from top of each potato. Carefully scoop out pulp, keeping skins intact. Blend butter, sour cream, salt, and pepper into potato pulp. Beat vigorously until smooth. Spoon pulp mixture into potato shells, or pipe in with pastry bag and star tip. Place filled shells in a ring along edge of microproof plate. Cook on HI, 4 minutes. Sprinkle with paprika.

4 servings

Potatoes, Sweet Potatoes, Carrots

ITALIAN POTATO SALAD

Cooking Time: 14 to 16 minutes

**2 pounds potatoes, peeled and
cut into 1-inch cubes**
½ cup water
¼ teaspoon salt
¼ cup Italian dressing
**6 large hard-cooked eggs, chopped,
divided**
½ cup chopped pimiento, divided
1 cup mayonnaise
1 stalk chopped celery
3 green onions
¼ teaspoon rosemary
**½ teaspoon Italian herb seasoning
Minced parsley**

Place potatoes, water, and salt in 4-quart microproof casserole. Cover with casserole lid and cook on HI, 4 minutes. Stir. Cover and cook on HI, 10 to 12 minutes, or until potatoes are tender.

Drain potatoes. Pour Italian dressing over potatoes and toss lightly. Set aside ¼ cup egg for garnish. Add remaining eggs to potatoes and toss lightly. Set aside 1 tablespoon pimiento. Add remaining pimiento to potato mixture. Blend in mayonnaise, celery, green onions, rosemary and Italian seasoning. Transfer to serving bowl. Garnish with reserved egg, pimiento, and parsley.

6 servings

GERMAN POTATO SALAD

Cooking Time: 4 to 6 minutes

**2 cans (16 ounces each) sliced
potatoes, drained**
¼ cup sliced celery
1 tablespoon chopped pimiento
½ teaspoon salt
**⅛ teaspoon pepper
Hot Bacon Sauce (page 146)**
1 tablespoon chopped fresh parsley

In a 1½-quart microproof casserole, combine potatoes, celery, pimiento, salt, and pepper. Pour Hot Bacon Sauce over potato mixture. Stir well. Cook on HI, 4 to 6 minutes, or until potatoes are hot. Stir in parsley.

6 to 8 servings

A glass measure and a whisk is all the equipment you need to master sauces with your microwave oven.

Basic White Sauce (page 144) can be the base for dozens of creative sauces. Just add your ingenuity, cheese, herbs, a bit of onion, etc.

Voila! See what a sauce can do for a beautiful vegetable platter (and your reputation as a skilled microwave cook).

SAUCES

Sauces *are* a cinch in your microwave oven. They are definitely a microwave success story. For those of us who have slaved over a hot stove with whisk in hand and double boiler at full speed, those days are gone forever. Sauces simply do not stick or scorch as they do when prepared on the stove top. They heat evenly and require less time and attention. You don't have to stir constantly and can simply retire that double boiler. Usually, just an occasional stirring is all that is required to prevent lumping. Sometimes a quick whisking after cooking can be added to make a sauce velvety-smooth. You can measure, mix, and cook all in the same glass measure or in the serving pitcher itself! Choose Tarragon Sauce (page 149) or Béarnaise Sauce (page 144) to perk up meat or vegetables, others for desserts. Just try making a sauce the microwave way and you'll turn an ordinary food into an elegant treat.

ADAPTING YOUR RECIPES

All those sauces generally considered too difficult for the average cook are easy in the microwave oven. When looking for a sauce recipe similar to the conventional one you want to convert, find a recipe with a similar quantity of liquid and similar main thickening ingredient such as cornstarch, flour, egg, cheese, or jelly. Read the directions carefully to determine procedure, timing, and power control setting. Then, when you stir, notice the progress of the sauce, and remove when the right consistency or doneness is reached. Keep notes to help you the next time.

Helpful Tips

Use a microproof container about twice the volume of ingredients to safeguard against the sauce boiling over — so easy with milk and cream-based sauces.

Sauces and salad dressings with ingredients not sensitive to rapid heating should be prepared on HI. Basic White Sauce is an example.

Bring cornstarch-thickened mixtures to a boil and remove as soon as thickened. Remember, overcooking will destroy the thickening agent.

You will notice that more flour or cornstarch is required in microwave cooking than in conventional cooking to thicken sauces and gravies, since they will not be reduced by evaporation.

Stirring quickly two or three times during cooking is sufficient to assure even cooking. Too many stirrings may slow cooking.

Did you know you can reheat sauces with the temperature probe? Reheat dessert sauces on HI with the temperature probe set at 125°F. Reheat main dish sauces, such as gravy or canned spaghetti sauce, on HI with the temperature probe set at 150°F.

When sauces require time to develop flavor or if they contain eggs, which might curdle, they should be cooked slowly, on 50 or even 30. Don't allow delicate egg yolk sauces to boil.

BASIC WHITE SAUCE
Cooking Time: 6¾ to 7¾ minutes

- **1 cup milk**
- **2 tablespoons butter**
- **2 tablespoons all-purpose flour**
  Dash white pepper
  Dash nutmeg

Place milk in 4-cup glass measure and cook on 70, 2 minutes. Set aside.

Place butter in 4-cup glass measure and cook on HI, 45 seconds. Stir in flour and continue to cook on HI, 1 minute.

Add milk, pepper, and nutmeg, to flour mixture and stir briskly. Cook on HI, 3 to 4 minutes, or until mixture boils, stirring once during cooking. Let stand 5 minutes before serving.

Serve with cooked broccoli or cauliflower.

1 cup

Invent your own sauce, using Basic White Sauce as a base. Try stirring in shredded cheese, or your favorite herbs, or a combination of both. Curry powder, saffron, or turmeric add their special colors and flavors. Use your imagination!

HERB SAUCE
Cooking Time: 2½ minutes

- **1 cup white wine or chicken broth**
- **½ cup butter or margarine**
- **2 teaspoons chopped chives**
- **½ teaspoon ground mustard**
- **½ teaspoon tarragon**
- **½ teaspoon rosemary**
- **⅛ teaspoon pepper**
- **2 eggs, beaten**

Combine wine, butter, chives, mustard, tarragon, rosemary and pepper in a 4-cup glass measure. Cook on HI, 2½ minutes.

Slowly beat wine mixture into eggs. Serve with meat, fish, or vegetables.

about 1½ cups

BEARNAISE SAUCE
Cooking Time: 1 to 2 minutes

- **4 egg yolks**
- **2 teaspoons tarragon vinegar**
- **1 teaspoon instant minced onion**
- **½ teaspoon chervil**
  Dash white pepper
- **½ cup butter**
- **1 teaspoon minced fresh parsley**

Place egg yolks, vinegar, onion, chervil, and pepper in blender container. Place butter in 1-cup glass measure and cook on HI, 1 to 2 minutes, or until bubbly.

Turn blender to high speed and gradually add butter through cover opening. Blend until sauce is thick and creamy. Stir in parsley.

Serve warm over broiled steak, cooked green vegetables, poached eggs, or fish.

½ cup

CHEF'S GRAVY

Cooking Time: 4 to 4½ minutes

- **⅓ cup meat or poultry drippings**
- **¼ cup all-purpose flour**
- **2 cups warm broth, water, or juice**
  Salt and pepper

Combine drippings and flour in 4-cup glass measure. Stir until smooth. Add broth and stir briskly until well blended. Cook on HI, 4 to 4½ minutes, or until mixture boils, stirring several times.

Season with salt and pepper. Beat until smooth. Add gravy enhancer to deepen color, if desired. Serve with meat, potatoes, or stuffing.

2½ cups

HOMEMADE SPAGHETTI SAUCE

Cooking Time: 23 to 28 minutes

- **1 medium onion, sliced**
- **6 medium mushrooms, sliced**
- **¼ cup sliced celery**
- **½ green pepper, sliced into thin strips**
- **2 cloves garlic, minced**
- **1½ tablespoons vegetable oil**
- **½ pound lean ground beef**
- **1 can (16 ounces) whole peeled tomatoes, chopped, liquid reserved**
- **1 can (6 ounces) tomato paste**
- **1 tablespoon chopped fresh parsley**
- **½ teaspoon oregano**

Combine onion, mushrooms, celery, green pepper, garlic, and oil in 2-quart microproof casserole. Cover with casserole lid and cook on HI, 5 minutes.

Stir in beef and cook on HI, 3 minutes. Stir through several times. Blend in tomatoes with liquid, tomato paste, parsley, and oregano. Cover and cook on HI, 15 to 20 minutes, or until sauce thickens.

about 4 cups

BARBECUE SAUCE

Cooking Time: 4½ to 5 minutes

- **1 cup ketchup**
- **¼ cup molasses**
- **¼ cup lemon juice**
- **¼ cup firmly packed brown sugar**
- **1 tablespoon Worcestershire sauce**
- **1 teaspoon Dijon-style mustard**
- **¼ teaspoon pepper**
- **1 clove garlic, minced**

Combine all ingredients in 1-quart glass measure. Cover with plastic wrap and cook on HI, 4½ to 5 minutes, stirring once.

about 1½ cups

HOT BACON SAUCE

Cooking Time: 3½ to 4½ minutes

- **3 tablespoons sugar**
- **3 teaspoons cornstarch**
- **6 tablespoons vinegar**
- **¼ cup water**
- **8 strips bacon, cooked, crumbled, fat reserved**
- **2 green onions, chopped**

Combine sugar, cornstarch, vinegar, water, and bacon fat in 2-cup glass measure. Cook on HI, 3½ to 4½ minutes, or until sauce boils. Stir in bacon and green onions.

about 1½ cups

This is the classic dressing used in making hot spinach salads and German Potato Salad (page 142). The salad pictured is a special one with purple kale and mandarin oranges added to the spinach. Give your own imagination free reign!

ORANGE SAUCE

Total Cooking Time: 2 to 3 minutes

- **⅔ cup orange juice**
- **3 tablespoons fat-free duckling juices**
- **2 tablespoons brown sugar**
- **1 tablespoon cornstarch**
- **2 teaspoons grated orange peel**
- **2 tablespoons orange-flavored liqueur**

Combine all ingredients except liqueur in 2-cup glass measure and stir well to dissolve cornstarch. Cook on HI, 2 to 3 minutes, or until mixture thickens. Add liqueur. Serve hot.

about 1¼ cups

Not having duck? Any poultry drippings will do. Or omit drippings, simply increase orange juice by 3 tablespoons and use as a dessert sauce!

HOLLANDAISE SAUCE

Cooking Time: 2 minutes

- **¼ cup butter or margarine**
- **¼ cup light cream**
- **2 egg yolks, well beaten**
- **1 tablespoon lemon juice**
- **½ teaspoon dry mustard**
- **¼ teaspoon salt**

Place butter in 4-cup glass measure and cook on HI, 1 minute, or until butter melts. Add cream, egg yolks, lemon juice, mustard, and salt. Beat with mixer or wire whisk until smooth. Cook on 70, 1 minute, beating well every 15 seconds until thickened.

Remove from oven and continue to beat until light and smooth. Serve immediately over cooked asparagus, broccoli, or Eggs Benedict (page 112).

¾ cup

If sauce curdles, beat in 1 teaspoon hot water and continue beating until mixture is smooth.

To reheat Hollandaise, cook on 20, 15 to 30 seconds. Stir, then let stand 1 minute. Repeat until sauce is hot.

Hot Bacon Sauce with salad

CLARIFIED BUTTER

Cooking Time: 2½ to 3 minutes

1 cup (½ pound) butter

Place butter in 2-cup glass measure and cook on 20, 2½ to 3 minutes, or until butter is completely melted and solids go to bottom, leaving clear liquid at top. Skim off any foam and discard. Carefully pour liquid into jar through a cheesecloth-lined strainer.

about ¼ cup

CREAMY DIJON SAUCE

Cooking Time: 2 to 3 minutes

¼ cup dry white wine
2 tablespoons whipping cream
2 tablespoons butter
2 teaspoons Dijon-style mustard
¼ teaspoon tarragon

Combine all ingredients in 1-cup glass measure. Cover with plastic wrap. Cook on 50, 2 to 3 minutes.

Serve with meat, spread on sandwiches, or stir into your favorite casserole.

about 1 cup

CITRUS SAUCE

Cooking Time: 1½ to 2½ minutes

½ cup sugar
1 egg, lightly beaten
   Juice of 1 lemon

Stir sugar, egg, and lemon juice together until blended. Cook on 50, 1½ to 2½ minutes, or until sauce thickens. Use to glaze Cornish hen, chicken, or duck.

about ½ cup

HOISIN SAUCE

Cooking Time: 4 to 4½ minutes

1 cup beef broth
¼ cup soy sauce
¼ cup dry sherry
2 tablespoons arrowroot or cornstarch
2 tablespoons molasses
2 tablespoons tomato paste
2 cloves garlic, minced
½ teaspoon ground ginger
⅛ teaspoon pepper

Combine all ingredients in 4-cup glass measure. Cover with plastic wrap and cook on HI, 4 to 4½ minutes, or until thickened, stirring once.

about 1¾ cups

We think you will enjoy this sauce with stir-fried vegetables, meat, poultry, or seafood. Try it with rice and with Western-style dishes, too.

LEMON BUTTER SAUCE

Cooking Time: 1½ to 2 minutes

½ cup butter or margarine
2 tablespoons lemon juice
⅛ teaspoon salt
⅛ teaspoon white pepper

Combine butter, lemon juice, salt, and pepper in 2-cup glass measure. Cook, uncovered, on HI, 1½ to 2 minutes, or until butter melts. Stir through.

Serve hot over seafood, green vegetables, or Easy Salmon Loaf (page 106).

⅔ cup

TARRAGON SAUCE

Cooking Time: 4 minutes

- ½ **cup unsalted butter**
- ⅓ **cup dry white wine**
- 1 **tablespoon tarragon vinegar**
- 2 **tablespoons minced fresh tarragon or**
    2 teaspoons dried tarragon
- 1 **tablespoon chopped chives**
- ½ **teaspoon salt**
- ¼ **teaspoon pepper**
    Dash hot pepper sauce
- 3 **egg yolks, beaten**

Combine all ingredients except egg yolks in 2-cup glass measure and blend well. Cook on HI, 2 minutes.

Stir a small amount of butter mixture into yolks, then stir yolks into butter mixture. Cook on 50, 2 minutes, stirring once. Beat through until smooth.

Serve over poached eggs, broiled meat, cauliflower, or carrots.

1 cup

LEMONY DILL SAUCE

Cooking Time: 3½ to 4½ minutes

- ½ **cup butter or margarine**
- 2 **tablespoons all-purpose flour**
- 1 **teaspoon instant chicken bouillon**
    crystals
- ½ **teaspoon dill**
- ½ **teaspoon salt**
- 1 **cup chicken broth**
- 2 **tablespoons lemon juice**

Place butter in 2-cup glass measure. Cook on HI, about 1½ minutes.

Blend in flour, bouillon, dill, and salt. Briskly stir in broth and mix until blended. Cook on HI, 2 to 3 minutes, or until mixture boils and thickens, stirring twice during cooking time. Stir in lemon juice.

Serve with broiled or poached salmon steaks.

1½ cups

Strawberry Sauce with cake

STRAWBERRY SAUCE

Cooking Time: 3 to 4 minutes

> 1 **pint fresh strawberries, hulled**
> ½ **cup sugar**
> 2 **tablespoons cornstarch**
> 1 **cup water**
> 2 **tablespoons butter or margarine**
> ½ **cup lemon juice**

Reserve a few of the best berries for garnish. Purée the remaining berries in a food processor or blender. Strain purée to remove seeds.

Place sugar, cornstarch, and water in 4-cup glass measure. Stir until blended. Cook on HI, 3 to 4 minutes, or until mixture boils and is thick and clear. Stir twice during cooking time.

Add butter and stir until melted. Stir in lemon juice and purée. Chill. Serve over pound cake, vanilla pudding, custard, or in parfaits.

2½ cups

VERMONT SAUCE

Cooking Time: 1½ to 2 minutes

> ½ **cup dark corn syrup**
> 2 **tablespoons brown sugar**
> 1 **tablespoon honey**
> 1 **tablespoon water**
> ¼ **teaspoon maple extract**

Combine all ingredients in 2-cup glass measure. Stir until blended. Cook on HI, 1½ to 2 minutes, or until syrup boils.

about ¾ cup

RUM CUSTARD SAUCE

Cooking Time: 10 to 12 minutes

> 1½ **cups milk**
> ½ **cup light cream**
> ⅓ **cup sugar**
> ⅛ **teaspoon salt**
> 3 **eggs, lightly beaten**
> 3 **tablespoons rum**

Place milk, cream, sugar, and salt in 4-cup glass measure. Cook on 70, 3 to 4 minutes, or just until mixture boils.

Stir ½ cup milk mixture slowly into eggs, then add to remaining milk mixture and stir until blended. Cook on 50, 3 minutes. Stir.

Cook on 30, 4 to 5 minutes, stirring once every minute, until thickened.

Cool to room temperature. Stir in rum. Serve with bread pudding, banana pudding, poached peaches, or poached pears.

2½ cups

CHOCO-PEANUT BUTTER SAUCE

Cooking Time: 2½ to 4 minutes

> 1 **square (1 ounce) unsweetened baking chocolate**
> ¼ **cup milk**
> 1 **cup sugar**
> ⅓ **cup peanut butter**
> ¼ **teaspoon vanilla**

Place chocolate and milk in 4-cup glass measure. Cook on HI, 1½ to 2 minutes. Stir until mixture is smooth. Add sugar, and stir again. Cook on HI, 1 to 2 minutes, or until mixture boils. Add peanut butter and vanilla, and stir until blended.

Serve hot or cold over ice cream, cake, or sliced bananas.

1 cup

HOT FUDGE SAUCE

Cooking Time: 5 minutes

- **⅓ cup water**
- **2 ounces unsweetened baking chocolate**
- **1 tablespoon butter or margarine**
- **1 cup sugar**
- **2 tablespoons corn syrup**
- **1 tablespoon vanilla**

Combine water, chocolate, and butter in 4-cup glass measure. Cook on HI, 2 minutes, or until chocolate is glossy.

Stir in sugar and corn syrup. Cook on 50, 3 minutes, stirring twice during cooking time. Blend in vanilla.

Let stand to cool slightly before serving.

about 1 cup

Serve over ice cream, chocolate cake, or fresh fruit, or use as a fondue for pound cake or fresh berries.

PEANUT COLADA SAUCE

Cooking Time: 3 to 5 minutes

- **½ cup chunky peanut butter**
- **½ cup cream of coconut**
- **1 tablespoon lime juice**
- **1 tablespoon orange juice**
- **1 teaspoon soy sauce**

Combine all ingredients in 2-cup glass measure. Blend well. Cover with plastic wrap and cook on 50, 3 to 5 minutes.

Serve warm.

about 1 cup

Cream of coconut is available in the beverage section of your grocery store, or at a liquor store. Use sauce on ice cream, cake, or bananas. Sprinkle shredded coconut on top for a truly special treat.

Homemade Pie Shell (page 165), plain (at top), and color-enhanced. Clockwise: cinnamon, egg yolk wash, vanilla, and yellow food coloring.

For microwave baking, cake pans and muffin cups are only filled halfway. Microwave baking provides higher rising than conventional.

You can speed the rising of dough by using the microwave oven. The method is explained under "Helpful Tips" on page 154.

BREADS, CAKES, & PIES

Quick breads, sweet rolls, muffins, coffee cakes, pies, and cookies are easy to prepare in the microwave oven. Many breads turn out with excellent texture and flavor, but since there is no heat in the microwave oven cavity, a crust does not develop and they do not brown. For that reason, we have selected recipes that are well-suited to microwave cooking and you may wish to experiment with your own.

Selection of *microproof* muffin rings, ring molds, cake dishes, cookie sheets, pie plates, and bundt pans is important. Fortunately, the availability and variety of such items, specially made for microwave cooking, has grown tremendously in recent years. But if you don't want to wait, there are some things you can do without special equipment. Surely, you must have at least one glass pie plate around, and other glass baking dishes. That's all you need for many of our recipes. Or you can place a small straight-sided glass inside a round microproof casserole to create your own "instant" microproof bundt pan or ring mold. Microwave baking is fun, and fun to watch. So much so that you can count on giggles from any youngsters who happen to catch your latest microwave magic act.

ADAPTING YOUR RECIPES

There's no need to retire your time-honored pie, cake, or other baked goods recipes. Most will adapt well to microwave cooking with a minimum of effort on your part. Some, of course, simply belong in your conventional oven. In the early years of microwave cooking, everyone thought it was necessary to cook *everything* in the microwave oven. Well, we've grown up, so feel free to choose the cooking method — microwave or conventional — that suits you best. At the same time, don't be shy about microwave baking. It really is excellent.

When adapting "quick bread" recipes, you will find it necessary to reduce the amount of leavening (baking powder or baking soda) by about one-quarter the normal amount. A bitter aftertaste is apparent if too much leavening is used in biscuits or muffins. Since foods rise higher in the microwave oven, you will not see a loss in volume from the reduction of baking soda or powder. If a recipe contains buttermilk or sour cream, do not change the amount of soda, since it serves to counteract the sour taste and does not act only as a leavening agent. When using a mix where leavening cannot be reduced, allow the batter or dough to stand about 10 minutes before cooking to reduce some of the air in the dough. Yeast doughs need not be changed but may cook more evenly if cooked in a bundt pan or ring mold rather than a loaf pan.

Helpful Tips

To raise yeast dough, half fill a 2-cup glass measure with water. Place it in the oven and bring to a boil on HI, 3 to 3½ minutes. Place dough in oven next to water. Set Power Control at "1" (lowest possible setting other than zero) and timer at 10 minutes. When timer beeps, leave dough in oven another 20 minutes, or until double in bulk.

Fill paper-lined muffin cups only half full to allow for muffins rising higher than they do when baked in a conventional oven.

You can prepare your own "brown 'n serve" rolls. Bake them in the microwave oven. Brown in the conventional oven just before serving.

When preparing yeast dough, use a glass measure and the temperature probe set at 120°F to heat liquids to the exact temperature needed to activate the yeast.

If a baked item appears done to you, open door and check with tester or toothpick, just as you do in conventional cooking. Interrupting the cooking does not erase the remaining cooking time. Touch START to resume cooking.

During cooking, some baked goods may begin to rise unevenly. When you notice this, open door and rotate dish about one-quarter turn. Uneven rising is seldom significant because many items are inverted onto a serving dish and the variation in rising disappears.

Small drop cookies and slice 'n bake cookies don't do as well as the larger bar cookies in the microwave oven. Drop cookies must be cooked in small batches and tend to cook unevenly. A serviceable cookie sheet can be made by covering cardboard with waxed paper.

A pie shell is cooked when the surface appears opaque and dry.

REHEATING GUIDE — BAKERY

Food	Power Control	Time	Special Notes
Bread, frozen 1 lb. loaf	30	2 - 3 min.	
Cheesecake, 17 - 19 oz.	30	4 - 5 min.	Remove from foil pan to plate. Let stand 1 minute.
Coffeecake, whole frozen 10 - 13 oz.	80	1½ - 2 min.	Place on paper plate or towel.
Cupcakes, crumb cakes, (1 or 2)	30	½ - 1 min.	Place on shallow microproof plate.
Doughnuts, (4)	80	35 - 40 sec.	Place on paper plate or towel. Add 15 seconds if frozen.
English muffins, waffles, frozen, (2)	HI	30 - 45 sec.	Place on paper towels.
Fruit pie. 2-crust, 9", 2½ - 3 lbs.	follow package directions		
Hamburger buns, hot dog rolls, frozen, 1 lb.	30	1 - 2 min.	Place on paper plate or towels.
Pound cake, frozen, 10¾ oz.	30	2 min.	Remove from foil pan to plate. Rotate once. Let stand 5 minutes.
Sweet rolls, muffins, (4)	20	35 - 45 sec.	Place on paper plate or towels. Add 15 seconds if frozen.

* Due to the tremendous variety in convenience food products available, times given here should be used only as guidelines. We suggest you cook food for the shortest recommended time and then check for doneness. Be sure to check the package for microwave instructions.

BLUEBERRY STREUSEL COFFEE CAKE

Cooking Time: 13½ to 15 minutes

- **2 cups all-purpose flour**
- **1 cup sugar**
- **2 teaspoons baking powder**
- **1½ teaspoons orange peel**
- **1 teaspoon salt**
- **½ cup butter or margarine**
- **2 eggs**
- **1 cup milk**
- **1 teaspoon vanilla**
- **2 cups fresh blueberries, raspberries, or 1 cup chopped dates**

Topping:

- **⅓ cup firmly packed brown sugar**
- **¼ cup flour**
- **1 teaspoon cinnamon**
- **½ cup chopped nuts**
- **2 tablespoons butter**

In large mixing bowl, combine flour, sugar, baking powder, orange peel, and salt. Set aside.

Place butter in 1-cup glass measure and cook on HI, 1 to 1½ minutes. Add to flour mixture. Add eggs, milk, and vanilla. Stir just until moistened. Pour into 8-cup microproof ring mold. Sprinkle fruit over batter.

To prepare topping, combine brown sugar, flour, cinnamon, and nuts. Cut in butter until mixture resembles coarse crumbs. Sprinkle topping over fruit. Cook on 50, 10 minutes.

Rotate dish one-half turn and cook on HI, 2½ to 3½ minutes, or until cake tests done.

Remove from oven and let cool 5 minutes before serving.

6 to 8 servings

SOUR CREAM COFFEE CAKE

Cooking Time: 8 minutes

- **½ cup butter or margarine, softened**
- **½ cup sugar**
- **2 eggs**
- **½ teaspoon vanilla**
- **1½ cups all-purpose flour**
- **½ teaspoon baking soda**
- **½ teaspoon baking powder**
- **½ cup dairy sour cream**

Topping:

- **½ cup chopped nuts**
- **⅓ cup firmly packed brown sugar**
- **2 tablespoons all-purpose flour**
- **¼ teaspoon cinnamon**
- **⅛ teaspoon salt**
- **2 tablespoons butter or margarine**

In large bowl, cream butter and sugar. Add eggs and vanilla, and blend well.

Combine flour, baking soda, and baking powder. Add to creamed mixture alternately with sour cream, stirring until well blended.

To prepare topping, combine nuts, brown sugar, flour, cinnamon, and salt. Cut in butter until mixture resembles coarse crumbs.

Spread half the batter in 8-inch microproof cake dish. Sprinkle half the topping over batter. Carefully add remaining batter and sprinkle with remaining topping. Cook on 60, 4 minutes. If cake is rising unevenly, rotate dish one-quarter turn.

Cook on HI, 4 minutes, or until cake tests done.

Remove from oven and let stand 3 minutes before serving.

9 servings

Oatmeal Granola Quick Bread

OATMEAL GRANOLA QUICK BREAD

Cooking Time: 13 to 14 minutes

- 2 **cups all-purpose flour**
- 1 **cup whole wheat flour**
- ½ **cup firmly packed brown sugar**
- 1½ **tablespoons baking powder**
- 1 **teaspooon salt**
- 1 **teaspoon cinnamon**
- ½ **teaspoon nutmeg**
- 1¼ **cups milk**
- 1¼ **cups quick-cooking rolled oats**
- 2 **eggs, beaten**
- ⅓ **cup vegetable oil**
- ⅓ **cup molasses or honey**

Topping:

- 1 **cup granola**
- ½ **cup chopped nuts**
- ¼ **cup firmly packed brown sugar**
- 3 **tablespoons butter**

Combine flours, brown sugar, baking powder, salt, cinnamon, and nutmeg in large mixing bowl. Set aside.

Pour milk into 4-cup glass measure. Cover and cook on HI, 2 minutes. Add oats and stir. Let stand 2 minutes. Stir beaten eggs, vegetable oil, and molasses into oatmeal mixture. Add to dry ingredients and stir just until moistened. Spoon batter into 8-cup microproof ring mold.

To prepare topping, combine granola, nuts, and brown sugar. Cut in butter until mixture resembles coarse crumbs. Sprinkle topping over batter. Cook on 50, 4 minutes. Rotate dish one-half turn. Continue to cook on 50, 4 minutes.

Cook on HI, 3 to 4 minutes, or until bread tests done.

Remove from oven and let stand 5 minutes. Turn out onto wire rack to cool completely.

8 to 10 servings

DANISH NUT BREAD

Cooking Time: 12 to 13 minutes

- 1 **envelope active dry yeast**
- ¼ **cup warm water (105°F to 115°F)**
- 1 **teaspoon sugar**
- 2 **cups all-purpose flour**
- ½ **teaspoon salt**
- ¾ **cup butter**
- 2 **egg yolks**

Filling:

- 1 **package (3 ounces) cream cheese**
- ½ **cup sugar**
- 1 **teaspoon grated lemon peel**
- 1 **teaspoon grated orange peel**
- ½ **cup chopped pecans**
  Powdered sugar

Combine yeast, warm water, and sugar in small glass mixing bowl. Let stand 10 minutes, or until yeast bubbles. Combine flour and salt in large mixing bowl. Cut in butter until mixture resembles coarse crumbs. Blend in egg yolks and yeast. Stir with wooden spoon until dough forms a ball around spoon. Divide dough in half; set aside.

To prepare filling, combine cream cheese, sugar, lemon peel, and orange peel until well mixed. Stir in pecans. Set aside.

Roll half the dough into a 12 × 9-inch rectangle. Spread with half the filling. Roll up jelly roll style. Place in 6-cup microproof ring mold and cook on 80, 6 to 6½ minutes.

Remove from oven and let stand 5 minutes. Sprinkle with powdered sugar. Repeat with remaining dough.

2 loaves

No rising time is required for this company-special yeast bread! This wonderful treat just looks complicated — it isn't at all. Plan to serve it soon after baking. That's when it is best. And your house will be filled with those wonderful baking aromas!

ZUCCHINI NUT BREAD

Cooking Time: 14 to 15 minutes

- **1 cup sugar, divided**
- **2 teaspoons cinnamon**
- **1 cup grated zucchini**
- **2 eggs**
- **½ cup vegetable oil**
- **½ cup yogurt**
- **1 teaspoon vanilla**
- **1¾ cups all-purpose flour**
- **1 teaspoon baking soda**
- **1 teaspoon salt**
- **⅔ cup chopped walnuts**

Butter an 8-cup microproof ring mold. Combine 2 teaspoons of the sugar with 2 teaspoons cinnamon, and sprinkle over butter, tilting mold to spread evenly. Discard excess sugar mixture.

Beat together zucchini, eggs, remaining sugar, oil, yogurt, and vanilla. Stir in flour, baking soda, and salt. Mix well. Stir in nuts.

Pour into prepared mold. Cook on 80, 14 to 15 minutes, or until bread tests done. Rotate dish one-quarter turn if bread appears to be rising unevenly.

Remove from oven and let stand 10 minutes before removing from pan. Cool completely before slicing.

12 to 18 servings

BANANA DATE BREAD

Cooking Time: 11½ minutes

- **½ cup butter or margarine**
- **2 cups sliced ripe bananas (2 medium)**
- **2 eggs**
- **½ cup firmly packed brown sugar**
- **2 cups all-purpose flour**
- **1 teaspoon cinnamon**
- **1 teaspoon baking powder**
- **½ teaspoon baking soda**
- **½ teaspoon salt**
- **½ cup chopped dates**

Place butter in large microproof bowl. Cook on HI, 1½ minutes. Add bananas, eggs, and brown sugar; beat until smooth. Add flour, cinnamon, baking powder, baking soda, and salt. Beat until batter is smooth. Stir in dates.

Pour batter into 10-cup microproof ring mold. Cook on 70, 10 minutes, or until bread

tests done. Rotate mold one-quarter turn if bread seems to be rising unevenly.

Remove from oven and let stand 10 minutes before inverting onto wire rack to cool completely.

8 to 10 servings

It's usually not necessary to grease the microproof pan for baked goods in the microwave oven. But if you want a sugar-, nut-, or crumb-coated cake or bread, grease the pan, sprinkle with desired ingredient, and proceed with the recipe.

WHOLE GRAIN QUICK BREAD

Cooking Time: 9½ to 10 minutes

- **½ cup cornmeal, divided**
- **½ cup whole wheat flour**
- **½ cup all-purpose flour**
- **¼ cup wheat germ**
- **1½ teaspoons baking powder**
- **½ teaspoon salt**
- **1 cup apple juice or orange juice**
- **¼ cup honey**
- **1 egg**
- **2 tablespoons vegetable oil**

Set aside 2 tablespoons cornmeal for topping. Combine remaining dry ingredients in large mixing bowl. Add juice, honey, egg, and oil. Stir just until moistened. Pour batter into 8-cup ring mold. Sprinkle reserved cornmeal over top. Cook on 80, 8 minutes.

Rotate dish one-half turn and cook on HI, 1½ to 2 minutes, or until bread tests done.

Remove from oven and let stand 10 minutes. Invert onto serving platter.

8 to 10 servings

To determine doneness for breads, cakes, and muffins, test just as you would when using a conventional oven. A toothpick inserted near the center should come out clean. The bread may look moist when it tests done — because it finishes cooking outside the oven, during standing time.

HONEY CORN BREAD

Cooking Time: 12 to 14 minutes

- 1 **cup yellow cornmeal**
- 1 **cup biscuit baking mix**
- 3 **teaspoons baking powder**
- 1 **cup milk**
- 2 **eggs, beaten**
- ⅓ **cup honey**
- 2 **tablespoons vegetable oil**

Mix cornmeal, biscuit mix, and baking powder in large bowl. Add milk, eggs, honey, and oil. Stir just until dry ingredients are moistened. Pour into 8-inch square microproof baking dish. Cook on 50, 10 minutes. Rotate dish if bread seems to be rising unevenly.

Cook on HI, 2 to 4 minutes, or until bread tests done.

Remove from oven and let stand 5 minutes. Serve warm.

8 servings

Flavored butters are wonderful with home-baked breads. Try these:

Honey Butter: ¼ cup honey, ¼ pound butter

Cinnamon Butter: 2 to 3 teaspoons cinnamon, ¼ pound butter

Stawberry Butter: ¼ cup strawberry jam, ¼ pound butter

RAISIN BRAN MUFFINS

Cooking Time: 6 to 9 minutes

- 1 **egg**
- 1 **cup buttermilk**
- 1¼ **cups all-purpose flour**
- 1 **cup raisin bran cereal**
- ¾ **cup firmly packed brown sugar**
- 1 **teaspoon baking soda**
- ¼ **teaspoon salt**
- ¼ **cup vegetable oil**
- ¼ **cup chopped nuts (optional)**

Beat egg and buttermilk together until well mixed. Stir in flour, cereal, brown sugar, baking soda, salt, and oil. Blend well. Stir in nuts. Let batter stand 5 minutes. Spoon batter into paper-lined microproof muffin pan, filling each compartment about half full. Cook on HI, 2 to 3 minutes, or until muffins test done.

Repeat with remaining batter.

18 muffins

You can make Banana Bran Muffins by adding 1 medium banana, mashed (about ½ cup) and reducing buttermilk from 1 cup to ¾ cup.

PEANUTTY CHOCOLATE CAKE

Cooking Time: 17 to 18 minutes

- 1 **package (18 ounces) yellow cake mix**
- ½ **cup creamy peanut butter**
- 4 **large eggs**
- ¾ **cup water**
- ⅓ **cup vegetable oil**
- 1 **cup chopped unsalted peanuts, divided**
- 1 **cup chocolate chips, divided**
  Caramel Glaze (below)

Combine cake mix, peanut butter, eggs, water, and oil in a large bowl. Beat on medium speed for 3 minutes. Pour one-third of the batter into a 12-cup microproof bundt pan. Sprinkle ⅓ cup each of the peanuts and chocolate chips over the batter. Pour another one-third of the batter carefully over peanuts and chocolate chips. Sprinkle another ⅓ cup each of the peanuts and chocolate chips over the batter. Repeat with remaining batter, peanuts and chocolate chips. Cook on 70, 17 to 18 minutes.

Let stand 10 minutes. Invert onto serving platter. Spoon warm Caramel Glaze over cake and let cool completely.

8 to 10 servings

CARAMEL GLAZE

Cooking Time: 3½ minutes

- 2 **tablespoons butter**
- ¾ **cup firmly packed brown sugar**
- 1 **teaspoon cornstarch**
- ⅛ **teaspoon salt**
- ¼ **cup milk or whipping cream**
- 1 **teaspoon vanilla extract**

Place butter in 4-cup glass measure and cook on HI, 1 minute. Stir in brown sugar, cornstarch, and salt. Gradually add milk, stirring to blend. Cook on HI, 2½ minutes. Stir in vanilla.

about 1¼ cups

DEVIL'S FOOD CAKE

Cooking Time: 23 to 25 minutes

- 2 **cups sifted all-purpose flour**
- 1¼ **teaspoons baking soda**
- ¼ **teaspoon salt**
- ½ **cup shortening**
- 2 **cups sugar**
- ½ **cup cocoa**
- 1 **teaspoon vanilla**
- 1 **cup water**
- ½ **cup buttermilk**
- 2 **eggs, beaten**

Grease bottoms of two 8-inch round microproof cake pans. Line bottoms with waxed paper cut to size. Set aside.

Sift together flour, baking soda, and salt in large bowl. Set aside.

Cream shortening, sugar, cocoa, and vanilla until light and fluffy. Pour water into 2-cup glass measure and cook on HI, 2½ minutes, or until water boils. Stir water, buttermilk, and eggs into creamed mixture. Beat well. Add dry ingredients and beat until smooth.

Pour batter into prepared cake pans. Cook, one pan at a time, on 50, 8 minutes. Rotate pan one-quarter turn.

Cook on HI, 1 to 2 minutes, or until cake tests done. Let stand 5 minutes. Invert onto cooling rack. Remove waxed paper. Let cool thoroughly before frosting.

8 to 10 servings

For frosting, try Chocolate Fudge Frosting (page 163) or White Frosting 163).

Peanutty Chocolate Cake

BUTTERSCOTCH CAKE

Cooking Time: 9¼ to 10¼ minutes

2 tablespoons butter or margarine
¾ cup firmly packed brown sugar, divided
¼ cup butterscotch chips
¼ cup chopped walnuts
¾ cup water
½ cup quick-cooking rolled oats
¼ cup butter or margarine, cut up
½ cup sugar
1 egg
¾ cup all-purpose flour
½ teaspoon baking soda
½ teaspoon salt
½ teaspoon cinnamon
½ teaspoon nutmeg

Place 2 tablespoons butter in 6-cup microproof ring mold. Cook on HI, 45 seconds. Tilt mold to coat bottom with melted butter. Set aside. Stir together ¼ cup of the brown sugar, butterscotch chips, and nuts. Spread evenly in bottom of mold.

Place water in microproof mixing bowl. Cook on HI, 2 minutes, or until water boils. Stir in oats. Add ¼ cup butter. Let stand until butter is softened. Beat in sugar, remaining brown sugar, and egg. Add flour, baking soda, salt, cinnamon, and nutmeg. Stir just until blended. Pour over nut mixture. Cook on HI, 6½ to 7½ minutes, or until cake tests done. Rotate mold during cooking time if cake seems to be rising unevenly. Let stand 5 minutes. Invert onto serving plate. Serve warm or chilled.

8 servings

CHOCOLATE FRUIT TORTE

Cooking Time: 4 to 6 minutes

Crust:

1¼ cups (about 10 whole) graham crackers, crushed
5 tablespoons butter or margarine, melted
2 tablespoons cocoa
1 tablespoon sugar

Filling:

1 cup semisweet chocolate chips
3 tablespoons butter or margarine
1 package (8 ounces) cream cheese
⅓ cup powdered sugar
¼ cup milk
1 teaspoon vanilla

Topping:

2 cups (1 pint) fresh fruit, sliced
¼ cup clear fruit jelly

Combine graham cracker crumbs, margarine, cocoa, and sugar in 9-inch microproof pie plate. Press into bottom of dish. Cook on HI, 1 to 1½ minutes, or until firm. Set aside.

To prepare filling, combine chocolate chips and margarine in 4-cup glass measure. Cook on HI, 1 minute. Remove cream cheese from package. Place on microproof plate and cook on 50, 1 to 1½ minutes.

Combine cream cheese, powdered sugar, milk, and vanilla, and stir briskly until blended. Pour into crust. Set aside.

To prepare topping, arrange fruit over cooled pie. Place jelly in small microproof bowl and cook on HI, 1 to 2 minutes, or until jelly is melted. Spoon warm jelly over fruit. Chill before serving.

6 servings

Seasonal fruits star on this pie. Strawberries, kiwi fruit, and bananas are very popular choices. Choose one fruit or combine several, keeping color and shape in mind.

CAKE MIX

Cooking Time: 7 to 7½ minutes

> **1 package (9 ounces) single-layer cake mix**

Line bottom of 9-inch round microproof baking dish with waxed paper. Prepare cake batter as directed on package. Pour into prepared baking dish. Cook on 50, 5 minutes. If cake seems to be rising unevenly, rotate dish one-quarter turn.

Cook on HI, 2 to 2½ minutes, or until cake tests done. Let cool in pan 3 to 5 minutes before inverting cake onto serving plate. Carefully peel off waxed paper.

1 layer

CHOCOLATE PUDDING CAKE

Cooking Time: 9¾ to 11¾ minutes

> **2 tablespoons butter**
> **1 cup all-purpose flour**
> **¾ cup sugar**
> **6 tablespoons cocoa, divided**
> **2 teaspoons baking powder**
> **½ teaspoon salt**
> **½ cup chopped nuts**
> **½ cup milk**
> **1 teaspoon vanilla**
> **¾ cup firmly packed light brown sugar**
> **1¼ cups water**
> **Whipped cream**

Place butter in 1-cup glass measure. Cook on HI, 45 seconds, or until butter melts. Set aside.

Combine flour, sugar, 2 tablespoons of the cocoa, baking powder, and salt. Stir in nuts, milk, melted butter, and vanilla. Pour into 8-inch round microproof baking dish. Set aside.

In 4-cup glass measure, combine brown sugar, remaining cocoa, and water. Mix well. Pour over batter. Do not stir. Cover with paper towel. Cook on HI, 9 to 11 minutes, or until cake tests done. Remove from oven and let stand 10 minutes. Top with whipped cream and serve.

9 servings

CHOCOLATE FUDGE FROSTING

Cooking Time: 3 minutes

> **1½ cups sugar**
> **⅓ cup milk**
> **¼ cup butter or margarine, cut into small pieces**
> **¾ cup semisweet chocolate chips**
> **¼ cup chopped nuts**
> **1 teaspoon vanilla**

Combine sugar, milk, and butter in 4-cup glass measure. Stir. Cook on HI, 1½ minutes. Stir. Cook on HI, 1½ minutes.

Add chocolate chips and beat until smooth. Add nuts and vanilla. Beat until mixture is of spreading consistency. Frosting will thicken as it cools.

1 cup

WHITE FROSTING

Cooking Time: 4 minutes

> **1 cup sugar**
> **½ cup water**
> **¼ teaspoon cream of tartar**
> **Dash salt**
> **2 egg whites**
> **1 teaspoon vanilla**

Combine sugar, water, cream of tartar, and salt in 2-cup glass measure. Cook on HI, 4 minutes.

Meanwhile, in small mixing bowl, beat egg whites until soft peaks form. Gradually add hot syrup to egg whites, beating constantly. Add vanilla. Continue beating 5 minutes, or until frosting is thick and fluffy.

1½ to 2 cups

CHOCOLATE CAKE FOR TWO

Cooking Time: 6 minutes

- **⅔ cup all-purpose flour**
- **½ cup sugar**
- **3 tablespoons unsweetened cocoa**
- **1 teaspoon baking powder**
- **⅓ cup water**
- **¼ cup oil**
- **1 egg, beaten**
- **½ teaspoon vanilla**
- **¼ cup chopped nuts**

Line bottom of a 1-quart shallow microproof dish with waxed paper. Set aside.

Stir together flour, sugar, cocoa, and baking powder in 2-quart mixing bowl. Stir in water, oil, egg, and vanilla; mix thoroughly. Stir in nuts.

Pour batter evenly into prepared dish. Cook on 70, 3 minutes.

Rotate dish. Cook on 70, 3 minutes.

Remove from oven and let cake cool in dish 5 minutes. Invert cake onto serving plate. Remove waxed paper.

Serve with ice cream and hot fudge sauce.

2 servings

APPLE CINNAMON CAKE

Cooking Time: 10½ to 11½ minutes

- **3 tablespoons butter**
- **½ cup firmly packed brown sugar**
- **¼ cup chopped walnuts**
- **1 teaspoon pumpkin pie spice**
- **1 medium cooking apple, cored and sliced**
- **1 package (9 ounces) yellow cake mix**

Place butter in 8-inch round microproof baking dish. Cook on HI, 1½ minutes. Stir in brown sugar, walnuts, and pumpkin pie spice. Spread evenly over bottom of dish. Arrange apple slices around edge of dish. Set aside.

Prepare cake mix according to package directions. Pour batter over apples. Cook on 50, 7 to 8 minutes, or until top begins to set. Rotate dish one-half turn and cook on HI, 2 minutes. Let stand 5 minutes before inverting onto serving platter.

4 servings

DUTCH APPLE PIE

Cooking Time: 14 to 16 minutes

- **7 cooking apples, peeled, cored, and sliced (6 cups)**
- **¾ cup sugar**
- **6 tablespoons all-purpose flour, divided**
- **¼ cup raisins**
- **1 teaspoon cinnamon**
- **⅛ teaspoon salt**
- **1 prebaked 9-inch Homemade Pie Shell (page 165)**
- **¼ cup firmly packed brown sugar**
- **2 tablespoons butter or margarine**

Place apple slices in large bowl. Mix sugar, 2 tablespoons of the flour, raisins, cinnamon, and salt. Add to apples and stir to coat. Pour apple mixture into pie shell and spread evenly. Combine remaining flour and brown sugar. Cut in butter until mixture resembles coarse crumbs. Sprinkle over apples. Cook on HI, 14 to 16 minutes, or until apples are fork-tender. Cool before serving.

6 to 8 servings

PECAN PIE

Cooking Time: 9½ to 10½ minutes

- ¼ **cup butter or margarine**
- 1¼ **cups pecan halves**
- 1 **cup sugar**
- 3 **eggs, lightly beaten**
- ½ **cup dark corn syrup**
- 1 **teaspoon vanilla**
- ⅛ **teaspoon salt**
- 1 **prebaked Homemade Pie Shell (right)**

Place butter in 4-cup glass measure. Cook on HI, 1½ minutes. Add remaining ingredients, except pie shell, and mix well. Pour into pie shell. Cook on HI, 8 to 9 minutes, or until center is set. Let cool to room temperature and serve.

8 servings

HOMEMADE PIE SHELL

Cooking Time: 5 to 6 minutes

- 1 **cup all-purpose flour**
- 1 **teaspoon salt**
- 6 **tablespoons shortening**
- 2 **tablespoons ice water**

Place flour and salt in small bowl. Cut in shortening until mixture resembles coarse crumbs. Sprinkle water over mixture. Stir with fork to form a ball. Roll out on floured pastry board to 12-inch circle. Fit into 9-inch microproof pie plate. Trim and flute edge. Prick pastry with fork. Cook on HI, 5 to 6 minutes. Pastry is done when it appears dry and blistered and is not doughy. Cool before filling.

one 9-inch pie shell

COCONUT CREAM PIE

Cooking Time: 8 to 9 minutes

- 1 **can (12 ounces) evaporated milk**
- ½ **cup milk**
- 1 **package (3⅛ ounces) coconut cream pudding or pie filling mix**
- ¾ **cup shredded coconut, divided**
- 2 **tablespoons butter or margarine**
- 1 **prebaked 8-inch Crumb Crust (right)**

Pour evaporated milk into 4-cup glass measure. Add milk, pudding mix, and ½ cup of the coconut. Stir briskly. Cook on HI, 6 to 7 minutes, stirring once. Pour into crumb crust. Set aside.

Place remaining coconut in 1-cup glass measure. Add butter. Cook on HI, 2 minutes. Remove from oven and stir thoroughly. Coconut should be lightly browned. Sprinkle coconut over pie filling. Refrigerate until firm.

6 servings

CRUMB CRUST

Cooking Time: 2½ to 3 minutes

- 5 **tablespoons butter or margarine**
- 1¼ **cups fine crumbs (vanilla wafers, graham crackers, gingersnaps, chocolate wafers)**
- 1 **tablespoon sugar**

Place butter in 8- or 9-inch microproof pie plate. Cook on HI, 1 minute. Blend in crumbs and sugar. Set aside 2 tablespoons crumb mixture to sprinkle over top of pie, if desired. Press crumb mixture firmly and evenly over bottom and sides of pie plate. Cook on HI, 1½ to 2 minutes. Cool before filling.

one 9-inch pie shell

Crumb crusts are adaptable. Make a familiar crust special by adding your choice of the following: 2 tablespoons cocoa, ¼ cup coconut, 2 tablespoons ground nuts, ¼ teaspoon pumpkin pie spice, or ½ teaspoon grated orange or lemon peel.

BANANA CREAM PIE

Cooking Time: 6 to 7 minutes

1 can (12 ounces) evaporated milk
½ cup milk
1 package (3 ounces) vanilla pudding
2 large ripe bananas
1 prebaked 9-inch Homemade
      Pie Shell (page 165)
2 tablespoons sliced almonds

Pour evaporated milk into 4-cup glass measure. Add milk and pudding mix. Stir briskly. Cook on HI, 6 to 7 minutes, stirring once.

Meanwhile, slice 1 banana into bottom of pie shell. Pour prepared pie filling over banana slices. Slice remaining banana around edge of pie. Garnish with whipped cream. Sprinkle sliced almonds over top of pie. Refrigerate until firm.

6 servings

STRAWBERRY RHUBARB PIE

Cooking Time: 5½ to 7 minutes

½ cup sugar
3 tablespoons cornstarch
1 cup water
1 pound rhubarb, cut into
      ½-inch pieces
1 pint strawberries, hulled
1 prebaked Homemade Pie Shell
      (page 165)

Combine sugar, cornstarch, and water in large microproof bowl. Stir until cornstarch is dissolved. Cook on HI, 2½ to 3 minutes, or until mixture is clear, stirring once during cooking time. Add rhubarb and strawberries. Stir. Cook on HI, 2 to 3 minutes, or until sauce begins to thicken. Stir. Continue to cook on HI, 1 minute, or just until sauce is thickened. Let stand 5 minutes. Pour into pie shell and cool to room temperature before serving.

6 to 8 servings

If you use frozen rhubarb and strawberries, thaw and drain well, reserving juice. Add water to juice to equal 1 cup as a substitute for water in recipe.

PERFECT LEMON MERINGUE PIE

Cooking Time: 12 to 15 minutes

⅓ cup cornstarch
½ cup cold water
1¾ cups sugar, divided
1 cup hot water
¼ teaspoon salt
5 eggs, separated
2 tablespoons butter or margarine
½ cup fresh lemon juice
2 tablespoons finely grated
      lemon peel
1 prebaked Homemade Pie Shell
      (page 165)
¼ teaspoon cream of tartar
½ teaspoon vanilla

Dissolve cornstarch in cold water in 2-quart microproof bowl. Add 1¼ cups of the sugar, hot water, and salt. Blend well. Cover with casserole lid and cook on HI, 6 to 7 minutes, or until mixture is thick and clear, stirring occasionally. Set aside.

Beat egg yolks in another bowl until thick. Gradually beat into cornstarch mixture. Cook, uncovered, on HI, 2 minutes. Add butter and stir until melted. Blend in lemon juice and peel. Pour into pie crust. Set aside to cool slightly.

Beat egg whites with cream of tartar in large bowl until foamy. Gradually beat in remaining sugar until whites are stiff and glossy. Blend in vanilla. Spread over cooled filling, sealing to edges.

Preheat conventional oven to 450°F. Place pie in conventional oven and cook at 450°F, 4 to 6 minutes, or until meringue is lightly browned. Let cool to room temperature before serving.

6 to 8 servings

Strawberry Rhubarb Pie, Perfect Lemon Meringue Pie, Banana Cream Pie

BLUEBERRY PIE

Cooking Time: 5½ to 7 minutes

- ½ **cup sugar**
- 3 **tablespoons cornstarch**
- 1 **cup water**
- 5 **cups blueberries**
- 1 **teaspoon grated lemon peel**
- 1 **teaspoon lemon juice**
- 1 **prebaked Homemade Pie Shell (page 165)**

Combine sugar, cornstarch, and water in large microproof bowl. Stir until cornstarch is dissolved. Cook on HI, 2½ to 3 minutes, or until mixture is clear, stirring once during cooking time. Stir in blueberries, lemon peel, and lemon juice. Cook on HI, 2 to 3 minutes, or until sauce begins to thicken. Stir. Continue to cook on HI, 1 minute, or just until sauce is thickened. Let stand 5 minutes. Pour into pie shell and cool to room temperature before serving.

6 to 8 servings

This "no fuss" fruit pie technique gives you several options. You can serve "as is," top with ice cream, or add a streusel topping.

CHOCOLATE CHIP BARS

Cooking Time: 8 to 8½ minutes

- ½ **cup butter or margarine**
- ¾ **cup firmly packed brown sugar**
- 2 **large eggs, lightly beaten**
- 1 **teaspoon vanilla**
- 1 **cup chopped nuts**
- 1 **cup semisweet chocolate chips**
- ½ **cup all-purpose flour**
- 1 **teaspoon baking powder**
  Confectioners sugar

Place butter in 2-quart microproof bowl. Cook on 80, 1 minute. Add brown sugar, eggs, and vanilla. Stir until blended. Add nuts, chocolate chips, flour, and baking powder. Mix well. Spread in 9-inch round microproof baking dish. Cook on HI, 3 minutes. Rotate dish one-quarter turn.

Cook on HI, 4 to 4½ minutes, or until cake tests done. Let stand in pan until cool. Sprinkle with confectioners sugar.

24 bars

PEANUT CRISPY BARS

Cooking Time: 3 to 3½ minutes

- ¼ **cup butter or margarine**
- 5 **cups miniature or 40 large marshmallows**
- ⅓ **cup peanut butter**
- 5 **cups crispy rice cereal**
- 1 **cup unsalted dry roasted peanuts**

Place butter in 3-quart microproof casserole. Cook on HI, 1 minute. Add marshmallows. Cover with casserole lid and cook on HI, 2 to 2½ minutes, or until soft, stirring once. Stir in peanut butter until blended. Mix in cereal and peanuts. Press warm mixture into lightly buttered 12 × 7 × 2-inch dish. Cool before cutting into bars.

36 bars

GRANOLA

Cooking Time: 5 minutes

- ½ **cup honey**
- ½ **cup vegetable oil**
- 3½ **cups oatmeal**
- ½ **cup all-purpose flour**
- ½ **cup wheat germ**
- ½ **cup sunflower seeds**
- ½ **cup sesame seeds**
- ½ **cup instant dry milk**
- ½ **cup chopped walnuts**
- 1 **teaspoon cinnamon**

In a 4-cup glass measure, combine honey and oil. Set aside. Combine oatmeal, flour, wheat germ, sunflower seeds, sesame seeds, milk, nuts, and cinnamon in 3-quart microproof casserole. Add honey mixture and stir until well mixed. Cook on HI, 5 minutes, stirring once.

Cool. Store in airtight container.

7½ cups

BROWNIE MIX

Cooking Time: 6 to 6½ minutes

- 1 **package (16 ounces) brownie mix**
- 1 **tablespoon confectioners sugar**

Butter 8-inch round microproof pie plate. Prepare brownie batter as directed on package. Pour into prepared pie plate. Place in oven. Cook on HI, 3 minutes.

Rotate pie plate one-quarter turn. Cook on HI, 3 to 3½ minutes, or until brownies test done. Let stand in pie plate until cool. Sprinkle with confectioners sugar and cut into wedges or squares.

16 brownies

GINGER BARS

Cooking Time: 3 to 4 minutes

- 6 **tablespoons all-purpose flour**
- 2 **tablespoons brown sugar**
- ½ **teaspoon baking powder**
- ½ **teaspoon pumpkin pie spice**
- ¼ **teaspoon ginger**
- 2 **tablespoons molasses**
- 1 **tablespoon hot coffee**
- 1 **egg**
- 2 **tablespoons butter or margarine**
  Confectioners sugar

Combine flour, sugar, baking powder, pumpkin pie spice, and ginger. Stir until well mixed. Add molasses, coffee, egg, and butter. Beat on medium speed, 1 minute. Pour into 8-inch microproof baking dish. Cook on HI, 2 minutes. Rotate dish one-half turn. Cook on HI, 1 to 2 minutes, or until bars test done. Let stand until cool. Dust with confectioners sugar, cut into bars, and serve.

16 bars

COCONUT SQUARES

Cooking Time: 8 minutes

- ¼ **cup butter or margarine**
- 1 **cup graham cracker crumbs**
- 1 **teaspoon sugar**
- 1 **cup flaked coconut**
- ½ **cup chopped nuts**
- ⅔ **cup sweetened condensed milk**
- 1 **cup semisweet chocolate bits**

Place butter in 9-inch round microproof baking dish. Cook on HI, 1 minute, or until melted. Stir in graham cracker crumbs and sugar. Pat mixture firmly and evenly in bottom of dish. Cook on HI, 2 minutes. Set aside.

Mix coconut, nuts, and milk. Spoon carefully over partially cooled graham cracker crust. Cook on HI, 4 minutes, rotating dish one-half turn once during cooking.

Sprinkle with chocolate bits. Cook on HI, 1 minute. Spread melted chocolate evenly over coconut mixture. Cool and cut into squares.

16 to 20 squares

THE ULTIMATE BROWNIE

Cooking Time: 8½ to 10½ minutes

- ½ **cup butter or margarine**
- 2 **ounces baking chocolate**
- 2 **eggs**
- ¾ **cup sugar**
- ½ **cup all-purpose flour**
- 1 **teaspoon baking powder**
- 1 **teaspoon vanilla**

Caramel Layer:

- 14 **vanilla caramels**
- 2 **tablespoons butter**
- 2 **tablespoons milk**

Chocolate Nut Layer:

- 1 **cup semisweet chocolate chips**
- 1 **cup coarsely chopped walnuts**

Place butter and chocolate in 2-cup glass measure. Cook on HI, 1½ minutes, or until butter melts. (Chocolate will not appear melted until stirred.) Beat eggs in large bowl until foamy. Stir in chocolate mixture, sugar, flour, baking powder, and vanilla. Pour into 9-inch microproof baking dish. Set aside.

To prepare caramel layer, combine caramels, butter, and milk in 2-cup glass measure. Cook on HI, 1 to 2 minutes, or until melted. Stir. Spoon over chocolate batter.

To prepare chocolate nut layer, sprinkle chocolate chips and nuts over caramel layer. Cook on HI, 6 to 7 minutes, or until brownies test done. Brownies will still be moist but will dry and firm as they cool. Cool before cutting into squares.

18 to 20 servings

The only description that really fits these special brownies is "outrageous." If you substitute pecans for the walnuts, you'll be reminded of those delicious caramel-chocolate-pecan candies called turtles.

DATE OATMEAL BARS

Cooking Time: 11 to 13 minutes

- 1 **cup chopped dates**
- ½ **cup raisins**
- ½ **cup water**
- 1 **tablespoon all-purpose flour**
- 2 **tablespoons sugar**
- ½ **cup chopped nuts**

Crust:

- ½ **cup butter or margarine**
- ¼ **teaspoon baking soda**
- 1 **tablespoon water**
- 1 **cup firmly packed brown sugar**
- 1 **cup unsifted all-purpose flour**
- 1 **cup quick cooking rolled oats**
- ¼ **teaspoon salt**
- 1 **teaspoon cinnamon**

Combine dates, raisins, water, flour, and sugar in microproof mixing bowl. Cook on HI, 3 to 4 minutes, or until mixture boils and thickens, stirring once. The date mixture should be the consistency of jam. Stir in nuts. Set aside.

To make crust, place butter in microproof bowl and cook on HI, 1 minute. Add baking soda and water; stir. Add brown sugar, flour, oats, and salt. Pat two-thirds of oats mixture into greased 9-inch round microproof baking dish. Spread with date mixture. Stir cinnamon into remaining oats mixture. Crumble oats mixture over top of dish. Cook on HI, 7 to 8 minutes. Rotate dish if bars seem to be cooking unevenly. Cool on flat surface before cutting into bars.

24 bars

Use conventional candy thermometer outside the oven or the traditional cold water test when making candy in your microwave oven.

Chocolate tends to hold its shape when melted in the microwave oven. Don't overcook. It will lose its shape as soon as it is stirred.

Fruit is amazingly easy to prepare in the microwave oven. Baked Apples (page 181) can be cooked 5 at a time. Double the recipe timing.

CANDIES, PUDDINGS, & FRUIT

Candies? Too much bother, you say? Well, this cookbook is not for conventional cooking methods, so please don't skip this chapter. We think you will be pleasantly surprised by the incredible convenience the microwave oven offers in making the tasty treats featured in this chapter. Candies are so much fun to make you may find yourself making them often as nearly last-minute gifts for your friends on special occasions, or just to say thank you. Believe it or not, you use one bowl, no double boiler, and scorching is gone forever. You won't need any special equipment, either, unless you really become a fan, as we think you might. Then, a special microwave candy thermometer would be a convenient aid. For now, you can test temperatures with a conventional candy thermometer, *outside the oven*, or by using the less reliable traditional testing method of dropping a spoonful of candy mixture into cold water. The temperature probe, incidentally, cannot be used for candy making because the temperatures are beyond the range of the probe's sensing abilities.

Chocolate-Dipped Fruit and Nuts (page 174) is one especially-easy recipe and would be a good one to select for your first candy-kitchen effort. You will also be delighted, we think, by the spectacular results provided by the Honeycomb recipe on page 172.

If you are looking for something lighter, yet wonderfully refreshing, you'll be delighted with fruit when it is touched with the wizardry of this oven. It retains its full color and, since virtually no moisture is lost, the flavor is outstanding. Glazed Pears in Custard Sauce (page 179) is an outrageous recipe. The Baked Apples (page 181) or Poached Pears (page 177) are a bit more tame but just as delicious.

Last but, as they say, by no means least are puddings. They don't need a water bath, and very little stirring is required. Now "instant" puddings can have the taste and texture we all prefer. We've taken two pudding recipes — Chocolate Walnut Pudding (page 181) and Maple Nut Pudding (page 181) — and fashioned a lovely parfait. Sneak a look at the photograph on page 180 for the results.

ADAPTING YOUR RECIPES

The best route to successful adaptation of your own candy, pudding, and fruit recipes is to find a recipe here that is similar to the one you want to try. The only caution is to compare the amount of any water, milk, or fruit juice that might be called for in the conventional recipe to the amount in the recipe here. You may need to reduce such liquids a bit because evaporation is such a minimal process in microwave cooking.

You can substitute fruits rather freely for those in the book. You will find better results if you select fruit of uniform size when cooking whole fruit.

Just one final note: Baked custards should be removed from the oven when centers are just nearly firm. They will set as they cool.

COOKING/REHEATING GUIDE
DESSERTS

Food	Power Control	Time	Special Notes
Egg custard 3 oz.	70	8 - 10 min.	Follow package directions. Stir every 3 minutes.
Fruit, frozen, 10 oz.	HI	5 - 5½ min.	Slit pouch. On microproof plate. Flex pouch halfway through cooking time to mix.
Pudding and pie filling mix 3¼ oz.	HI	6½ - 7 min.	Follow package directions. Stir every 3 minutes.
Tapioca 3¼ oz.	HI	6 - 7 min.	Follow package directions. Stir every 3 minutes. Use 4-cup glass measure.

*Due to the tremendous variety in convenience food products available, times should be used only as guidelines. We suggest you cook food for the shortest recommended time and then check for doneness. Most packages have instructions for microwave and conventional ovens.

HONEYCOMB

Cooking Time: 12 to 15 minutes

   1 **cup sugar**
   1 **cup dark corn syrup**
   1 **tablespoon white vinegar**
   1 **tablespoon baking soda**
   1 **package (12 ounces) semisweet chocolate chips**
   2 **tablespoons vegetable shortening**
   1 **ounce unsweetened baking chocolate, broken into small pieces**

Line 8-inch square microproof dish with aluminum foil; grease generously. Set aside.

Combine sugar, corn syrup, and vinegar in 2-quart glass measure or microproof bowl. Cook on HI, 3 minutes. Stir through several times. Continue to cook on HI, 7 to 10 minutes, or until mixture has thickened and microwave candy thermometer registers 300°F (a small amount of mixture will separate into hard and brittle threads when dropped into very cold water). Quickly stir in baking soda, blending completely. Pour into baking dish, tilting to cover bottom evenly. Let cool until firm, about 1 hour.

Break honeycomb into pieces and set aside. Combine chocolate chips, shortening, and baking chocolate in 2-quart glass measure or microproof bowl. Cook on HI, 2 minutes. Using wooden spoon, stir through to melt thoroughly. Dip honeycomb pieces into chocolate, covering completely. Let cool on waxed paper. Store in airtight container.

about 1 pound

When baking soda is added, mixture will increase in volume greatly. It will puff up above sides of baking dish but will sink somewhat as it cools.

DIVINITY

Cooking Time: 12 to 15 minutes

> **2⅔ cups sugar**
> **⅔ cup light corn syrup**
> **½ cup water**
> **3 egg whites**
>   **Pinch salt**
> **¾ cup unsalted chopped nuts**

Combine sugar, corn syrup, and water in 2-quart glass measure or microproof bowl. Cook on HI, 12 to 15 minutes, or until microwave candy thermometer registers 260°F (a small amount of mixture will form a ball hard enough to hold its shape but it will remain pliable when dropped into bowl of very cold water).

Meanwhile, beat egg whites with salt in large bowl until stiff. Gradually pour hot syrup into whites, beating constantly until mixture is very stiff, about 2 to 3 minutes. Stir in nuts. Let stand 1 minute. Quickly drop by tablespoonfuls onto waxed paper. Let cool completely. Store in airtight container in cool place.

about 3 dozen

Do not stir down sugar from sides of bowl as this will affect the texture of the candy.

PARTY MINTS

Cooking Time: 6 minutes

> **2 cups sugar**
> **¼ cup light corn syrup**
> **¼ cup milk**
> **¼ teaspoon cream of tartar**
> **8 to 10 drops peppermint extract**
>   **Red, green, or yellow food coloring**

Combine sugar, corn syrup, milk, and cream of tartar in 2-quart glass measure. Cook on HI, 6 minutes. Let stand 3 to 4 minutes, or until slightly cooled.

Beat vigorously until creamy. Add peppermint extract and food coloring. Drop by teaspoonfuls onto sheets of foil. Let stand until cool and firm. Store in airtight container.

about 36 mints

CHOCOLATE CASHEW CLUSTER

Cooking Time: 2½ to 3½ minutes

> **1 pound semisweet chocolate**
> **1 cup cashews**

Place chocolate in 2-quart glass measure. Cook on HI, 2½ to 3½ minutes.

Add cashews; stir until blended. Drop mixture by teaspoonfuls onto waxed paper. Let stand until firm. (If mixture in bowl becomes too firm, cook on 30, 1 to 2 minutes.)

1½ pounds

If you like, add ½ cup plump raisins to this candy.

CHOCOLATE-DIPPED FRUIT AND NUTS

Cooking Time: 2 to 3 minutes

- ½ **pound dark chocolate**
- ½ **pound white chocolate**
- ½ **pound milk chocolate**
-   **Assorted fruit and nuts**

Place dark chocolate in 4-cup glass measure. Cook on HI, 2 to 3 minutes, or just until chocolate appears shiny. (Chocolate will hold its shape.) Stir until smooth.

Dip fruit or nuts into chocolate, one at a time, leaving part of fruit uncovered. Place in candy cups or on waxed paper while chocolate sets.

Repeat with remaining white chocolate, milk chocolate, fruit, and nuts.

about 70

One-half pound chocolate yields about 16 large dipped strawberries, 32 maraschino cherries, 32 pineapple spears, etc.

PEANUT BRITTLE

Cooking Time: 9½ minutes

- 1 **cup sugar**
- ½ **cup corn syrup**
- 1¾ **to 2 cups unsalted dry-roasted peanuts**
- 1 **teaspoon butter or margarine**
- 1 **teaspoon vanilla**
- 1 **teaspoon baking soda**

Generously grease large baking sheet; set aside. Combine sugar and corn syrup in 2-quart glass measure. Cook on HI, 4 minutes.

Stir in peanuts with wooden spoon and cook on HI, 4 minutes.

Stir in butter and vanilla and cook on HI, 1½ minutes.

Add baking soda; stir until mixture is light and foamy. Pour onto prepared baking sheet. Spread quickly to edges, using back of wooden spoon. As candy cools, stretch to a thin sheet, using palms of hands. Cool completely before breaking into pieces. Store in airtight container in cool place.

1 pound

ROCKY ROAD CANDY

Cooking Time: 5 to 6 minutes

- 1 **package (12 ounces) semisweet chocolate chips**
- 1 **package (12 ounces) butterscotch chips**
- ½ **cup butter**
- 1 **package (10½ ounces) miniature marshmallows**
- 1 **cup nuts**

Combine chocolate, butterscotch, and butter in 3-quart microproof casserole. Cook on 70, 5 to 6 minutes, or until melted. Stir to blend. Fold in marshmallows and nuts. Spread on buttered 13 × 9-inch pan. Refrigerate until set (about 2 hours). Cut into squares.

45 servings

Try these variations: Substitute ½ cup nuts and ½ cup chopped dried fruit for 1 cup nuts. Dried apricots, pitted prunes, or candied fruit would be delicious.

ALMOND BARK

Cooking Time: 7 to 9 minutes

- 1 **cup whole blanched almonds**
- 1 **teaspoon butter or margarine**
- 1 **pound white chocolate**

Place almonds and butter in 9-inch glass pie plate. Cook on HI, 4 to 5½ minutes, or until almonds are toasted, stirring twice during cooking time. Set aside.

Place chocolate in large microproof mixing bowl and cook on HI, 3 to 3½ minutes, or until softened. Stir in almonds and pour onto waxed paper-lined baking sheet. Spread to desired thickness and refrigerate until set. Break into pieces.

1½ pounds

Chocolate-Dipped Fruit and Nuts

RICH CHOCOLATE FUDGE

Cooking Time: 20 to 22 minutes

- **4   cups sugar**
- **1   can (14 ounces) evaporated milk**
- **1   cup butter or margarine**
- **1   package (12 ounces) semisweet chocolate chips**
- **1   jar (7 ounces) marshmallow creme**
- **1   cup chopped nuts**
- **1   teaspoon vanilla**

Combine sugar, milk, and butter in 3-quart microproof bowl. Cook on HI, 20 to 22 minutes, or until a drop of mixture dropped into cold water forms a soft ball (234°F to 240°F on a candy thermometer. A small amount of syrup dropped into ice water forms a ball that does not fall apart, but flattens out when picked up.) Do not leave thermometer in oven during cooking.

Stir in chocolate chips and marshmallow creme until mixture is well blended. Stir in nuts and vanilla. Pour into buttered 9-inch square dish for thick pieces or 12 × 7 × 2-inch dish for thinner pieces. Cool before cutting into squares.

48 pieces

EGG CUSTARD

Cooking Time: 11 to 17½ minutes

- **3   tablespoons sugar**
- **¼   teaspoon salt**
- **¼   teaspoon nutmeg**
- **3   eggs, beaten**
- **1½ cups milk**
- **1   teaspoon almond extract**

Stir sugar, salt, and nutmeg into beaten eggs. Set aside.

Pour milk into 1-quart microproof casserole. Cook on HI, 3 to 3½ minutes, or until hot.

Stir egg mixture into hot milk. Stir in almond extract. Cook on 50, 8 to 14 minutes, or until set. Rotate dish one-half turn if custard seems to be rising unevenly. Let stand 5 minutes.

5 to 6 servings

CARAMEL NUT CANDY

Cooking Time: 2 to 3 minutes

- **1   pound light caramels**
- **2   tablespoons water**
- **1   can (12 ounces) mixed nuts (about 2 cups)**

Lightly butter 8-inch square baking pan. Set aside.

Combine caramels and water in 2-quart glass measure. Cook on HI, 2 to 3 minutes, or until caramels soften slightly. Stir through with a wooden spoon until caramels are smooth. Stir in nuts. Pour into prepared pan. Refrigerate until firm. Cut into 1-inch squares before serving.

about 7 dozen

LEMON PINEAPPLE CREME

Cooking Time: 6 to 7 minutes

- **¾   cup sugar, divided**
- **3   tablespoons cornstarch**
- **1   can (8 ounces) crushed pineapple, undrained**
- **⅔   cup water**
- **2   eggs, separated**
- **1   teaspoon grated lemon peel**
- **2   tablespoons lemon juice**
- **1   package (3 ounces) cream cheese, cubed**

Combine ½ cup of the sugar, cornstarch, pineapple with juice, and water in 4-cup glass measure. Cook on HI, 4 to 5 minutes, or until mixture boils. Stir twice during cooking time. Set aside.

Beat egg yolks. Add to pineapple mixture. Stir in lemon peel and lemon juice. Stir in cream cheese. Cook on 80, 2 minutes. Beat vigorously to blend in cream cheese. Set aside to cool.

Beat egg whites until frothy. Continue to beat, adding remaining sugar gradually. Beat until soft peaks form.

Fold egg whites into cooled pudding. Spoon into dessert dishes and refrigerate.

5 to 6 servings

RAISIN BREAD PUDDING

Cooking Time: 14½ to 17 minutes

- **4 slices raisin bread, cubed (about 4 cups)**
- **¼ cup raisins**
- **3 eggs**
- **½ cup firmly packed brown sugar**
- **1 teaspoon vanilla**
   Dash salt
- **2 cups milk**
- **2 tablespoons butter or margarine**
   Cinnamon or nutmeg

Combine bread and raisins in 2-quart round microproof dish. Set aside.

Beat eggs, brown sugar, vanilla, and salt until well blended.

Place milk and butter in 4-cup glass measure. Cook on HI, 4½ to 5 minutes, or until steaming hot. Gradually stir in egg mixture.

Pour milk mixture over bread and raisins. Sprinkle with cinnamon. Cover with waxed paper. Cook on 50, 10 to 12 minutes, or until set. Center may be slightly soft at end of cooking time. It will set as pudding cools. Serve warm or chilled.

6 servings

POACHED PEARS

Cooking Time: 22 to 28 minutes

- **1½ cups sugar**
- **4 whole cloves**
- **1 stick cinnamon**
- **4 cups cranberry juice**
- **¼ cup lemon juice**
- **4 firm, ripe pears (6 to 8 ounces each)**

Combine sugar, cloves, cinnamon, cranberry juice, and lemon juice in 3-quart microproof casserole. Stir. Cover with casserole lid and cook on HI, 12 to 14 minutes, or until liquid boils and sugar dissolves.

Peel and core pears. Place pears on their sides in hot syrup. Cover and cook on 50, 6 minutes.

Turn pears over, cover, and cook on 50, 4 to 8 minutes, or just until pears are tender. Let stand 20 minutes. Drain. Chill before serving.

4 servings

RASPBERRY COBBLER

Cooking Time: 7½ to 8 minutes

- **1 package (10 ounces) frozen raspberries, thawed**
- **¼ cup sugar**
- **2 tablespoons cornstarch**
- **1 teaspoon pumpkin pie spice**
- **½ cup biscuit mix**
- **1 tablespoon sugar**
- **3 tablespoons sour cream or yogurt**
- **1 egg yolk**

Combine raspberries, sugar, cornstarch, and pumpkin pie spice in 1-quart microproof casserole. Cover with casserole lid and cook on HI, 4 to 5 minutes, or until thickened, stirring once. Stir and set aside.

Stir together biscuit mix, sugar, sour cream, and egg yolk. Spoon batter over fruit mixture around outside edge of casserole. Cook on HI, 3½ to 4 minutes, or until set.

2 servings

Glazed Pears in Custard Sauce

GLAZED PEARS IN CUSTARD SAUCE

Cooking Time: 22 to 30 minutes

- ½ **cup dry sherry**
- ½ **cup cream sherry**
- ½ **cup water**
- 2 **tablespoons lemon juice**
- 4 **whole cloves**
- 1 **stick cinnamon**
- 2 **firm, ripe Anjou or Bosc pears (6 to 8 ounces each)**
  Vermont Sauce (page 151)
  Rum Custard Sauce (page 151)

Combine dry sherry, cream sherry, water, lemon juice, cloves, and cinnamon in 3-quart microproof casserole. Cut pears in half but do not separate. Place pears in casserole. Cover with casserole lid and cook on HI, 6 to 8 minutes, or until pears are barely poached. Drain pears, reserving liquid. Set aside.

Prepare Vermont Sauce, substituting 1 tablespoon of the reserved pear liquid for the water. Pour Vermont Sauce into the 3-quart microproof casserole. Carefully separate pears and place halves, skin-side down, in casserole. Cook, uncovered, on 50, 6 to 8 minutes, or until tender.

Turn pears over and cook on HI, 1 minute.

Arrange pear halves, cut-side down, on serving plates. Pour Rum Custard Sauce around each pear half.

4 servings

APPLESAUCE

Cooking Time: 6 to 7 minutes

- 3 **cups peeled, cored, and sliced cooking apples**
- ¼ **cup apple juice**
- 1 **teaspoon lemon juice**
- 2 **tablespoons sugar**
- ¼ **teaspoon cinnamon or nutmeg**

Combine apples, apple juice, and lemon juice in 1-quart microproof casserole. Cover with casserole lid and cook on HI, 6 to 7 minutes, or until apples are tender. Stir once during cooking time.

Add sugar and cinnamon. Stir until applesauce is smooth. Serve warm or cold.

2 servings

FRUIT COMPOTE FOR TWO

Cooking Time: 5 minutes

- 1 **can (8½ ounces) pineapple chunks, drained**
- 1 **apple, cut into chunks**
- 1 **banana, cut into thick slices**
- 5 **maraschino cherries, halved**
- 1 **tablespoon brown sugar**
- ¼ **teaspoon cinnamon**
  Dash nutmeg
  Dash cloves
- 2 **tablespoons orange juice concentrate**
- 1 **teaspoon butter**

Combine all ingredients in 2-quart glass measure. Cover with plastic wrap. Cook on 50, 2 minutes. Stir.

Cover and cook on 50, 3 minutes. Let stand 2 minutes before serving.

Serve hot for breakfast, or as an accompaniment with ham or pork.

2 servings

FRESH STRAWBERRY JAM

Cooking Time: 20 to 23 minutes

- 5 **cups crushed strawberries**
- 2 **teaspoons lemon juice**
- 1 **package (1¾ ounces) powdered fruit pectin**
- 7 **cups sugar**

Combine strawberries, lemon juice, and pectin in 3-quart microproof bowl. Cover with plastic wrap and cook on HI, 10 to 11 minutes, or until mixture boils. Stir once during cooking time.

Stir in sugar. Cook on HI, 10 to 12 minutes, or until mixture boils hard for at least 1 minute. Skim off foam. Pour into 8-ounce hot sterilized jelly glasses and seal with two-piece vacuum-type lids, according to manufacturer's directions.

Eight 8-ounce jars

Chocolate Maple Parfait

CHOCOLATE WALNUT PUDDING

Cooking Time: 8 minutes

- ⅓ **cup sugar**
- 1 **cup chocolate chips**
- 3 **tablespoons cornstarch**
- 1 **tablespoon butter**
- 2 **cups milk**
- 1 **teaspoon vanilla**
- ½ **cup chopped walnuts**
- 2 **egg yolks, beaten**

Combine sugar, chocolate chips, and cornstarch in 1-quart glass measure. Stir. Add butter and milk. Cook on HI, 6 minutes, stirring once.

Slowly stir ½ cup milk mixture into egg yolks. Whisk egg mixture back into milk. Cover and cook on 50, 2 minutes.

Stir in vanilla and walnuts. Set aside to cool. Pudding thickens as it cools.

4 servings

You can create a luscious parfait by combining Chocolate Walnut Pudding and Maple Nut Pudding (right) for a Chocolate Maple Parfait!

MAPLE NUT PUDDING

Cooking Time: 8 minutes

- ½ **cup firmly packed brown sugar**
- 3 **tablespoons cornstarch**
- 2 **cups half and half**
- 4 **egg yolks**
- 1 **tablespoon butter**
- 2 **tablespoons maple syrup**
- 1 **teaspoon maple extract**
- ½ **cup almond slices**

Mix sugar, cornstarch and half and half in 1-quart microproof casserole. Cook on HI, 6 minutes, stirring once. Set aside.

Beat egg yolks in small mixing bowl. Slowly add ½ cup of the hot cream mixture to eggs. Whisk egg mixture back into hot cream mixture. Cover with casserole lid and cook on 50, 2 minutes, or until thick and creamy. Stir in butter, maple syrup, maple extract, and nuts. Pour into serving dishes. Pudding will thicken as it cools.

4 servings

BAKED APPLES

Cooking Time: 4½ to 5½ minutes

- 2 **large baking apples**
- 2 **teaspoons butter or margarine**
- ¼ **cup firmly packed brown sugar**
- ¼ **teaspoon cinnamon**
- 2 **teaspoon golden raisins**

Core apples and slit skin around the middle of each apple to prevent skin from bursting. Place apples in small individual microproof baking dishes. Place butter in 1-cup glass measure. Cook on 50, 30 seconds. Stir in sugar, cinnamon, and raisins. Fill each apple with sugar mixture. Cover each dish with plastic wrap. Place dishes in oven and cook on HI, 4 to 5 minutes, or until tender.

2 servings

Try this recipe with two firm pears instead of apples for a special treat.

Chicken Dinner

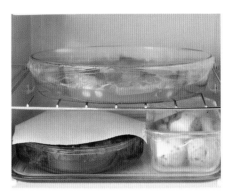

Easy Salmon Loaf cooks on the wire rack. Broccoli Spears and Frozen Fruit are placed on the glass tray to cook more slowly.

Special Swiss Steak starts cooking on the glass tray and finishes on the wire rack. A loaf pan and cake dish fit snugly on the bottom glass tray during the second cooking stage.

Temperature probe menus are flexible. Halfway through the cooking time, turn meat and rearrange or add other dishes.

WHOLE MEAL COOKING

Dinner's in the oven! Who doesn't look forward to hearing this familiar saying as mealtime approaches? You'll find that just as in conventional cooking you can prepare a whole two- or three-dish meal at the same time in your microwave oven. For the most successful whole meal, it is important to consider the placement of dishes in the oven, the size and shape of the microproof containers, the kinds of food you select, the timing, and the sequence of cooking. This chapter provides you with all the necessary information and step-by-step instructions for organizing your own whole meals. Start by reading the following basic tips on how to approach whole meal planning.

Helpful Tips

Since microwaves enter from the top of the oven, they are primarily attracted to food placed on the wire rack in the upper guides; a smaller amount reaches the bottom tray. It is logical then to place delicate quick-cooking food on the bottom glass tray and longer cooking food on the wire rack.

Whenever the wire rack is not being used, remove it from the oven.

When the browning dish or grill is used, place it on the glass tray. Do not cook other foods on the glass tray at the same time.

An ideal procedure for whole-meal cooking is to place two foods with similar cooking times on the wire rack and one shorter-cooking food on the glass tray.

If all foods require the same cooking time, reverse the location of dishes in the oven halfway through cooking time.

While the wire rack can be used in two positions, the upper position is generally best. Use the lower position whenever greater capacity on the top is needed. This does limit the useable space below.

Check your cooking dishes to be sure they will fit together in the oven before filling with food.

Often covers with knobs are too high to fit easily when the wire rack is used. Use plastic wrap instead of casserole lids when necessary.

IMPORTANT GUIDELINES FOR TIMING AND PLANNING

■ If all foods take less than 15 minutes individually, add cooking times together and program the menu for the total time.
■ If all foods take 5 to 35 minutes individually, add cooking times together and subtract about 5 minutes.
■ If any one food takes over 35 minutes, all the food can be cooked in the time suggested for food taking the longest time.

PLANNING A MENU

To make timing and planning easier, we have divided the menus into three types. For one-stage menus, all dishes are cooked for the same length of time. Two-stage menus require that the dishes on the wire rack and ceramic tray exchange positions halfway through cooking. Probe menus require cooking the meat first with the temperature probe, cooking the remaining dishes, then bringing the whole meal to serving temperature.

Choose a menu from the chart and review the individual recipes. Occasionally you will find that an ingredient should be prepared ahead. For example, squash is precooked 2 minutes to be more easily cut for Apple Stuffed Acorn Squash (page 136).

Place dishes in oven with food from column "A" on the wire rack; "B" and "C" are placed on the glass tray.

Apply the rules in "Important Guidelines for Timing and Planning." Cooking time for each recipe follows the recipe title in the menu charts.

Most recipes in whole-meal cooking benefit from stirring, rearranging, turning, and reversing position of dishes in the oven halfway through cooking time.

ONE-STAGE MENUS

To demonstrate one-stage menu planning, we have chosen:

(A) Easy Salmon Loaf
       page 106 .... 27 minutes
(B) Broccoli Spears
       page 129 .... 9 minutes
(C) Frozen Fruit
       page 172 .... 5 minutes

Note that individual cooking times range from 5 to 27 minutes. Using the "Guidelines" (above left), this one-stage meal will cook in about 36 minutes.

Let's take it step by step:

1. Prepare the Easy Salmon Loaf according to the recipe. Cover with plastic wrap and set aside.
2. Prepare Broccoli Spears in 1-quart microproof casserole. Cover with plastic wrap and set aside.
3. Prepare Frozen Fruit in 2-cup microproof serving dish. Cover with plastic wrap and set aside.
4. Place the wire rack in the upper guides. Place the salmon loaf on the wire rack. Place broccoli dish and frozen fruit dish on the glass tray. (See the photograph on page 183.) Cook on HI, 36 minutes.
5. Remove all dishes from oven. Let stand, still covered, on heat-resistant surface for 5 minutes before serving.

ONE-STAGE MENUS
Pick one dish from each column in any combination.

A	B	C
Idaho Meatballs (15) (page 72)	Dilled Zucchini and Corn (6) (page 134)	Sweet-Sour Red Cabbage (23) (page 139)
Family Meat Loaf Ring (16) (page 68)	Parsley New Potatoes (10) (page 140)	Frozen Fruit 10 oz. (5) (page 172)
Easy Salmon Loaf (27) (page 106)	Broccoli Spears 10 oz. Frozen (9) (page 129)	Baked Apple (5) (page 181)
Sauerbraten (45) (page 66)	Pan-Baked Potatoes (11) (page 140)	Raspberry Cobbler (7) (page 177)
Beef Rouladen (18) (page 63)	Calexico Bean Bake (10) (page 138)	Carrots 10 oz. Frozen (9) (page 129)
Barbecued Chicken (18) (page 89)	Far East Celery (10) (page 134)	Chopped Broccoli 10 oz. Frozen (8) (page 129)

TWO-STAGE MENUS

Pick one dish from each column in any combination.

A	B	C
Special Swiss Steak (57) (page 68)	Parsley New Potatoes (11) (page 140)	Butterscotch Cake (9) (page 162)
Lamb Ragout (40) (page 74)	Honey Corn Bread (12) (page 159)	Frozen Fruit 16 oz. (9) (page 172)
Baked Ham with Pineapple (29) (page 77)	Apple-Stuffed Acorn Squash (17) (page 136)	Raspberry Cobbler (7) (page 177)
Chicken Breasts with Vegetables (20) (page 88)	Baked Apples (5) (page 181)	Cake Mix - single layer (7) (page 163)

TWO-STAGE MENUS

The Two-Stage procedure is designed to give one recipe a longer time to cook. To demonstrate this we have chosen:

(A) Special Swiss Steak
     page 68 .... 57 minutes
(B) Parsley New Potatoes
     page 140 .... 11 minutes
(C) Butterscotch Cake
     page 162 .... 9 minutes

Using the "Guidelines" (page 184), all foods will be cooked in the time it takes Special Swiss Steak, 57 minutes.

Let's take it step by step:

1. Melt butter for cake and set aside.
2. Prepare Special Swiss Steak, reserving cherry tomatoes, green beans, and onions to add in step 7. Set aside.
3. Meanwhile, prepare Parsley New Potatoes. Place in 8 × 5-inch loaf pan. Cover with plastic wrap and set aside.
4. Place a small glass in center of an 8-inch round baking dish. Prepare Butterscotch Cake. Pour into prepared dish.
5. Place wire rack on upper guides. Place steak on wire rack, potatoes and cake on glass tray. (See photograph on page 183.)
6. Cook on HI, 35 minutes. Rearrange steak. Add cherry tomatoes, green beans, and onions. Cover. Stir potatoes. Cover. If cake is rising unevenly, rotate dish.
7. Place steak on glass tray, potatoes and cake on wire rack. Cook on HI, 22 minutes. Remove from oven. Drain potatoes. Stir butter, parsley, salt, and pepper into potatoes. Cover. Let all dishes stand, covered, 5 minutes before serving.

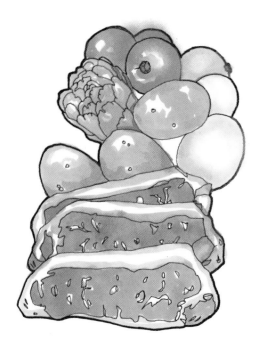

TEMPERATURE PROBE MENUS

Another whole meal method uses the temperature probe. HI is used, even though the individual recipes may call for lower power settings. Temperature setting to use follows the meat recipe title.

Protect top of meat with a narrow strip of foil. Insert probe into meat. Place wire rack in upper position. Place meat on wire rack. Plug in probe. Set temperature control. At Pause, turn meat over, being careful not to dislodge probe. The probe may be unplugged while turning meat. At Pause, remove meat and cover with aluminum foil. Place one dish on wire rack and one dish on the ceramic tray. Cook for shortest length of time given for any dish. Place meat, without probe, on wire rack. Place remaining dishes on ceramic tray. Cook on HI, about 5 minutes or until all dishes are at serving temperature.

To demonstrate the temperature probe method, we have chosen:

(A) Chicken with Herbs
     page 89 .... 34 minutes

(B) Peas Francine
     page 139 .... 9 minutes

(C) Twice-Baked Potatoes
     (pre-bake potatoes)
     page 140 .... 18 minutes

Let's take it step by step:

1. Prepare Chicken with Herbs. Place in oven on glass tray. Cook on HI with temperature probe set at 180°F.
2. At Pause, turn chicken over, being careful not to dislodge temperature probe. Continue to cook on HI to 180°F.
3. Prepare Peas Francine. Cover with casserole lid and set aside.
4. Finish preparation of Twice-Baked Potatoes. Place on microproof plate.
5. At Pause, remove chicken from oven. Remove temperature probe. Cover tightly with aluminum foil. Place wire rack in upper position. Place potatoes on wire rack and peas on ceramic tray. Cook on HI, 10 minutes.
6. Uncover chicken and place on wire rack. Place lettuce leaves over peas. Cover. Place peas and potatoes on ceramic tray. Cook on HI, 5 minutes. Let dishes stand, covered, 5 minutes before serving.

TEMPERATURE PROBE MENUS
Pick one dish from each column in any combination.

A	B	C
Pork Loin, boneless (165°F) 3 to 4 lbs. (page 62)	Far East Celery (10) (page 134)	Applesauce (6) (page 179)
Beef Rib roast (130°F) boneless, 2½ to 3 lbs. (page 61)	Pan-Baked Potatoes (11) (page 140)	Green Beans, fresh (12) (page 129)
Tenderloin of Beef Supreme (130°F) 2 to 2½ lbs. (page 64)	Twice-Baked Potatoes (18) (page 140)	Peas Francine (9) (page 139)
Turkey Roast, thawed (150°F) 2 to 3 lbs. (page 83)	Simple Herbed Rice (12) (page 119)	Harvard Beets (9) (page 138)
Chicken with Herbs (180°F) 3 lbs. (page 89)	Vegetable Trio (7) (page 138)	Neapolitan Green Beans (12) (page 132)

INDEX